BLUES FROM LAUREL CANYON

MY LIFE AS A BLUESMAN

John Mayall

with Joel McIver

OMNIBUS PRESS
London / New York / Paris / Sydney / Copenhagen / Berlin / Madrid / Tokyo

Visit Omnibus Press at www.omnibuspress.com

This book is dedicated to my family and friends, as well as to the fans who have always believed in my music and stuck with me.

Thank you from the bottom of my heart.

FOREWORD

The importance of the role of John Mayall & The Bluesbreakers, when it comes to British music, is beyond belief. John's history is indelibly marked throughout the ranks of rock'n'roll, not just the blues.

Many of The Bluesbreakers went on to experiment with different forms of music, but their roots were always steeped in the boot camp of John's band. Historically, their music was unbelievably dynamic in terms of how it was taken out of England into the United States. Look at the work that Mick Taylor did with The Rolling Stones. Look at what Peter Green and John McVie and Jeremy Spencer and I did with Fleetwood Mac. Look at the success which Eric Clapton and Jack Bruce had with Cream, whose mutated blues formula was inherited from John Mayall. It's no wonder that John is known as the godfather of British blues.

I first met John in 1964, when a band that I was in, The Cheynes, opened up for The Bluesbreakers at the original Marquee. In my world, meeting John was like meeting a star, because he was so revered. We got to know each other when Peter Green recommended to John that I join The Bluesbreakers to take over from Aynsley Dunbar. Of course, Aynsley was and remains an incredibly talented drummer, so I couldn't understand why they would want me in his place, because I play in a simple style. At the time, I think John was looking for a way to uncomplicate The Bluesbreakers, so I got the gig, and soon got to know him both as a mentor and as a boss.

John was way ahead of his time in terms of being organised about running the band. You had to do as you were told, but at the same time he became known for allowing anyone in his band – including me – to be who they were as a musician. That is the legacy of John Mayall's Bluesbreakers. He allowed us to blossom within a safe zone – *his* zone. The same thing happened in Fleetwood Mac, because Peter Green and I learned from John.

What do people need to know about John Mayall? I would say the most important thing is to preserve his legacy. He created a platform, a stage, for musicians – me being one of them – that needs not to be forgotten. John's legacy is that he has been true to his schooling as a blues player. He has never compromised that, and he has never pretended to be anything other than that. He has stuck to his guns, and he has placed his love of the blues above anything else. That is his legacy.

I'm just one listener among millions who have enjoyed John's music, and we should all be grateful that he chose to take the path which he has taken.

Mick Fleetwood
January 2019

CONTENTS

INTRODUCTION

Welcome to my autobiography! I've titled it *Blues From Laurel Canyon* for two reasons – firstly, because that's the title of an album I recorded in 1968; it was the first LP I released after I retired the name of my band, The Bluesbreakers. Secondly, and more importantly, the period of my life which this book covers leads up to a particularly golden era in the sixties and seventies, when I lived in a beautiful house in the equally gorgeous Laurel Canyon in Los Angeles.

It's difficult for me to describe, in words on paper, what it was like to be a touring and recording musician in that exact part of the world at that exact time. So much of that period was about sensations and emotions – the California sun above my swimming pool; the chink of ice in the cocktails; the tanned skin of the beautiful people who populated my life. Although my mother and my four children lived in England, they were regular visitors, and it was a family home.

At the same time, my house in Laurel Canyon was the location of the infamous Brain Damage Club, the bar where anything could (and did) happen. I damn near killed myself a couple of times, as you'll read in this book, and I still struggle to believe the things we got up to behind closed doors.

This was my life back then, and although I'm a different man nowadays, I have nothing but affection for the world I used to inhabit and the friends I made. Read on, and I hope you enjoy the ride.

John Mayall
Los Angeles, 2019

CHAPTER 1

KEY TO LOVE:
MY FAMILY TREE

Let me introduce you to my family, with as much information as I can recall about them and their lives.

My dear maternal grandfather Fred Leeson, known to all as Grandad, died of a stroke in his beloved garden on May 29, 1964. He took a lifetime's worth of memories to the grave – but I'll always remember the stories he told us.

Born on February 12, 1877, Fred was one of the eight sons and two daughters of his mother Sarah and father Edmund, a country labourer. There was a ninth brother, but he drowned at an early age. Life was hard and there were many mouths to feed: only a strong belief in God kept Sarah going, as she tried to control her brood. Grandad told us that discipline was very severe, and for serious infractions of house rules or unruly behaviour, his father would not only beat them with his hefty leather belt, he would take them by their collars and hang them up on meat hooks, suspended from the kitchen ceiling, for hours on end. These seemed like medieval punishments to me.

Despite Grandad's rugged childhood, I never heard him complain about his early life. He was raised within sight of Mow Cop on the border of Cheshire and Staffordshire: this was an eleventh-century feudal fort built by the squire of the nearby parish of Lawton so that he could keep an eye on his barons and peasants from the lookout tower. Life in Lawton at the end of the nineteenth century hadn't changed a great deal in the intervening years, and young Fred used to walk to school across the village green.

In those days it was accepted that country children would finish school at twelve and go into an apprenticeship of some sort. Fred was taken in by a butcher, and he began to learn the trade by working long hours as an errand boy, delivering meat to the gentry on foot. Sometimes he had to walk several miles, which motivated him to be successful in his own right. As the years passed, he acquired enough practical experience to strike out on his own, and by the time he got married in 1902 he was a merchant with a huge country estate called Aidenswood.

According to all reports, Fred was a bit of a Casanova in his youth and was always in the company of the village lasses, but he put these affairs behind him when he met Rose Hannah Wilson and began a serious courtship. This was regarded as marrying above his station, as they used to say in those days, as Rose had been educated to be a genteel lady by her upwardly mobile parents, Samuel, a collier from Edinburgh, and Mary Ellen, a schoolteacher. Following in her mother's footsteps, Rose also became a teacher. I suppose Fred thought that he was coming up in the world. However, it ultimately proved to be a poor match, although he remained with Rose for the rest of her life.

It often bothered Fred in his later years that he hadn't married his former sweetheart, a local girl called Alice Band. In fact, I believe he once returned to Lawton and contacted her. She wasn't ready to put out the welcome mat for him, though, and that door remained closed. It hurt his vanity to be dismissed in this way, but she could hardly be blamed; he'd ditched her without a word of warning some years before.

The birth of a daughter improved the domestic chemistry between Fred and Rose. My mother was born on August 3, 1906 and was named Beryl Veronica Leeson. Fred now had a more receptive member of the family on whom he could bestow affection and love.

By coincidence, she happened to be born, as I was myself, six years before the outbreak of a World War. Each of us, in our own time, was able to experience a countryside childhood in a period of peace.

Beryl once wrote me a letter containing memories of her days at Aidenswood. What follows is fairly long, but I include it here for several reasons. The letter evokes a time and a place that no longer exist, and a memory which I loved; as one of the last remaining British musicians of my generation, I think it's important to record it for posterity. My mother's words also reveal the background against which I discovered American blues – music from an entirely different setting. For those reasons, Beryl's memories perfectly illustrate the events which followed later in my life.

This is what she wrote:

"I'm back in my childhood and I shed a few tears for my lost paradise. I was lucky enough to have been born in the heart of the English countryside in lovely Old England, born with a passion for flowers and the green fields – a child of the soil. Looking back on the sunny days of my childhood, I was wilful and unpredictable; a lone child but never lonely, loving life.

"I remember every stick and stone, every stream and field: even now the glorious perfume of lilac or the sight of a wood full of bluebells brings it all back to me. I see myself sitting in the grass making daisy chains, necklaces, bracelets and a crown for my head. I think of all the people I knew who by now are all dead. These were the golden days. I hadn't learned of the evanescence of life. Sorrow hadn't touched me.

"The house we lived in was very large, circa Queen Anne. It stood in its own grounds, surrounded by a thick belt of horse chestnut trees, laden with candles of pink and white in the late spring. In front of the house was a big lawn with a circular drive. Through the wrought-iron gates, the main drive went straight to the back of the house, to a stone archway that led into a cobbled courtyard, where there were stables and lofts. Behind the courtyard, a pergola of white and deep purple lilac – a breathless, beautiful sight – led into a walled kitchen garden. I used to stand under the arch, looking up and imagining that heaven must be like this.

"The kitchen garden was full of apple, plum and pear trees, as well as vegetables. I used to stand with my mouth open under a plum tree, waiting for one to pop in. Further on was a croquet lawn, then a tennis court and finally a wilderness of wild roses, bracken and blackberry bushes – a wonderful place to play in.

"This was Aidenswood, the first house to capture my heart. The roots are still with me. I often used to wonder who 'Aiden' was, and what became of his wood, but I never found out, alas. Inside the house, besides my parents, lived Alice the maid, a buxom country girl with the stamina of an ox. The kitchen was her special domain, with its gleaming kitchen range that had to be black-leaded once a week – a fearsome task. A young farmer's daughter came to help out, three times a week. I was fascinated by her bright red face and hands to match.

"Friday was baking day, when Alice would bake huge amounts of delicious pies, cakes and bread to last the whole week. The hall had a vast curving oak staircase, which was wonderful for sliding down. The bedrooms were too many for me to count at first. The one used as the apple room where all the fruit was stored was my favourite. The smell was delicious, of autumn leaves and cider.

"As I grew older, education had to be considered. The village school was miles away, so an angular spinster, Miss Moore, was detailed to give me lessons when I could be found, which wasn't often! I'm really sorry now that I made her life so miserable. I learned to read very quickly, for which I'm grateful to her. Books and the magic of English language and literature became very important to me. Arithmetic I never mastered, and I wasn't even prepared to try.

"I was only a baby when we first came to live at Aidenswood. I arrived sitting on Grandad's shoulders, the way he always carried me. Most men seem to want a boy first, but he always wanted a girl. Maybe that's why he spoiled me so outrageously – although, thinking back, when you were born, I think he realised what he had missed by not having a son to carry on his name.

"Life in the country miles from anywhere was wonderful, but it did mean that I hadn't any playmates. It didn't bother me at all – my playmates were the flowers and the trees. I lived in an imaginary world of people I made up. My doll 'Arabella Maud' – a name I thought most elegant – was a great help, but my greatest friend was 'Our Fan'. She didn't exist, of course, but to me she was very special. I can't even tell you what I thought she looked like, but we did everything together.

"Relatives who came to visit thought I was an exceedingly odd child, always talking to someone who wasn't there. Our Fan and I would sit together among the bluebells and ragged robin in the wood. I would be a princess and Fan was the prince rescuing me. At one time I was a little worried, because all the best princesses I had read about had long yellow hair and blue eyes, and I had neither. I asked Grandad about this but he said that princesses with dark curls were very rare: after all, Snow White was dark, so I felt quite reassured.

"I'm afraid, to my mother, I was a complete enigma. Although she loved me, she'd look at me sometimes and wonder how she could possibly have produced such a contradiction of all she expected a little girl to be. All she'd wanted was a well-behaved, nicely dressed and above all clean child, and what she'd got was a ragamuffin who tore her dresses and was never tidy. Then she'd say, 'Of course, you're just like your father,' which seemed to absolve her from blame."

My mother loved it when the gypsies came to the nearby fields, she told me.

"I loved playing with their children, with their brown skin, black hair and brown eyes. Like their children, the women were dark and most of them wore gold earrings, except one who wore a pair that had a stone in them that glinted and blazed in the light, like shafts of red fire. I watched them all the time and thought how lovely they were – you must have guessed, this was my first introduction to garnets. I had never seen anything so beautiful.

"We played wonderful games, sailing my socks and shoes in the stream, fishing with bent pins in the canal and climbing trees in the bluebell wood. I invariably mislaid one or both of my socks and shoes. We ate stewed rabbit and hedgehog and made blackberry tea over the campfires: life was such fun. I had a governess who used to say, 'If you're a naughty girl, I shall give you to the gypsies,' and I thought, 'I can't wait. When can I go?' I never minded the frequent smackings or the de-nittings I had to endure.

"Grandad was on good terms with them, even when they once sold him a blind horse! They really got the better of him that time. He went to them and they said they'd got a good one for sale, so he said, 'Fine, I'll come round and have a look at it.' He thought it was in great shape and so he bought it. It was only after he'd got it home that he noticed it didn't want to leave the stable, and so he had his friend Jack Connolly come over and take a look at it. It was then that Jack told Grandad that the poor bugger was totally blind and couldn't see a thing! He laughed about it so many times, blaming his own gullibility, yet admiring the gypsies' business prowess.

"At midnight on Christmas Eve every year, the church choir came to sing carols, with their lanterns to light the way. This was always a big occasion: Grandad always invited them in for port and refreshments. He would carry me downstairs and I would sit on his knee wrapped in a blanket, listening to their chatter and laughter as they ate vast quantities of pies and cake which Alice had spent all morning baking. I was asleep long before they went to their next call, and Grandad would carry me back to bed and tuck me in. It was a happy night.

"My mother was the most fastidious and particular person, who tried her absolute best to keep me looking clean and presentable. I'd be all dressed up in starched clothes, never a mark on me. Everything was white and all frilled and pleated, and I was never allowed to get dirty or play. She used to invite my cousin Sybil to come and stay at horribly regular intervals – a very dull child. She never got dirty or lost her hair ribbons: I suppose Mother hoped some of Sybil's goodness would rub off onto me.

"At the top of my roly-poly bank was the canal – a magical place of beauty. I knew many of the water gypsies, who languidly sailed along in their painted, horse-drawn barges, travelling from mysterious places to others that I'd never heard of. The canal was an endless source of amusement to me, picking wild flowers and fishing. I remember that one of my favourite games was playing Moses in the bull rushes, with the game based on King Herod and the Slaughter of the Innocents. I was Miriam and dear long-suffering Arabella

Maud was Moses, which entailed me crouching amongst the bull rushes in my knickers, rather wet and muddy.

"Sometimes on rainy days I would climb into the loft, to roll about in the sweet-smelling hay and listen to the horses shaking their heads and jingling their harnesses. Alice would bring me great wedges of bread and jam which tasted so good.

"Life was so secure and predictable – until at one fell swoop my whole world collapsed. We were to leave to go to live in Manchester. Aidenswood was lost, and the years of happiness were over: it was almost more than I could bear. The city was hateful and ugly, with endless streets and houses. I fretted and grew thin, but as it is said, 'One door shuts, another opens,' and that is how it was for me. Through my door was the beauty of Wales, and the happiness at school which was my salvation.

"On to my schooldays and a new chapter. I was still a little girl around six years old, and I had been hurt – but the nuns at school healed that hurt."

I pick up the story with the assistance of some taped memories recorded in 1980. Coupled with my own occasional remembrances, my mother's tale emerges and moves forward.

The move to Manchester was apparently seen as a better opportunity for her father's business, and happened to coincide with the outbreak of the Great War in August 1914. There was a huge push for volunteers for the army: recruiters were ready and eager to grab up all the healthy young men they could lay eyes on. A great sense of patriotism was in the air and, because the fighting was predicted to be over by Christmas, there was no shortage of volunteers. Sometimes whole streets went happily to the recruiting stations, little realising that unprecedented slaughter lay ahead. Who could have known?

There were, however, many non-believers, and among them was young Fred Leeson, who did all he could to dodge the scooping up of Britain's male population. He told tales of hiding in side streets as the parades went by, with Lord Kitchener's finger pointing everywhere from the famous poster. He avoided the draft with bribes, or by claiming his importance to the country in keeping the meat supply moving to the home front.

In November 1918 the war ended, and everyone began the readjustment to peacetime. Unfortunately, Fred and Rose didn't have much in common. In fact, because he was an uneducated man, she was rather ashamed of him, and reluctant to tell her friends that he was on the lowest rung of the professions – a common butcher.

To give you an example, when my mother Beryl was happily farmed out to Loreto College, a convent school in Llandudno run by nuns, her mother would come to visit once a term and stay at the Grand Hotel: this was the poshest hotel in town, right on the seafront. However, her father was never allowed to come when she was there because he might 'let the side down'. It was amazing that he stood for this. There was an accepted social division between them that he did not challenge; this resonated with me when I started studying music of black origin, steeped as it was in racial tensions.

My mother missed her parents when she was away at school, but when she was with them, she found that together they were extremely tiresome. Whenever possible, she tried to avoid going out in their company, as they would invariably end up quarrelling and fighting over her. She rather enjoyed them separately, though; her father would always let her get dirty, go fishing and be naughty and free-spirited, while her mother would dress her up and take her out to afternoon tea in smart places.

Beryl knew that her mother had boyfriends. Rose was a very attractive woman back in the twenties, and was a great one for mixing with the upper classes. One of her boyfriends was an army major called Jimmy Reynolds, and there was another gentleman called Teddy Whittaker who was always hanging round with his hopes up and used to come to tea regularly. Rose always let Beryl know that if it hadn't been for her, she could have been in India as part of the ruling class. Perhaps that was a little harsh, in retrospect.

Beryl also suspected that her mother was having an affair with a wealthy potter from Staffordshire. On one occasion Rose went down to London and stayed for a month with the sister of Rab Butler, later the Chancellor of the Exchequer – so who knew what she'd been up to, given her access to any number of admirers?

Meanwhile, Grandad was also busy on the home front: there was hell to pay when Rose returned and discovered traces of semen on the hearth rug in the front room. She never let him live this down, which was perhaps a little unfair. After all, he got into trouble because he didn't cover his tracks properly, while Rose was careful enough to keep her dealings discreet. Apparently what was good for the goose wasn't good for the gander.

No wonder Beryl dreaded the holiday homecomings, when there was so much latent hostility between her parents; they now slept in separate bedrooms. There was no family life to speak of, so it was always a happy day for her when the holidays were over and she could get back to school and her friends.

Beryl loved school, and the nuns whom she thought of as her salvation, although she was a rebel. They used to say to her, "Surely you'll wheedle awie past St Peter and sith," their rural Welsh way of indicating that she would persuade her way into heaven, as a comment on her lack of interest in conforming to the rules. She used to climb out of dormitory windows and leave the school to wander in the wilderness, simply to escape the unpleasant daily rituals of school. She hated hockey and found running round a cold field with a stick utterly pointless. Totally bored, she would make up all kinds of illnesses – stomach ache one day, a headache the next, and any other ailment she could think of.

Eventually the nuns got wise to these ruses because of their unnatural frequency and put her in the infirmary, where she was given heavy doses of castor oil. It didn't take long before they gave up and accepted her for who she was, however, and allowed her more or less to do what she wanted. Beryl loved their liberated attitude, an unusual one for nuns: in fact, they spoiled her dreadfully. In the end she learned only elocution and dancing, although she regretted this later; she would have been a beautiful French speaker.

At the age of eighteen, Beryl enrolled at a famous dancing school, Miss Radcliff's at Accleby Lodge. As part of the students' education, they attended various dance halls to give exhibitions, and at one of these events she met a fetching undergraduate from Cambridge. His name was Frederick Murray Hyde Mayall.

Murray, as he was known, was a good-looking, charming man from a very upper-class family background. His people had been titans in the British cotton industry and were still a major force in commerce. He was an accomplished banjo and guitar player and a member of a band called The Cam Collegians, who had a large, diverse line-up featuring two saxophones plus violin, trombone, piano and drums. This group was inspired by the success of the Original Dixieland Jazz Band, an all-white outfit from New York City. Perhaps curiously in hindsight, this group had attained worldwide recognition long before the black masters of the genre – Louis Armstrong, Kid Ory, Sidney Bechet and Jelly Roll Morton among them – became known.

My father pursued his music throughout his life, occasionally as a paid member of semi-professional dance bands. There was a Spanish pianist named Fred Elizalde who became very famous in Europe during the twenties and thirties and who also attended Cambridge. Murray became quite close to him, and they played together in many a jam session.

Murray was also a dedicated drinker. While at Cambridge, he and his friends would race down to London at weekends and drink the hours away at the 43 Club, a notorious dive on Gerrard Street in Soho run by an infamous club-owner, Kate Meyrick. They would drink till they dropped, and then stagger back to college.

When his godfather, Sir Edward Tootal Broadhurst of the Manchester textile firm Tootal Broadhurst Lee, secured him a job at the company's main London branch after he finished Cambridge – with all sorts of degrees, including a master's in Latin – his fondness for the bottle didn't go unnoticed. Ultimately it stood in the way of him getting a directorship in the firm.

My father, his friends the Pattenham Baldwins and his best pal Jack Pitchford – who later became my godfather – frequently went on serious benders. He would sometimes disappear for days and fail to show up for work. His mother, Mary Hyde Mayall – née Brumwell, and usually known as May – and Beryl's mother grew concerned once they got word of what was going on. Rose had never liked Murray, because he was such an incorrigible drunk: both ladies highly disapproved of his reckless behaviour.

They duly got their heads together and formulated a plan. "Let us go down to London and find him!" they said, and the search began.

11

After investigating all the known after-hours drinking dens, they eventually discovered Murray in Charlie Brown's in Limehouse, where he had been imbibing for days on end.

Before my father had time to sober up, his mother decided that the only way he was ever going to find salvation, give up drinking and settle down to a proper lifestyle befitting the Mayall name was for him to marry Beryl. The matter was soon settled, and Beryl and Murray were duly wed at Isleworth Registry Office on November 28, 1928.

My father duly promised his mother that he'd be a good boy and drink no more: as she adored him, despite him being the black sheep of the family, she went home satisfied that all would be well. His godfather got in touch with Tootals and arranged for all to be forgiven, because it was now understood that as a responsible married man he'd buckle down and behave himself.

The young couple moved into lodgings with a family in Ealing, but soon decided that this wasn't really what living in London was all about. They wanted to see the bright lights and be involved in the social whirl with their wealthy friends. When they moved into a flat with a French window overlooking a nice garden in Howley Place just off Warwick Avenue, it didn't seem to be a problem that they had little or no money. This was the Jazz Age, after all.

As Murray was a guitarist, he soon found the right crowd, but his old habits returned and he lost his job at Tootals for the last time. There was no turning back, and in order to raise cash, he talked Beryl into them both taking a job selling vacuum cleaners door to door. He would send her on ahead to knock on doors and make appointments with unsuspecting souls who had neither a need nor the money for such devices: the only carpet they might have would be a narrow strip down the hallway.

However, the job lasted quite some time, some cash was generated, and in the evenings my parents made the rounds of the nightclubs, acquiring new friends with both wealth and position. These included Margot Brown, a millionaire's daughter from Scotland, and Sargent Stone, an aristocrat's niece who used to give tennis parties in Wimbledon.

Murray and Beryl would dress up in their best clothes, and even though they hadn't a bean to their name, they would attend these parties and mingle with the aristocracy. However, they didn't fool everybody: Margot Brown felt so sorry for them that she once put a rabbit through the front window with a note to say that she wanted to offer a contribution to the larder. Apparently this rabbit came from the Browns' Scottish estate: it was a tradition to share the bounty with friends.

Despite the Brown family fortune, there was little to show for it once it reached the new generation. It turned out that Margot and her husband, a failing stockbroker, were living it up on credit. What a lot of happy ne'er-do-wells, loafing around together and having a lovely time with absolutely no money at all...

The newlyweds' marriage was soon under threat, although Murray knew nothing of it. One morning, after he had been drinking all night in Covent Garden, he stumbled into the fresh produce marketplace: perhaps the bright light of day affected his eyesight, but instead of a bunch of flowers, he arrived home to present Beryl with a bunch of spring onions. More significantly, he also brought home a drinking companion named Michael Doyle, a good-looking Irishman.

Michael and Beryl were attracted to each other from the first glance, and, as she told me, one thing led to another. As my father was generally inebriated and out doing whatever he had a mind to do, Beryl and her new lover found the opportunity to sleep together. Love was professed on both sides. This remained forever Beryl's secret from Murray.

However, before any further intimacy could develop, the money trickled away to nothing and my parents could no longer afford to live in London's West End. Having exhausted their connections and benefactors, their only recourse was to move back to the family estate in Saddleworth. Michael was left behind in London and soon drifted out of their lives.

In Saddleworth, the couple's lifestyle revolved more than ever around my father's drinking excesses. How could it have been otherwise? In that town, the Mayall family were among the most prominent in the whole county. The pubs wouldn't think of refusing a Mayall a drink, whatever the time of day or night. This wasn't necessarily a good thing.

My mother was at her wits' end. Life on the family estate was intolerable for her, as it meant living under the same roof as Murray's mother May and his sister Eileen, who strongly disapproved of his conduct. She felt that she couldn't turn to her parents: Rose had strongly disapproved of Murray from the start, and she was ashamed to have to admit defeat to her dear father Fred. May was a respectable person of sterling quality, but very strict. With her, everything had to be just so.

It was time to look for other options. My grandmothers May and Rose put their heads together once more. They thought, "This is no good at all. We've got to get Murray out of this place. He's drunk all the time and never home. The disgrace of it all! What on earth will Uncle Murray think?"

They were also concerned about the effect it would have on the maiden aunts on the Isle of Wight. Murray had offended them once before – and they subsequently left a fortune of £45,000 to a cats' home!

It transpired that one of Rose's boyfriends, a well-to-do British gentleman known as 'Uncle Jack', had recently lost a lot of money in the Wall Street crash of 1929, having invested heavily in US stocks and bonds. Jack had owned an estate in Windermere, but then moved to Bramhall to enjoy a more frugal life in the country and was living in a house in Grove Lane. He was very fond of Beryl and even fonder of her mother, so was eager to help out with this dilemma.

My parents went to visit Jack one day and he showed them a bungalow on the corner of Acre Lane. Although it was very run down, and quite the filthiest of dwellings – because the eccentric old lady who had lived there had moved a lot of goats, of all things, into the house – the place had possibilities. The goats had shat all over the place, and although the smell hadn't seemed to bother the old lady one bit, the floors were in a very bad state. However, the bungalow offered a solution to the embarrassment of Murray's presence in

Saddleworth, and so it came to pass that May bought the house for her son for three or four hundred pounds and they moved in.

The new home had little effect on Murray's habits: he soon found a lovely new set of drinking friends and the cycle began all over again. He got himself a job as a wages clerk in the local engineering firm of Simon Carves, something of a lowly position for a brilliant man with a fellowship in English literature and a master's degree from Cambridge.

My father had some interesting habits, in retrospect. He was a keen book collector, eventually amassing an extremely valuable collection of first editions of rare books, many of them in the original Latin. He also collected pornography, which in those days was an underground, undesirable pursuit. I suppose my mother turned a blind eye to this side of his literary interests as long as he kept these items under lock and key.

Everything in the realm of pornography was in very limited supply, and photographs and literature from the Victorian era were considered valuable rarities. My father's collection included nude postcards from France that had served the armed forces well in the First World War; the writings of Rabelais; bedroom snapshots of enthusiastic amateurs – with the gentlemen usually wearing black socks and shoes and little else; and all kinds of humorous limericks. This stuff was kept in a cupboard in the front room library and only brought out for viewing and trading with his friends, most of whom Beryl didn't care for. Today, we would regard these items as quaint relics of a bygone, repressed age, and very timid by modern standards.

At the beginning of 1933, the twenty-five-year-old Beryl discovered that she was pregnant. My father was very much against the idea of having children, and proposed to take care of this 'accident' before it went too far. Over the ensuing months, he did everything he could to prevent the prospect of fatherhood by going to shady back-street shops in Hulme and buying medications that were supposed to bring the pregnancy – and me – to an early end.

Fortunately these had no effect on Beryl, who was in the best of health and stamina. Even my father's suggestions that she should skip excessively and jump off stepladders failed to dislodge me. Once it was perceived that my arrival was inevitable, Beryl put her foot down and said, "I'm not going any further with this."

He responded, "What about an abor–," but didn't get to finish the sentence.

"No way! I'm going to have this baby, and that's that!"

Beryl now went about her life with an ever-growing belly. Little information about pregnancy was available in those days, and she had to guess about most of the mysterious changes her body was undergoing. She later told me that, among her adventures during this time, she became stuck under the bed while dusting. Luckily, her cries for help were heard by the milkman, Charlie Downing; he was able to rescue her by lifting up the bed and returning her to freedom.

As my mother's due date in November was drawing closer, my father decided that if his wife was going to have a baby, they might as well be in a more suitable locale to help the time pass more pleasantly – and what better place to be than Macclesfield, where there was a terrific old pub called the Spread Eagle, run by a very good friend of his named Old Barnes. Murray had recently used this establishment as his headquarters for a major drinking bout, and so off they went to stay at the pub in Chestergate.

They were there for three weeks – and, as Beryl told it, "Murray nearly drank himself silly, and I was doing my best to keep up. By now I was a fortnight overdue. There was nothing going on but drinking and sitting around waiting for something to happen, and I thought, 'My God, I can't stand this any longer,' and came home on the train. I cleaned the bungalow from top to toe. I polished, washed and cleaned everything like a new pin and then got back on the train to Macclesfield."

She continued:

"Back at the Spread Eagle, I took a couple of drinks of port, which was what we were all drinking that night. I have no idea why it was port, because I absolutely loathe it. Suddenly my waters broke and I thought, 'God, I've pissed myself!' Not knowing a thing about having babies, because in those days no one told you anything that might help you prepare for the event, I thought to myself, 'This is very odd. Maybe it's time to go to the hospital.'

"By this time, Murray was staggering but still coherent: he and Old Barnes rallied to the mission and we set off on foot to West Park Hospital. We had no money for a taxi and it was a mile or so to go. The streets of Macclesfield were black as pitch, wet and very cold. I hung on to Old Barnes like a limpet: without him I'd never have got there. I didn't think having a baby would be like this. It was like something out of Dickens! I simply pretended I was walking through a field of buttercups with a shining sun, although it was difficult. I suppose I was lucky I didn't deposit you in the street, although that never occurred to me, fortunately. With their wobbly support, the two men delivered me to the ward, where I lay for three days enduring an extremely uncomfortable and tortuous labour."

It was probably little compensation to be told by the sister in charge that nothing worthwhile came easily, but eventually an end to my mother's efforts came on November 29, when I popped out into the world. They named me John, with the middle name of Brumwell, which had been my maternal grandmother May's family name. I'd already been referred to as John for months, as she'd wanted another John Mayall to carry on the line.

CHAPTER 2

BRAND NEW START: CHILDHOOD DAYS

For two more weeks, my mother Beryl remained in hospital, recovering from the difficult birth. She then returned home to begin learning what to do with a baby. As she said, "The head and legs were easy. There were the right amount at both ends – but the middle bit was a complete mystery!"

She remembered sitting by the fire in the kitchen at Acre Lane with me – just a little scrap – on her knee, saying to me: "We're on our own now, mate. Forgive me any shortcomings I have."

After the birth, my tiny presence gave Beryl the excuse she needed to cut down on my father Murray's sexual attentions: life in the bungalow took on a new pattern of baby care, with nappy changing and all the attendant chores involved with nurturing a new baby.

My christening took place in a modest ceremony back in Saddleworth, so that the esteemed relatives on Murray's side could be present. His sister Eileen was there with her new fiancé George, and the family were very happy to know that there was another John Mayall to add to the long line of predecessors.

My grandmother May died just after I was born, which meant that my father now had an inheritance. The affluent Mayalls owned a considerable part of Mossley and Saddleworth, and had built Mossley Town Hall, which they also owned. When my grandmother died, the estate was sold and provided an income for Murray and his sister Eileen.

Things took a strange turn in 1934, when Murray joined the Cheadle Hulme Operatic Society. This seemed like a suspicious move for someone so dedicated to jazz, and indeed there was more to it than arias and arpeggios. He had met a lady called Doris Mitchell at the society, and their casual acquaintance soon grew into a serious affair.

This really irritated Beryl. There she was at home, struggling with a small baby, and there he was, out carousing with a woman on the side in addition to his regular hangouts with his friends. Quite naturally, things were never the same after that.

I asked my mother how she learned of my father's affair with Doris, to which she replied, "I can't remember how, but I do know that I felt pretty good about it, because she was little and fat. I thought it was great, because I looked better than she did, and that really did a lot for my ego. Of course, he was still telling me he loved me, but he fancied her. A fat lot of good that did me."

In fact, she and Murray were still sleeping together, although with a lot less intimacy. Beryl gave my father an ultimatum: if he wanted to resume his husbandly privileges, he would have to give up Doris. He agreed, and as far as Beryl knew, he never saw her again. I suspect he'd grown weary of her anyway.

My mother soon became pregnant again, in spite of precautions and infrequent sex. By now she had become an excellent, caring mother of one – and was well prepared for another.

On January 20, 1936, King George V died: this is my earliest memory of a major news event. I remember hearing it reported on the wireless and the king's death being discussed by saddened family members. A couple of months afterwards, on March 2, my brother Philip was born and was given the middle name of Leeson, which put an extra smile on my grandfather's face.

There was a funny mix-up regarding the identity of Philip's father. My father used to give guitar lessons to a Mr Etherington, a friend from Cheadle Hulme. When my mother's waters broke, it was this Mr Etherington who took her to hospital, as Murray was in a state of intoxication. The admitting nurse assumed that the man accompanying Beryl was the father. When Murray turned up and said who he was, the staff said, "Oh no, we've met Mr Mayall, and he definitely isn't you." It took quite a bit of explaining before they grasped who everyone actually was. They'd written my father off as an odd stranger with some sort of mad quirk.

When Beryl returned home with her new babe in her arms, I said to her, "Mummy, when's he going back? He's really not much use at all."

After Philip came into the picture, Beryl acquired a double-sized pram to push us both around in. I still vaguely recall how secure and dreamy I felt within it, soothed by the rocking motion and the sight of the deep blue sky beyond the canopy.

The arrival of another child in the Mayall family didn't change Murray's basic lack of interest in fatherhood. He became even more erratic and unreliable in his job, and would sometimes end up with an empty wage packet after a weekend of drinking.

Despite my father's unreliable nature, my early childhood was pretty idyllic. We still went on summer holidays as a family; I have memories of us all together on the pebbled beaches at Aldeburgh. At the age of three, my mother began reading Beatrix Potter books to me, and I became so used to them that if she deviated from the text at all, I would instantly point out the correct sentences from memory. Thanks to Peter Rabbit, I grew up with visions of country animals and those unforgettable wildlife characters, so accurately and beautifully drawn by the author.

The sights and sounds of childhood are still vivid today. I was very much adored by and spoilt by a Mrs Barber, who owned a small farm behind our back garden hedge. I remember watching her pluck freshly killed chickens, the blood still running from the chopping block, accompanied by the smell of burnt feathers. She used to make milk jellies for me if she got the slightest inkling of me coming round the corner for a visit.

We always had Persian cats, one at a time. We had one called Ginger who lived a really long time, until he was run over on the corner outside the front gate. I was also very attached to a blue budgie called Peter, whose death from an unknown ailment put me in mourning. I made a small coffin lined with cotton wool and buried him in it in the garden under an oak tree. I believe we got another budgie, but I never grew to love it as much as Peter.

There was the occasional accident, of course. Riding my tricycle down the cobblestone path in the back garden, I sustained my first injury when the front wheel jammed and I went over the handlebars and cut my head open. I have the scar near my hairline to this day.

Life seemed very peaceful and happy to me, but beyond my narrow, protected world, awful events were happening. Hitler came to power the year I was born, and Dachau became the Nazis' first concentration camp. Kristallnacht followed, along with the suppression and liquidation of the Jews under Hitler's direction.

Meanwhile, lynchings were an everyday event in America. In 1937, the great blues singer Bessie Smith died of injuries sustained in a car accident in Mississippi, because no whites-only hospital would admit her. There was civil war in Spain; and in Russia, Stalin was engaged in terrible purges, exterminating millions sent to Siberia.

All manner of ghastly events were building on the world stage, and yet I never knew a thing about it. My small world was a safe place, and my mother was my protector and nurturer. Music quickly became a part of my life thanks to Murray's collection of 78rpm records, housed in a deep chest to the left of the fireplace in the front room. It was also where his huge book collection filled the shelves, alongside a Hogarthian picture showing a bacchanalian scene with a fat guy devouring handfuls of grapes and a nude cherub peeing happily in the foreground. We boys weren't allowed to touch the records in case we broke them, so it was a treat to see these treasures being put on the turntable and played.

As Murray was a guitarist, the bulk of the collection centred round that instrument: this wonderful music was to be a major influence in my life. There was a twelve-inch blue label HMV record by Segovia that I never tired of listening to, with Bach's 'Gavotte' on one side and 'Theme Varie' on the other. I think it got broken at some point, but Murray was an expert at gluing the pieces back together. There was also a banjo record by Harry Reser featuring the songs 'Crackerjack' and 'Flapperette'.

Eventually I talked Murray into giving me a 78rpm record by the American quartet The Mills Brothers: it was called 'How'm I Doin', Hey Hey'. I particularly loved The Mills Brothers' records and played them over and over again after my mother gave me her HMV wind-up gramophone.

This came in useful during a particularly rough domestic patch, when Beryl sent me to Scholar Green to stay for a few days with her childhood friend Ethel Saunders, who we would always call Auntie Ethel. She and Uncle Roy would always talk about me being able to find my favourite records just by the look of the labels, before I had learned to read. I chose as my favourite record Victor Young's 'Sweet Sue, Just You', simply because I liked the way the words looked.

I was four years old in November 1937, and since Edward VIII had abdicated the crown the year before in favour of the American divorcee Mrs Simpson – what a scandal that was! – we had a new king. I never thought his younger brother George VI looked at all well: he seemed more fragile as a leader than his forebears. But my thoughts didn't linger on heads of state for long: I was more interested in the simple pleasures of childhood.

Sweets, for example. A penny went a long way in those times, and even a farthing with the cute little robin embossed on it would buy something at Mrs Brunt's. Old Mr Brunt was very fond of Philip and me, and when we'd come in asking for a penn'orth of liquorice allsorts or toffee, he always gave us good value, despite the effort it took him to move his ladder around to get down the sweet jars from the top shelf. We also loved Tizer ('The Appetizer'), Stone's ginger beer in squat brown bottles, and paper packets of lemon sherbet sucked out through a straw – and we used to chew liquorice root until our gums bled.

At weekends, the sound of a particular bicycle bell would have us rushing to the front gate: it was the ice-cream man, coming along Acre Lane on his tricycle. The special, sherbet-like taste of that ice cream on a hot summer day was never recaptured after the war.

The favourite among all my toys was my precious teddy bear, Edward. I never did anything without him: I took him for rides in little pull carts and out in the snow to build snowmen. I loved and squeezed him so much that in time the whole of his face became lopsided. One fateful day, we'd been out in the snow and he'd got wet, so I sat him in front of the electric fire: he fell forward into it and caught fire. Beryl smelled the burning and rescued him in time. We took him to a doll's hospital somewhere, although they were unable to exactly match the fabric and he looked like a wounded soldier from then on.

Sometimes we visited the circus, but I was absolutely terrified of the clowns. It seemed to me that they were coming right for me with their frightening make-up, and every sudden move they made would be accompanied by the loudest bangs I'd ever heard. I'd be reduced to tears, huddling down between the seats and begging to be taken home. I had to cover my face and ears until the clowns' portion of the show was over and the danger went away.

I was also afraid of dentists, for good reason. In this rural area the dentist made house calls. He came round and set up a foot-powered drill and other paraphernalia in the nursery. I struggled mightily as he clamped a mask over my nose and mouth and poured chloroform on it until I passed out. It was an evil, frightening smell.

I soon got to know the locals in our area. Every village seemed to have its own eccentric resident back then, and ours was no exception. I was fascinated – and not a little scared – by a little old lady called Addie Hickson. She was very thin and wan, and always wore a pulled-down black felt hat and a funeral dress with button boots. Addie would mutter and rant to herself as she weaved with brisk steps down the lane. Every once in a while she would pause for a loud monologue before beating herself about the head and attacking the hedge with her handbag then going on her way. I always kept to the other side of the road.

At the age of five I started primary school, where Mrs Buckley was my teacher. I loved the order and fun of it all right from the beginning, but for Philip it was a different story. At the end of his first day there, he commented, "It was quite nice, but I don't think I'll go any more."

In early 1939, we had no idea that everything was about to change. The countryside was so beautiful when I was young. You could spend a whole day in our lane, getting your fingers pricked and stained purple from gathering blackberries. I rarely saw a car pass by from one week to the next, so the sounds of birds were dominant, complementing the smell of flowers and the delicious aroma of freshly cut lawns. The sound of the farmer's huge horse clip-clopping along would bring us out onto the pavement to watch it pass: it pulled a long cart full of manure, or, at harvest time, bales of new-mown hay back to the barn.

I loved haymaking time. We'd been forbidden entrance beyond the farm's five-bar gates for so long that when the harvesting began, we were always around to help. The wigwam-like hay sheaves made wonderful dens. I used to help with the milk round too. That was special, because I'd climb aboard the pony and trap and set off to the farm, where I'd watch the fresh milk being poured into the huge metal urns. I would help measure the right amounts with a ladle into the bottles that people would leave on their doorsteps. I'd watch the pony chewing happily on the hay and chaff in his nosebag, and away we'd go with a tinkling rattle and a trot to the next group of cottages. It was a great ride.

On May 25, 1939, my sister Caroline was born; she was given the middle name of Dawn for no other reason than that it sounded pretty. She was christened in a dual ceremony with Christine White, George and Eileen's daughter. Now we were three kids, all unaware that a storm was coming over the horizon.

Just over four months later, war was declared and the beginning of a new way of life began for the British people. Its first impact on us was rationing, which began in January 1940 with ration books being issued to every household for sugar, butter and meat. As Grandad was a butcher, we were very fortunate that he could bend the rules where family was concerned. With meat being so much in demand, he was able to trade with other retailers. For me, this meant that I could still get my weekly comics despite paper rationing leading to shorter print runs of these publications. I read *Dandy*, *Beano*, *Knockout*, *Film Fun*, *Radio Fun* and *Comic Cuts*, and at Christmas our pillowcases were sure to contain the annuals.

Winston Churchill was voted in as prime minister on May 10, 1940 and we listened to his speeches on the wireless, urging everyone to 'do their bit'. Air raid shelters were being dug; corrugated iron domes covered with sod were seen everywhere. You entered them through a doorway at one end and sat patiently with gas masks on, upon the long wooden benches that ran along either side. There was always a dank smell in there as we held our candles and waited for the all-clear siren. Did we feel any fear? I think we were still too young.

In the summer, the pace of the war intensified. At school we always had to carry our gas masks in a bag with a shoulder strap. These clumsy gadgets were made more attractive to children with Mickey Mouse designs. Air-raid warnings became more and more frequent. Bombs fell and casualties mounted on the home front. In London, Buckingham Palace was hit and St Paul's Cathedral was badly damaged, and in the north of England, Coventry Cathedral was all but levelled.

As we lived only twelve miles from Manchester, we witnessed the fiery red skies above it when the city was badly shelled. Later that year, Grandad's house in Whalley Range was hit. He and Ma Leeson had to move.

In the spirit of keeping a stiff upper lip, 'You Are My Sunshine' was the most popular song of the day. As the USA hadn't yet entered the war, the songs we heard in our hit parade were mainly of the bland and cheery variety, such as 'Deep In The Heart Of Texas', 'Bewitched, Bothered And Bewildered' and 'Chattanooga Choo Choo'.

We continued to take family seaside holidays, visiting Aldeburgh shortly after Caroline was born. We used to stay at a boarding house run by a Mrs Leydon, who had a dozen cats that constantly urinated in the house. At seven years old, I walked in, inhaled deeply and pronounced loudly, "Hmm, same old smell!" Not the most diplomatic thing to say in front of a testy landlady.

The bleak east coast outpost of Aldeburgh was selected because Owen Barker, one of my father's old drinking friends from Cambridge, lived there, which meant that he and Murray could spend time in the pubs while Beryl took care of the three of us. It must have been a trial for my mother, as her marriage was on the rocks by now – as indeed were we when we hobbled painfully down to the seashore.

I used to hate walking on the stony beach, but once I was allowed to go out on the lifeboat and help the men haul it back up onto the beach after they'd done a practice launch. The smell of tar on the ropes that pulled the craft in and out of the water was exhilarating. I watched the staunch seamen in their sou'westers, with their gnarled hands honed by years of blustery cold weather, and wished I had their strength.

The cinema became a passion of mine when I was eight or nine years old. The 1934 movie *Treasure Island*, starring Wallace Beery, finally made it to the Tudor Cinema in Bramhall and Ma Leeson took me to see it. It was the first film I ever saw, and launched my lifelong dedication to the movies. Favourites of my childhood included such terrific dramas as *Mutiny On The Bounty*, *The Lives Of A Bengal Lancer*, *The Charge Of The Light Brigade* and *David Copperfield*. Errol Flynn was the undisputed hero of his time in *The Adventures Of Robin Hood*, *The Sea Hawk* and many more, while Basil Rathbone was always the top villain. After seeing *Beau Geste*, I became fascinated with horror art, and drew a very elaborate depiction of a legionnaire with an arrow through his head.

In the real world, my father's drinking continued. My mother's life was one long pattern of frustration, with neighbours bringing him home in a stupor from the pub or the gutter. He had a motorbike with a sidecar that I remember riding in. Inevitably, he once had a bad accident and nearly died. A significant portion of his internal organs was removed, and he carried large scars on his abdomen and forehead for the rest of his life.

He later acquired a tandem with a pillion seat, and I have a memory of him cycling all the way to a suburb of Manchester with me strapped on the back to see the movie *Stormy Weather*. I also remember that there wasn't much jazz in it, despite its title. Movies of this era didn't feature black people unless they were in the roles of maids, servants or savages – so I avidly sought out any movie that had even a hint of jazz or swing in it.

There was a time during Beryl's marital woes when she disappeared and left us in the care of a woman called Winnie Thomas. She had once been a ladies' maid to the nobility in the south of England and was the stepdaughter of the woman who used to be Beryl's home help. I can only recall that she was very strict, rather nasty and the least motherly sort imaginable, totally lacking in humour or compassion. Days and nights were miserable for Philip and me, as we pined for the return of our mother. Eventually she came back.

At nine years old I went to Bramhall Primary School, which was fairly easy to get to from Acre Lane. By now I'd learned to ride a bike, after several falls a couple of years before. I still remember my first unaided ride, when Beryl let go of the saddle: I felt so elated and free. I could cycle to school and feel somewhat grown-up as I travelled through Bluebell Woods, with its glorious smells and the bright blue swathes of colour lining the pathway.

I occasionally acted up in class and got summoned to the front of the room, where I would have to hold my hand out and get the cane. The teacher would sometimes use a long wooden ruler to hit us, and, because of its sharp edge, this would hurt even more than the regulation cane. God, did that sting!

The war came a step closer to home when the field next door was commandeered by the Air Force and bulldozers disturbed the tranquillity of Acre Lane. They ripped up the front hedge, laid a wide concrete driveway and surrounded acres of farmland with barbed-wire fencing. I've no idea what they used the camp for, because there never seemed to be much activity – just ugliness.

The local double-decker bus conductor was a friendly guy called Fred, who always helped us with our collections of cigarette cards. As the bus used to wait ten minutes before returning to Stockport, we got to sit with Fred and feel connected to worldly places. Cigarette cards came in many series, usually numbering fifty to a set: they covered subjects ranging from the flowers of England to military uniforms of all countries. I loved them.

As my interest in music grew, I discovered that my father kept a banjo, a mandolin and a couple of guitars in felt-lined cases under the bed. I used to lift the lid and pluck the strings, but wasn't allowed full access without supervision. He also had a ukulele, which was more my size: as I was devoted to George Formby, he allowed me to take it out and strum its four strings. I once heard him play a duet with Beryl with him on guitar and her on mandolin. They must have practised a lot in the college days.

Another favourite pastime among boys of my age group was trainspotting. This meant going to Grove Lane railway bridge a mile away, and with pencil and official book we'd watch for hours for any 'namers' to tick off in the manual: these were the express passenger trains. Due to the fame of the Mayall cotton-spinning empire in the previous century, there was even a John Mayall train plate. I was really thrilled on the day that I saw it swoosh by at a high speed with a double puff of smoke.

One day, on the way back from trainspotting at the railway bridge, Philip and I met a local tramp who we'd often seen hanging around the neighbourhood. We weren't unduly worried when he asked us to follow him into a nearby field, where he said there were some great blackberries. However, once we were out of sight of the main road, he reached for his flies and revealed his penis, which he invited us to inspect. He referred to it as his 'spotted dick' and asked us to play with the nice 'dolly'.

At this point we realised that something definitely didn't feel right, and we fled at high speed. We duly reported it to Beryl, who warned us to stay clear of all and any strangers in the future. We didn't need to be reminded again after that incident: the experience couldn't have been a more appropriate deterrent.

But nothing could stop us from enjoying the countryside. When winter came around, we always hoped there would be snow. When it came, we would pile on our scarves and gloves and run out to the lawn. I still remember the sound of crunching snow as we tried to build the biggest snowmen in the world. I really enjoyed playing with Philip, but I soon got frustrated by his unwillingness to stay out for very long. One snowball strike was usually enough to send him scurrying back into the house, where it was warm. He absolutely hated the cold, which used to infuriate me. I'd yell and shout, but to no avail. It got so bad that I used to hate him in the wintertime.

We had a copse, or small wood, just across the road, which was a great place to play adventure games of the Robin Hood variety. There were quite a few monkey-puzzle trees, which were exotic but impossible to climb, because of the sharp scales on their bark. In one of the darker sections of the woods, an owl once attacked me. I remember looking up, and the next thing I knew, it came out of nowhere and pecked me on the forehead. There was lots of blood, but my tears came more from fright than actual injury. Still, I was lucky its beak missed my eye.

We also enjoyed the suburbs. Philip and I would go into town to spend the day at Grandad's butcher's shop. It may sound strange, but we used to inhale the aroma of the fresh animal carcasses in the huge walk-in freezer, and time ourselves to see how long we could stay inside in the cold, with the door closed. I helped Grandad wrap the meat as he cut it up to order, and during the quiet times we'd go and sit together by the fire in the back room and keep it topped up with coke, coal being in limited supply. There were the latest comics to read, and he taught me a rhythmic trick like a mambo with hand slaps, handclaps and elbow thumps. It took me a while to get it down like he did, but once it was learned I've never forgotten it – and it has served me well in impressing drummers all my life.

A few blocks down the road was a fascinating antique shop whose name alone was guaranteed to capture my imagination – 'J. Blood'. I was interested in weaponry, and the shop stocked many of these items. To this day I don't know where the money came from, but thanks to Christmas and birthday presents I eventually owned a cavalier's sword with an ivory handle; a Russian executioner's sword; a nineteenth-century gentleman's sword stick; a chainmail vest; and a couple of antique daggers in exotic scabbards. My friends and I were therefore fully armed, with real weapons, when we played our games – and this inevitably led to an accident.

I can't remember exactly what happened, but one day one of our gang threw the executioner's sword at Philip: it went sailing at him point first and hit him just above the ear. Blood flowed, but luckily I was carrying a World War One army first aid kit containing a cushioned bandage. I applied a field dressing and led the injured soldier home. It was a nasty, triangular wound, and stitches were required at Stockport Infirmary.

Another mishap occurred when I climbed a tree across from Baldwin's Post Office and the branch I was hanging from, parallel to the ground, snapped. I plunged ten feet and, still clutching the broken branch, landed heavily on my back and was severely winded. I lay there, stunned and unable to move. It felt as if I'd broken every bone in my body.

Philip ran home with the alarming news. "Mummy?" he said. "John's fallen out of a tree, although I don't think he's dead!" By the time she arrived on the scene, I'd got my breath back and realised that there was nothing broken.

Another accident took place in the back garden of the bungalow, which I'd converted into a 'Red Indian' camp complete with firepit, lookout post and a couple of tents. We used to dress up as authentically as possible, with loincloths, home-made feathered headdresses, bows and arrows and capes that flowed behind us as we rode bareback round Acre Lane on our bikes.

One day, my friend Rodney Goodchild started to fool around, making a big show out of lighting the campfire. When it didn't seem to be burning fast enough, he began to fan it with the long chintz cloak that was tied round his shoulder and one armpit.

All of a sudden the edge of his cape caught fire, and within seconds flames were shooting up his back. As he screamed in agony, I rolled him round in the dirt until the flames were extinguished. Afterwards, the sight was pretty horrifying. Black and red flakes of peeling flesh fluttered from his back and sides; when he was taken to hospital, I was told that I'd probably saved his life. Rodney was in the burns unit for quite some time and had to have serious skin grafts.

Safely away from such danger and ensconced in a cinema seat, I thought Elizabeth Taylor was the most gorgeous girl on the silver screen; her *Lassie Come Home* was a real tearjerker for all ages, and I fell in love with her. The following year she got me again with *National Velvet*.

My hero George Formby ruled once more in *Get Cracking* and *Bell-Bottom George*. By now, I'd got Formby's *Ukulele–Banjo Tutor Book* and, using my father's donated instrument, I began to learn the basic four-string chords that later became the basis of my guitar style.

In November, at the age of ten, I got my first records – two twelve-inch 78s with Ravel's 'Bolero' on three sides and de Falla's 'Ritual Fire Dance' on the final side. With my father's help, I gradually began to build my own record collection. At nights I was lulled to sleep by the records of Eddie Lang, Lonnie Johnson and Django Reinhardt.

Domestic drama resumed when my mother's old flame Michael Doyle, from the partying days and nights in London, showed up out of the blue at the front door. He brought with him a Swiss nobleman, Count Kurt Vehensler, who I realise sounds like a character from a romantic novel. Obviously Beryl's genius for attracting scoundrels hadn't lost its power. A no-good Irishman and an unpredictable count from an estate in Lugano – just what my already disrupted family in suburban Bramhall needed.

Curiously, my father didn't seem to mind too much when they moved in with us – at least, not until it became apparent that Mr Doyle had serious designs on his wife. As the romance rekindled, Doyle painted a rosy picture of them running off together to London, where they would look for a place and send for the children when they were settled. Blinded by love, Beryl made up her mind to go with him, which meant that arrangements needed to be made for the care of we three kids.

Obviously, there was no way in the world that Murray could manage us alone, but after much discussion he agreed to let Beryl go with Doyle. The plan was that Philip and I would be put into a boarding school for an indefinite period, while Caroline – still only three years old – would go to Cornwall to stay with Murray's sister, our Auntie Eileen.

Now, it was 1943 and London was in chaos, with bombs being dropped and all sorts of wartime upheaval. Nonetheless, Beryl,

Michael and the count packed their bags and headed south to stay in a hotel until more permanent accommodation could be found. My mother was cut up at the prospect of losing her children: letting us go almost broke her heart.

Philip and I were sent to boarding school in Alderley Edge. It was a grim place called the Ryleys Preparatory School for Boys. This was the beginning of a pretty unhappy year for me, dominated by the dreadful internment at Ryleys. I missed home terribly and couldn't find any kindness or humanity in the teachers. The headmaster was a Mr Eaton Woodhouse, who was dominated by his wife, a real battleaxe of a school matron. She was built like a battleship and was the terror of my life, especially one night in the dormitory when she busted me in the act of reciting crude poems to my contemporaries.

My knowledge of rude limericks and bawdy verse stemmed from my father's collection of naughty seaside postcards and scrapbooks. I copied out the funniest material into a little notebook of my own. These recitals made me quite a popular kid after the lights were out.

This particular evening I was standing on the window ledge with the curtains drawn in front of me; for each presentation I would sweep aside the drapes with a great flourish, shouting, "For my next verse..." and then launch into a rhyme. This time I failed to notice that the dorm had gone quiet: when I threw back the curtains there was Mrs Woodhouse in all her outrage. I think I'd just started to recite a scatological version of 'There's a one-eyed yellow idol to the north of Kathmandu' which began as 'There's a dirty gent's urinal to the south of Waterloo'.

This was hardly explicit material, but nonetheless it meant a trip to the headmaster's study for six of the best. "Bend down and touch your toes," I was told, and then the carefully selected cane would slash across my bare buttocks, leaving behind six red welts. Afterwards, I couldn't sit or lie down on my back for hours. I was in tears. I thought it was all so unjust – after all, I was only trying to be popular in the only way that seemed to work.

Of the subjects I was taught, the one I loathed most was Latin. I could never see what point there was in learning a dead language, and I didn't care for the teacher either. He was a portly old guy with a crusty skin condition: he always smelled funny from the boric powder that he put on his face and which left a white film on his black jacket. He was highly unsavoury. Rumour had it that he was drunk a lot of the time, which didn't surprise me.

It's hard to say which I hated most – Latin, arithmetic, football or cricket. The last of these was certainly the most tiresome, and also the most dangerous. If I was posted at silly mid-off – a well-named position, I think – there was every chance that the hard leather ball would hit me right in the face. I still remember what it felt like when one got me at point-blank range in the groin. I had to feign illness or incompetence to avoid as many games as I could. When summer ended, we had to play football – a wet and dirty game, and essentially one more chance to get cold and bedraggled.

Mealtimes were another bane of my life. Thanks to wartime food shortages, leftovers on our plates were not tolerated. Everything had to be eaten, and for me this became a threat every morning at breakfast when the inevitable rashers of bacon were served. English bacon is rarely crispy at the best of times, but the stuff we were given was barely cooked at all and was mostly fat. My only hope was to smuggle the rancid stuff out of the dining hall in my jacket pocket. In time, the pockets became so clotted with congealed fat that the garment became known as the 'bacon suit'.

The local wildlife wasn't too pleasant either. There was a barn near the gym, infested with vermin. One day, a gang of us hunted down a huge rat and I was the brave lad among us who bludgeoned it with a shovel. I didn't let on that I was scared to death of it.

The one bright side to the Ryleys experience was the deep pond in the grounds that was used as a swimming pool, and it was there that I learned to swim. I'd seen other boys having fun jumping in and swimming, so I chose a time when no one was around and struck out from the side. I was confident that I'd make it across because, once at the deep end, I'd have no other choice. Luckily, I didn't think about the possible consequences of not being able to swim.

I was so miserable that I tried to run away from school, despite having no idea where home was. I was once at large for all of fifteen minutes after climbing out of the headmaster's study window and pelting as fast as I could to freedom. By the time I reached the front gates and found them open, I thought I'd made it – but I'd been seen. Mr Woodhouse's legs were longer than mine and he caught up with me about a hundred yards down the lane. I hadn't even cleared the school grounds when I was dragged back to renew my sentence, with detention thrown in to add to my misery. I cried my eyes out.

In 1944, the war accelerated and Hitler began assaulting London with new weapons that were fiendish in that they didn't have to be dropped from planes. They were the V1 and V2 rocket bombs, and the casualties they inflicted were enormous. Over 3,000 Londoners died in the first few weeks, and evacuations began in earnest. Every day, children with their labelled nametags were being put on trains to the country.

On June 6, D-Day took place in Europe. With the Americans adding their mighty force to the Allies, there was quite a lot of hope among the populace. This was reflected in the music on the airwaves. We were listening to The Andrews Sisters doing 'Don't Fence Me In', 'Rum And Coca Cola' and 'Boogie Woogie Bugle Boy'. Many prominent showbusiness people were doing their bit for the war effort, either as entertainers of the troops or as active servicemen – sometimes with sad consequences. The actor Leslie Howard became an Air Force pilot and was shot down, while Glenn Miller's plane went missing.

Back home, or rather back at the two homes that my mother and father now inhabited, things were going from bad to worse. Murray was unable to face the thought of Beryl and her lover Michael living in London, and decided to seek revenge. He forbade her from seeing Philip and me, even instructing the headmaster at Ryleys that she wasn't allowed to visit us.

She and Michael subsequently broke up. As she later recalled: "My Irishman was unreliable and didn't have a care in the world, so I didn't know what to do. I thought, 'I'll not stay with Michael Doyle any longer. It's so fruitless and there's no end to it.' I saw no way of getting anywhere, because he just wasn't interested in getting a place."

In the meantime, the mighty Count Kurt Vehensler had been waiting on the sidelines, so to speak. When Beryl split with Michael, he took the opportunity to pounce, using his wealth, influence and charm to get her fixed up in a gorgeous and expensive flat in Queen's Gate Terrace with a very nice friend of his called Joan. Its location, just round the corner from Hyde Park, was very pleasant indeed – but without her children, my mother's life became increasingly miserable.

To give an example of how empty her days had become, she once took the train up to Alderley Edge and stayed for a weekend at a hotel there, hoping to get a glimpse of Philip and me on a school hike to the village. Seeing us so near, without us knowing she was there, broke her heart. Only her fear that Murray would find out about her illicit visit stopped her from crying out to us. She had no idea what new punishment he might devise if he knew she'd disobeyed him.

We had to stay at Ryleys over Christmas 1944. I had been given the present of a Santa Claus outfit and decided to make the rounds of each boy's bed on Christmas Eve, asking each of them what they wanted for Christmas. As I stood there, matron burst through the door and I was marched in my red costume down to Mr Woodhouse's study. I had to wait in silence for what seemed like an eternity for him and his wife to return from whatever festive occasion they'd been attending. It was doubly humiliating to have to lift up my Santa costume, bend over and receive six stinging slashes of the cane. I have never felt more lonely and homesick than at that moment.

On May 7, 1945, the war in Europe ended and VE Day was celebrated. A flood of documentation revealed the horrors of the Nazi concentration camps. At the cinema we were shocked to see the dreadful, staring eyes of the emaciated living dead in the camps – our first revelation of the Holocaust. Corpses, white and skeletal, were strewn about like discarded trash across the barren wastelands of Buchenwald and Treblinka.

By the time I left Ryleys that summer, President Truman had authorised the dropping of atomic bombs on Hiroshima and Nagasaki. VJ Day was the finale to the dreadful years of warfare.

Before saying farewell to the war years, I'd like to make a list of common items that will forever be connected with my childhood. Most of these products, slogans, occupations and objects are now gone and all but forgotten, but I wish to preserve their memory here.

Air raid wardens, Andrews Liver Salts, ATS, barrage balloons, Bemax, Bile Beans, Bird's Custard, blackout curtains, Bournville Cocoa, Cadbury Milk Tray, Camp Coffee with chicory, Champion, Churchman's No. 1, cod liver oil, Duraglit, Everybody's, Gert and Daisy, Home Guard, Kensitas, *Knockout*, *Lilliput* 9d, Lux Pure Soap Flakes, McDougalls Self Raising Flour, *Men Only* 1/3d, Ovaltine, Oxydol, *Picture Post*, Players Navy Cut Cork Tipped, *Punch*, Rinso, Rowntrees Cocoa, Sloan's Liniment, Swan Vestas: The Smoker's Match, *Tatler*, *Tiger Tim's Weekly* 2d, *Tiny Tots* 2 1/2d, Triumph, Typhoo Tea, Vim, WAAFs, Wheat Flakes, *Woman's Own*, WRNS... It's impressive to think that a few of these names are still around! That's longevity for you.

CHAPTER 3

OPEN UP A NEW DOOR:
WAR AND THE BLUES

The war ended, and so did our imprisonment at the dreaded prep school. Back at the bungalow, Auntie Eileen delivered our sister Caroline into our mother's arms, and Philip and I were liberated from the depressing drudgery of Ryleys. Never did the word 'home' mean so much.

I believe we went to the seaside that summer. I'll always remember the boarding house breakfast in St Anne's-on-Sea when, lo and behold, we were served cornflakes, which tasted delicious after five years of plain wheat flakes. We also got to see bananas again, which had been sorely missed.

The family drama didn't abate just because World War Two was over, of course. Back in London, Count Vehensler confessed to my mother Beryl that he'd always worshipped her from afar and promised her a chance for happiness with him back in Switzerland. We children would have a home, he said, and apparently life would be wonderful. The only snag was that Beryl didn't love him, but this matter wasn't about to stand in the count's way. If anything, it made him even more persistent. His attentions grew more unwelcome and eventually he went too far: Beryl said that he nearly raped her one night, although fortunately she managed to fend him off. I think he realised that he'd crossed a line at that point.

My mother's room-mate, Joan, emerged as the voice of reason and came to Beryl's aid with some sensible advice. She urged her to call my father Murray and get something sorted out. Putting aside her pride, Beryl duly phoned him and called a truce. He came down to London on the train and she promised to come back home to him, with all forgiven. She was desperate to reunite with us children and was ready to agree to any condition that would accomplish that end. For his part, Murray promised to reform his habits in order to keep his job. He did make an effort – at first.

So now we were all together again at the bungalow. The marital situation didn't improve, however. Beryl moved in with Philip and Caroline and I moved into the nursery, when things between my parents became too horrible. My mother took to locking the door at night so we wouldn't be disturbed.

By now, I think my father had got used to the idea that his marriage was over. He was already getting involved with the woman who would later become his second wife. Ten years younger than Beryl, her name was Gwen, and she seemed much more in tune with him, as she too liked to have a drink.

Beryl was also looking for a way out and told her father how bad things had become. In a second he told her, "Come and live with us."

This didn't appeal to Ma Leeson at all, who had hysterics at the thought of all the extra work, but there was no other solution but to make the move from 1 Acre Lane to number 23 on the same road. Beryl wanted nothing from the bungalow but our clothes and toys, so our possessions easily fit on Charley Downing's horse-drawn cart and a wheelbarrow.

We children didn't know the reasons for the exodus and found it pretty exciting. In spite of the years of trial caused by our inebriated dad, we'd been amazingly well shielded from the worst of it by Beryl. I imagine most of the quarrels between them took place after we were asleep.

Once we'd unloaded our things at Grandad's, Philip and I shared the front upstairs bedroom, Beryl and Ma Leeson shared the middle room's double bed, and Caroline slept in an annex to their room. Grandad, who hadn't slept with his wife in years, set up in the tiny back bedroom above the kitchen. Ma Leeson didn't particularly like the new arrangements, but she had no other choice.

I began smoking this year, inspired by the more sophisticated movie characters and also by Murray and Grandad, both of whom smoked pipes. Ma Leeson didn't smoke, but she kept a box of expensive Passing Clouds cigarettes for the benefit of her friends, who moved in upper-class circles and for whom showing off was everything.

I found the contents of the box very tempting, and it wasn't long before I was dipping in there for one or two, assuming that they wouldn't be missed. Of course, you can't do that indefinitely, so I had to find other sources of nicotine. I got a cheap Rizla roll-up device which wasn't very efficient but had to suffice. I obtained a packet of papers and began to go round to the three local bus stops and collect people's dog-ends in order to get the tobacco from them. Some people stubbed theirs out only halfway smoked, and these were a big help. All along the gutters I trudged, collecting my fixings. Attractive image, isn't it?

Later, when I could buy my own cigarettes, the first brand I got addicted to was Wild Woodbines, the cheapest on the market and five to a packet. Other popular brands of cigarettes were Park Drive, Turf, Capstan, Craven 'A' and Senior Service, but these were more expensive. I didn't care about the difference in quality, as you'll have gathered from my satisfaction with the treasures of the gutter.

At summer's end my new school was to be Woods Lane Secondary. After the masculinity of Ryleys, the experience of a coeducational environment was just heaven. I enjoyed the art classes: from the time I could hold a pencil, drawing and painting had been my first love. I was also interested in English and woodwork. The latter teacher was very particular about accuracy and was full of verbal tips repeated like mantras throughout the day, such as "Measure twice, cut once" and "A little bit and often".

I learned to use a gouge, a plane, a saw, hot glue, hand drill, brace and bit, varnish and the sanding block. There was no hurrying the procedures and, in all my time at school, I finished only three projects: a blotter, an octagonal teapot stand and a table lamp. These were much appreciated by Beryl, who found a place in the home for them all.

I had the usual teenage hobbies of the day. My friend across the road was Peter Taylor, who showed me how to make a crystal radio set which miraculously picked up the BBC after careful twiddling of the 'cat's whisker'. We also made our own 'telephone' by connecting two empty tin cans with a long piece of string and stretching it across the road to link our two bedroom windows. One of us would speak into the can while the recipient would hold the responding can to his ear. Luckily, there was little traffic along Acre Lane, otherwise we'd have been yanked out of our seats by a passing vehicle.

A Mr Darlington owned a farm and two fields to the left of our house, and it was while playing there that one of his horses kicked me in the balls when I was once foolish enough to stand behind it. Because of this painful incident, I always kept a watchful eye on its hooves' whereabouts when helping with the haymaking or milking.

The larger of Darlington's two fields was massive and had a pond. Around the edges at a certain time of year there was plenty of frogspawn, which we kept in jars. In the garden we had an old porcelain sink filled with water, so that, when the spawn were about to turn into frogs, there would be more room for them. Newts were much harder to catch, but having one of those in your mini-pond carried prestige galore.

In the spring of 1947, as I began my last term at Woods Lane Secondary Modern School, I applied for a scholarship to the Junior Art School in Manchester. Art was my favourite subject, and it was always thought that I was destined to pursue a career in that field. I had built up a small portfolio of paintings and drawings at school and, with these tucked under my arm, I got on the 31 bus to the city and went for my interview.

The one thing I had against me was that the minimum age for acceptance was fourteen, and so I wouldn't qualify until well after the term started in September. However, I must have made a good enough impression on the headmaster, Mr Mayer, for him to let me start there while I was still thirteen.

I was thrilled to be accepted: here was a place where art-related subjects would be on the schedule every day alongside a few token subjects such as English, geography, history and maths. Nothing could have suited me better and I couldn't wait for September to roll around.

On American Independence Day, July 4, Beryl officially gained her own freedom when her divorce became final. My father had been living with Gwen for quite some time, and they lost no time getting married because she was very pregnant with my half-brother Roderick, who was born on September 17. By now our old bungalow had lost its sparkle without Beryl's meticulous attentions, and it began to deteriorate a whole lot more as time went by. Murray and Gwen's lifestyle was more focused on entertaining and drinking than on parenting and cleanliness. In addition, Gwen was a heavy smoker, and the house became victim to rising damp, which couldn't have been healthy.

By the time Roderick's brother Stephen was born on December 27 the following year, things were looking pretty rough for the poor babes. They were left unsupervised most of the time, dressed rather scruffily in what looked like hand-me-down clothing from jumble sales. We often saw them playing in the gutters outside their house with sad eyes and runny noses.

We felt sorry for the two boys, but there was nothing we could do. Since our move to Grandad's we had been under strict instructions never to speak to Murray or have anything to do with him. This was a rather uneasy situation because he and I both had to use the 31 bus once I started at Junior Art School.

My new school was fabulous. From Monday to Thursday, the mornings were taken up with English, geography, history and arithmetic – but because it was an art school, the standards were pretty loose. In my worst subject, maths, I had a kindly teacher named Mr Yates who noticed what a tangle I was getting into with algebra. He patted me on the shoulder and said, "Well, John. Why don't we try some addition instead?" It was very lenient of him, and I'm still grateful, because in the age of calculators I have never needed any maths.

For some unexplained reason, I underwent something of a religious conversion at the age of fifteen and began attending Sunday school. The nice Methodist couple who ran it inducted me into their flock with open arms when I first showed up out of curiosity, or perhaps Sunday boredom. I seem to remember that their sermons were fairly short in length and told Bible tales in a digestible format. I never missed a single Sunday that year and, for my diligence, I was presented with a prize for the best attendance of 1948. It was a hardback copy of *Uncle Tom's Cabin* by Harriet Beecher Stowe, and the flyleaf was commemorated to note my achievement.

I don't think I'd done much serious reading until I got into this book. I found it very supportive of the way I felt about the horrible injustices of slavery, and the sorry plight of the African-American population at the time. This proved highly influential on my views when I became a professional musician.

Up to this point I'd been raised on Murray's record collection, which centred mainly on guitar players and big bands, but in 1948 I came across volumes of school yearbooks that contained a wide variety of articles by past students on many subjects, including one on the birth of boogie-woogie. I felt I'd stumbled into a goldmine as I copied down the exotic-sounding names of Pinetop Smith, Albert Ammons, Meade Lux Lewis, Cow Cow Davenport, Montana Taylor, Jimmy Yancey and Roosevelt Sykes.

As my knowledge grew of who was who in the history of blues and boogie-woogie, I became more and more drawn to this music, heart and soul. I was in awe of the world of America where the music was born: it was hard to compare my lifestyle with the honky-tonks, bars, juke joints and house rent parties that I read about. I read with sadness the story of Pinetop Smith, who was shot to death in a saloon while playing a gig. He was a straight young man, and the shooting was an accident – and so we lost the pioneer who claimed to have invented boogie-woogie.

Now that I had some names to go on, I began to frequent Hime & Addison's record shop on the way to the bus stop, and started to build a collection in this field. My first prized 78 by one of these masters was 'Shout For Joy' by Albert Ammons on one side of a Parlophone record, and 'Bear Cat Crawl' by Meade Lux on the other. This precious disc became my starting point as I waited for my turn on the school piano. I managed to get my fingers in the right positions for the left-hand pattern of a standard boogie in the key of C.

I also played the piano at home, but I was very nervous about doing it when anyone was around, so it took me years to get anywhere close to presentable. Once I got my left hand playing accurately, I added the right hand with a percussive pattern – and I was on my way. I often wonder how I would have played if I'd ever learned to read music and been taught correctly, but a couple of music lessons at Ryleys had long since turned me against this course. I also revered the black American blues players who, being self-taught, developed a style that could never have evolved any other way.

My record collection reflected my obsession with the piano, and I rounded up any record that had the word 'boogie' in it. Most were disappointing, but among the big band names a few stood out: Tommy Dorsey, Freddy Martin, Ray McKinley and some really interesting sides by Freddie Slack.

After heavy persuasion and a tidy offer from my savings, Peter Taylor parted with an RCA Victor American set of four 78s containing eight classic boogie piano duets by Albert Ammons and Pete Johnson. The title was *Eight To The Bar* and I played each piece over and over again until I could pick out a basic facsimile of 'Sixth Avenue Express' on the school piano.

For extra practice I used to go to the home of two sisters and their mother in Bramhall. They let me come round on my bike and shut myself up in the front room to plod away at the keys of their baby grand. It was slow work, because I was conscious that they might be hearing my stumbling attempts to play Ammons and Johnson's 'Pine Creek'.

My record collection began to grow with the addition of some eclectic choices. Sons Of The Pioneers had a big hit with 'Riders In The Sky' and 'Tumbling Tumbleweeds', which I liked because I was into westerns and the cowboy lifestyle of the movies. Teddy Powell had a record featuring a drum solo that filled one side of the disc, and my drummer friend Nev Taylor never tired of listening to it. Ern Pettifer – of whom few people have ever heard – played an amazing clarinet solo on a broken 78 that Murray had discarded. Joe Loss's version of 'In The Mood' made us crack up when the honking tenor sax break came around.

On July 15, Ma Leeson died, quite without warning. Unknown to us, she'd been suffering horribly for quite some time from cancer of the uterus; all we'd been aware of was that she often complained of severe pains and went to bed early. I remember coming home from school one evening and being told that she had died that morning.

The house felt empty without her and, although we were advised not to go into the front room, I nevertheless had to see her for myself. Her body was laid out on the couch and it was an eerie sight. This was my first encounter with a dead body. Nothing can prepare you for seeing someone you know looking like a wax effigy, or a poor imitation of one. When I touched her hand, the flesh was ice cold. It was disturbing, and I left the room and closed the door.

As my final weeks at Manchester Junior Art School drew to a close, we students were sent on job interviews. I was accepted at a large advertising agency, prominently situated in the heart of Piccadilly. I took a week off before showing up bright and early on a Monday morning, eager to make a good impression. The boss showed me round three floors of desks and tables, where I saw people bent over their chores, engrossed in their tasks. I hoped there would be a desk for me somewhere, but soon found out that this wasn't what they had in mind for me. By the time I clocked out at five o'clock, all I'd been required to do was brew tea, tie up parcels, run errands and empty the wastepaper baskets. It was misery with a capital M.

I went home heavy-hearted. After two years of learning to be an artist in society, all I seemed useful for was not getting anyone's lunch orders mixed up. On Friday, I received my wage packet: it amounted to one pound, five shillings and sixpence for a six-day week. I resolved there and then that I wasn't going back.

I felt no guilt at all for failing to show up on Saturday morning. Instead, I sat around at home wondering what on earth I was going to do for a living. I realised that any other job open in this field would end up being the same story, with me doing the same menial tasks at the bottom of the employment ladder.

"Bugger this," I thought. "I'm going to have a summer holiday before figuring out my next move."

So off I went to Rhyl with Beryl, Philip and Caroline, where we had a fortnight to enjoy the sandy beaches, pony rides, pier attractions and the cinema. It helped me to forget my failed career and to get over the loss of Ma Leeson.

After our return, a new era in my social life blossomed at Bramhall Baths. Teenagers gathered there from miles around and good friendships were born. My friends Mike Horrobin, Nev Taylor, Tubby Gator, 'Pooh' Angus and I were the show-off daredevils who used to climb up onto the roof of the indoor swimming pool and drop through the skylight when the attendant wasn't looking. We also used to do running dives off the changing room roofs and dress up in an assortment of wild garments to perform 'Crazy Gang' dives and sight gags off the high board.

One of the special dives I exhibited was called a 'half-pint'. You did this by doubling up and, holding onto one ankle, toppling into the pool. The last time I did this stunt, I forgot to straighten out under water and smashed into the bottom of the shallow end, busting my nose. It was diagnosed as a deviated septum and looked and felt terrible for weeks. I'd performed it with the intention of showing off to the girls, but I don't think it really achieved the magnetic effect I'd hoped for.

It was an age when most boys' talk involved tales of female conquest. To strengthen our belief in ourselves as potential studs, we fixed cardboard strips to our bicycles so that they caught the spokes and made a noise like that of a motor bike. We had a gang of ten and called ourselves 'The Oatmen', as a reference to the ones lucky enough to 'get their oats' – or, in other words, make out with a girl. Although some successes were claimed, it was all bravado based on wishful thinking.

Summer doesn't last forever and, as September 1949 approached, I began job hunting. Having made up my mind that I wasn't going to join another ad agency, I somehow got the idea of pursuing a career in window dressing. I'd always been inspired by the artistic way Kendal Milne, the big department store on Deansgate, designed their Christmas grottos and other displays around the store, so I applied for a position as a junior and was accepted.

I started work at Kendals almost immediately. I was introduced to a dozen interesting people who made up the display department; right off the bat, they seemed extremely friendly and eager to have a lad of fifteen to impress. I could tell straight away that I'd be happy to join them. As a team they set themselves apart from the regular employees of the store, who spent all of their working hours stuck behind a counter waiting on customers. We, on the other hand, were free to wander around from floor to floor, window to window and building to building as often as we pleased, in the course of getting a window display completed.

With wages coming in, I was able to increase my spending power on more records from Hime & Addison's. This was the year when I saw the first long-playing record displayed in the front window, but for now I was finding all the treasures on 78 that I wanted down in the smoky basement. It was a terrific atmosphere in which to flip through the latest releases and second-hand mark-downs. I found a rare copy of Pete Johnson's 'Basement Boogie' backed with 'Death Ray Boogie', and Jimmy Yancey's marvellous piano sides 'Five O'Clock Blues', 'Tell 'Em About Me' and 'Yancey Special'.

Piano blues wasn't my only interest. Ever since hearing Murray's guitar records as a child, I had also found a pathway into this area. His records leaned more towards the jazz side, with people like Django Reinhardt, Teddy Bunn, Charlie Christian, Eddie Lang and Lonnie Johnson. A classic pair of duets by the latter called 'Bullfrog Moan', backed with 'A Handful Of Riffs', led me to finding out about other powerful blues singers.

Lead Belly, for example, had written and recorded 'Goodnight Irene', which was enjoying international acclaim: it sometimes escaped most people's notice that he was a major blues singer and twelve-string guitarist. He had been convicted of first-degree murder and had only avoided a life sentence because of his contributions to American folk music. I had a collection of four 78s with great songs like 'Backwater Blues' – a song that I later incorporated into my own live set – 'On A Christmas Day' and 'Ella Speed'.

Josh White was also popular in Europe, and although he was sometimes unfairly dismissed because he had a smooth style suited to a more sophisticated audience, he was an accomplished player who had, as a youth, been an apprentice to Blind Lemon Jefferson. White recorded some incredible sides on the Asch label. I later performed many of them myself.

In finding out more about these guys, my research led me to their own influences. In Brownie McGhee's case it was Blind Boy Fuller, and in Josh's case it was Blind Lemon Jefferson. I got into the raw music of Jefferson with a record or two containing 'Hangman's Blues', 'Lockstep Blues' and 'Matchbox Blues'. All of these 'race' records of the twenties graphically illustrated the vile racial injustices that were a black man's reality in the American south during the first half of the century.

At the other extreme, I got my first exposure to modern jazz when I bought Charles Mingus's *Shuffle Bass Boogie* for the title track, and found it to be light years ahead of tradition. Johnny Otis's 'Harlem Nocturne' was featured on the B-side: I guess they didn't want to scare people off with too much advanced Mingus.

At Kendals, I was promoted to the position of personal assistant to a chap called Jim Pennington; his department specialised in events of a seasonal nature, such as Christmas and Easter-themed displays – although when I say 'department', it was really just a small room upstairs with a large work table and Jim sitting on a high stool.

I couldn't have been happier. Jim was not only the greatest raconteur I'd ever met, he was gifted with a sense of deadpan humour that kept me constantly amused as we performed the absolute minimum workload. Because our job descriptions were so vague, we could disappear for hours without having our absence noticed. I occasionally left the firm entirely at lunchtime and went to the cinema for a full show at the Manchester News Theatre. This place showed news shorts interspersed with cartoons and comedies. It was here that I first saw several shorts by The Three Stooges and laughed until tears rolled down my face.

Jim quickly became not only my mentor in artistic matters but also my hero, by virtue of his carefree attitude to authority. I had never heard anyone use obscene language in such a humorous way. His sentences were peppered with a veritable gamut of adjectives of the 'bloody-fucking-buggering-shit-bastard-bleeding' variety. He was also into the same sort of literature as I was: horror stories from the pages of the American pulp magazine *Weird Tales*.

On another occasion I found some American comics I'd never heard of before. They were issues 9 and 17 of *Mad* magazine. It was hilarious satire of a kind I'd never seen, and had great artwork by Will Elder and Jack Davis. Inside the front cover there were advertisements for other EC comics, such as *Tales From The Crypt*, *The Vault Of Horror* and *The Haunt Of Fear*. It was a long time before I was able to get my hands on these, and by then they cost a fortune.

I made one or two attempts to secure a girlfriend while working at Kendals. The first was a diminutive girl named Jean Shepherd who worked on the accessories counter on the ground floor. As the windows were almost next to where she worked, there was plenty of opportunity to make myself known to her, see her at coffee breaks and wait for her at the back door to walk her up Market Street to her bus stop in Piccadilly. It was a long enough walk to be able to pluck up courage to hold her hand or link arms.

This was a very big deal for me and I thought I was getting closer to her when she accepted an invitation to visit me. She arrived, we had cups of tea and chatted a while, and then she got the bus back home to Manchester. That was about it. No kisses, and no future.

Another girl named Brenda was rather a flirt, but that was as far as it went. There was also a redhead called Pauline who worked in the toy department: unfortunately, she didn't have much in the way of brains. Conversations of more than five sentences went nowhere. I once arranged a date with her but she didn't show up, so I went home, put 'Pavane For A Dead Princess' on the gramophone, and quietly wept over my inability to be a success with the ladies.

Still, there was always music. My piano playing was coming along nicely by now; I used to go and practise on the pianos in the store windows when nobody needed me for anything. It must have looked weird from the street.

Around this time, Murray took me to Stockport to a dance hall where The Ray Ellington Quartet was playing. I had bought every record they'd released, and I was familiar enough with their repertoire to be allowed to bring a pianist marionette and miniature piano to the show and operate it while Dick Katz took a piano solo. I realise this sounds like an odd thing to do, and I can't imagine how I plucked up the nerve to get up there on stage – but I did it, and people responded politely. Through this stunt I was able to meet Ray and his great musicians Coleridge Goode on bass, Katz on piano and Lauderic Caton on guitar.

This was the year when traditional jazz got into full stride; it was the thing to do to support your local trad band. Manchester's pride and joy was The Saints Jazz Band; I couldn't believe how amazing they were, and didn't understand why they weren't more popular nationally. Humphrey Lyttelton was the most famous bandleader in the country and always the most adventurous when it came to broadening the range of styles in his book. He used saxophones and had a big hit with 'Bad Penny Blues', a rip-roaring boogie-woogie piece featuring Johnny Parker, who I later came to know when he worked with Alexis Korner in 1962.

Other London bands who came up to play at our local venue, the Star Hotel, included Chris Barber and Mick Mulligan with George Melly. Chris was a charming bandleader who had such dedication to his music that he used his own money to bring over American bluesman Jesse Fuller, the one-man band. Chris's wife Ottilie Patterson was the singer, and Lonnie Donegan got his first opportunity to play a few tunes within the show. His music quickly developed into a new phenomenon – skiffle.

Mick Mulligan was the drunkest trumpeter-bandleader I'd ever seen, and I was impressed that he could still play in the state he was in off stage. George Melly sang some great humorous blues songs such as 'Send Me To The 'Lectric Chair'. However, he was rather lecherous: I didn't know he had a thing for boys until he tried to sneak me away from the crowd with his arm round me. I didn't care for that one bit.

As I reached the age of seventeen, Lead Belly's original version of 'Goodnight Irene' was top of the hit parade alongside other biggies of 1950 such as 'C'Est Si Bon' by Louis Armstrong, 'Music! Music! Music!' by Teresa Brewer and an annoying polka called 'Tzena Tzena Tzena'. It was sad that in the very year 'Goodnight Irene' became so well known, its composer never got to reap the benefits of what must have been enormous royalties. Lead Belly had died the previous year and left a hole in blues music that would never be filled.

The good news was that Big Bill Broonzy came over to Europe and settled in Paris for a while. He recorded a new catalogue of solo pieces that exposed him to a new generation unfamiliar with his role in the history of Chicago blues. He had been a major catalyst in the music, kickstarting the careers of Washboard Sam, Jazz Gillum, Memphis Minnie, Josh Altheimer, Memphis Slim and 'Big Maceo' Merriweather. These new songs were released in the UK and I was first in line to add them to my collection. I learned many of these songs and added them to my own repertoire.

My love life finally began looking up when I discovered that a girl called Pat found me somewhat attractive; I took her to the pictures a couple of times. I had built a treehouse in the garden and moved into it, for reasons which are now no longer clear to me, and she joined me at a few parties there. However, these events soon came to an end when the parents of a girl I knew discovered that she was sleeping with her boyfriend. Not under my roof, I might add, but somehow I got the blame, as if I was some sort of corrupting influence. Other parents put the word out that their sons and daughters were hanging out at the Mayall treehouse and therefore we all had to be up to no good. I found myself friendless almost overnight when they banned their kids from coming round to our house.

I was upset and lonely, and turned my thoughts and attention to blues and jazz for solace. I could definitely identify with these guys, who obviously knew what it meant to be unlucky in love and expressed their pain through music. I still hung out at Bramhall

Baths; Nev Taylor and Mike Horrobin were still my best buddies; and most of the regular gang were hanging out there, so my social life wasn't entirely dead.

By September 1951, I had completed my second year at Kendals. I was very happy and settled in, but once more things were about to change. This happened when an ominous brown envelope arrived, bearing the stamp 'On Her Majesty's Service'. It was the dreaded letter summoning me to report for my National Service.

CHAPTER 4

KILLING TIME: NATIONAL SERVICE AND KOREA

Until 1960, all British men were called up to do two years in the army when they reached the age of eighteen – and now my time had come. I heard that the alternative was to be a conscientious objector, but no one I knew had any idea how one went about doing this – and I was worried that I might have to go to jail instead. I didn't consider that to be a fun option.

In early December I responded to the draft and was herded into a small lecture room where a smart, fresh-faced lieutenant began to outline the life of a Royal Engineer. He pointed out that, although National Service was compulsory, there was a new scheme in force to make the package more attractive. By signing on as a regular soldier for a third year, the benefits far exceeded anything the draft had to offer. You would be entitled to twice the amount of leave per year, the pay was almost a third more than that received by ordinary servicemen, and there would be an almost certain guarantee of early promotion.

I was very impressed by this, and began to pity the poor idiots who were going to put up with the obviously inferior two-year deal. I absorbed all the convincing rhetoric outlining the three-year offer's advantages, and after half an hour I was ready to sign my life away. I strutted back to Kendals, confident that I'd done the best thing – although Jim Pennington's downcast face made me wonder if I'd done something I would regret.

The army recruiters had told me they would notify me when they were ready for me, and so I settled in for a Christmas at home. Before we took our break, Jim and I made a beautiful and extremely elaborate miniature of the Swiss Alps to constitute the main theme of the Santa Claus grotto on the top floor. The project took several weeks, and we took pride in constructing everything meticulously to scale. I made some highly detailed cardboard Swiss chalets that were very much admired; Kendals let me take them home afterwards. They ended up as part of Beryl's treasure trove.

By now, I couldn't tolerate the popular songs that made the current hit parade, such as Johnnie Ray's 'Cry', so I avoided the radio, turned to my records even more, and buried myself in blues and jazz. Given the popular music climate, it was little wonder that few people could relate to the boogie-woogie and blues I was playing on the piano. By now Murray had given me one of his guitars, but it had a pretty high action, so I took off the fifth and sixth strings. This allowed me to master the chords I'd learned from George Formby's *Ukulele–Banjo Tutor Book*.

On March 15, 1952 I received my notice to appear for National Service, and packed a suitcase containing the permitted items listed on the form they sent me. With an army train pass in hand, I said goodbye to Beryl and Grandad and headed for the railway station.

I had to change trains twice in order to get to Great Malvern, where the basic training was to take place, and I was already homesick. I found myself close to tears as I stared out of the window at the English countryside flashing by. I don't think I could have felt more alone than I did at that point.

At my destination, I was met by the sight of other hapless youths, milling around on the platform and waiting to load into the trucks that would take us to the Royal Engineers' transit camp. What a cold and desolate place that was. We were herded into huge Quonset hangars containing rows of beds to which we were assigned, in no particular order.

Immediately, the only question on everyone's lips was "How many days are left to do?" Most of the guys had calculated the number of days they needed to complete in their two-year service period and were already counting down. At that moment, it sank in that I'd sealed my doom by signing on for three years. The thought of 365 extra days trapped in the army seemed akin to a life sentence. There were one or two other gullible lads like me, and we were mocked unanimously by the short-term conscripts. I guess it made them feel superior.

After a couple of days, 'volunteers' were asked to shovel coal or peel mountains of potatoes; the rest of the time we lay around on our beds waiting for something to happen. We were eventually issued with uniforms, greatcoats, pay-books, medical records and a number. I was now the property of the British Army and had become #22796042 Sapper Mayall, J. of the Royal Engineers. Perhaps this sounds impressive: in fact, it was just the first step in the process of turning us into robots.

Once our paperwork was in order, we received our postings to various training camps dotted around the country. I was assigned to Farnborough in Hampshire, and was fairly happy with that location until I actually got there. I was swept into a whirlwind of radical discipline and disorientation, with the first stop on our road to debasement the barber shop, where we were shorn of all our hair. I'd had what I considered a short haircut before I left home, thinking that it would be acceptable, but these guys were merciless. They pressed the electric clippers close to the napes of our necks and didn't let up the pressure until way past the top of our heads. Great clumps of hair fell to the floor, and minutes later our heads resembled hard-boiled eggs.

I was assigned to a billet that housed about twenty-four 'sprogs' – the term for raw recruits – and a lance corporal, who had his own room at the end of the barrack. From four in the morning until the lights went out at ten o'clock at night, we were screamed at and ordered around until we were dizzy and wracked with fatigue and confusion. No sooner had you drifted into a deep sleep than the blazing lights went on and yells of reveille wrenched you into a living nightmare.

Shouts of "Hands off cocks and on socks!" had us scrambling around, trying to get washed in cold water, get dressed and be

Pretty standard procedure for young babes totally unaware of what is happening.

I was born to be climbing trees from an early age and totally fearless of great heights.

I seem to be giving my faithful teddy bear Edward a ride in our driveway. I always loved my bike too!

My sister, Caroline, pointing out the camera as brother Philip and I try to look good. I always wore my red cap in those days.

Beryl almost gets cut off in this family photo at home with Grandad, Ma Leeson, Philip, Caroline and me.

Philip and me with Beryl on a pebbly beach summer holiday in Aldeburgh.

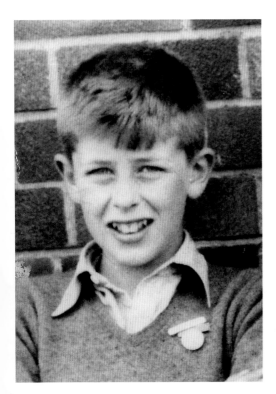

An early school photo with me trying to look grown up.

I prided myself as an acrobat swinging from the heights of the oak tree below my treehouse.

At home in my treehouse playing guitar with pin-up photos adorning every wall surface. Loved those pictures!

I was totally crazy to be risking my life standing on the roof of my treehouse! Only did this once for the camera!

Family album photo of Grandad and Ma Leeson on their wedding day.

An early photo of Beryl on a beach in Aldeburgh with her favourite spaniel dog before I was born.

My father, Murray, with his favourite guitar and a banjo he rarely played.

Trying to appear casual in these pre-army days photos.

1954

Posing with a couple of snakes wrapped round my arms outside my tent in Korea.

Me with my squadron before the army shipped me to Korea.

An army photo from my time in Korea before the hard winter set in.

Standing outside the army camp gates in Haslemere. Note my freshly painted shoes and neat appearance!

outside with rifles on parade while it was still dark. Roll call was designed to last as long as possible for our discomfort, and then we were quick-marched to breakfast in the canteen before being rushed back to barracks, where we made our beds in the regulation manner and stood by for inspection by the sergeant major. We hoped and prayed that we'd remembered to lay out our kit in exactly the way it was supposed to be.

There was plenty of tension and loud reprimands to put the fear of God into us, and then we were rushed outside to the parade ground for more inspection and drill, until our feet were blistered from the unforgiving new boots. Out on the parade ground, we were taught how to slope arms, order arms, present arms, stand at ease and stand easy, in addition to learning everything there was to know about the M1 rifle and how it was now your best friend.

We learned how to form three ranks, make left, right and about turns, left and right wheels, halt and "By the left quick march". It was laughable to see us getting our directions mixed up and to see some poor blighter separated from the column by making a left turn instead of a right. As for the slow march, we were truly a pitiful sight, creeping about like zombies until the drill sergeant would berate us with cries of "You 'orrible shower of shit!"

Days and nights quickly became a blur. The four weeks devoted to basic training encompassed weapon training and the use of rifles, grenades and mortars. We were also made to endure obstacle courses, crawling in mud under barbed wire, scaling high walls and climbing ropes. We peeled potatoes until our hands withered from the cold water, not forgetting the endless task of 'bulling' boots. We were given two pairs with surfaces that were initially rough and bumpy: we were required to make them so smooth that you could use them as a mirror. The method was to take a hot iron and gradually sear the leather until the bumps were gone, and then apply spit and polish until they reached the acceptable look. This required hours and hours of patience.

At the end of each day, after dinner was over, you bought your cigarettes from the NAAFI and wearily returned to your barrack room. All you would see were rows and rows of worn-out recruits, endlessly rubbing their toecaps with rotating applications of boot polish and water until the last scream of the day announced "Lights out in five minutes!"

We were issued with two battle dresses: one for everyday wear and the other – your 'best BD' – for parades and special occasions. They were made out of serge, and knife-edged pleats and creases were supposed to be the correct look, although the thickness of the material made these almost impossible to accomplish. We used to get razor blades and 'comb' as much excess fluff off as we could in order to make the fabric thinner. It was a hellish, monotonous task.

In addition to the constant ritual of keeping our boots gleaming and our uniforms pressed, we had to spend an hour every night applying Blanco to our belts. This was a pale green liquid that, when dry, left a chalky matte finish that got dirty easily and showed up the slightest mark or scuff. Belt, buckles, badges and buttons all had to be cleaned and polished with Brasso or Duraglit, and you had to be careful that none of these cleaning agents got on the fabric of your jacket or beret.

Somehow I survived the drilling, the route marches with thirty-pound backpacks and rifles, and the constant abuse. At the end of basic training, we had evolved into fully trained, mindless soldiers who could now look down on the next batch of raw recruits with scorn and superiority. After the ceremonial graduation parade, we were granted thirty-six hours' leave; I headed home, even though the travel time ate into my free time considerably. The taste of home-cooked meals was welcome, and there was nothing like a proper cup of tea after the bromide-laced stewed brew we had got used to at camp.

Around this time, a newspaper called the *Weekly Overseas Mail* printed a story about me. It didn't mention that I was in the army, instead implying that I was still happily living in my treehouse.

JOHN'S HOUSE IS UP A TREE
by Harry Giltrap

EIGHTEEN-YEAR-OLD John Mayall is often missing from his Cheadle Hulme home in Cheshire – but his mother doesn't worry. For she knows he is quite safe up in the tree-top house he has built for himself. Safe did I say? Well, almost. I climbed a rickety 30ft ladder, struggled through a trapdoor and found myself in a snug little den perched precariously among the branches of an old oak tree.

"Don't worry," John reassured me with a smile, as the wind gave the illusion that we were in a ship at sea. "The house has been up for four years without any serious mishap."

The house that John built is made of scrap wood, corrugated iron, glass and tarpaulin. It is 15ft long by 6ft wide and took only a week to construct. It can accommodate 15 people and there are bunks to sleep four. Here without interference, John and his friends carry out their hobbies – listening to jazz records, painting, puppetry and horror make-ups. While searching through his 300 records, John found that I was not the only visitor for a house martin had nested in one of the shelves that line the walls. Spare space on the walls is decorated with artist John's own murals and 250 pin-ups.

The next four weeks were rather different, because we now began the specialised training that would determine our future occupations, although we had only two choices. You could be a field engineer or a clerk. The former required you to be out in all weathers, building bridges, putting up and taking down fences, clearing minefields and generally being ahead of the front-line troops, making it safe for them to advance towards the enemy. The latter would qualify you to sit in a warm office shuffling papers.

I instantly knew which one I preferred.

Without a moment's hesitation, my hand shot up to volunteer immediately for office work. This was not only the easiest decision I ever made while in service, but also the only time I was allowed to decide anything.

We had to learn a great deal about the usage of army forms, how the administration worked and, most important of all, how to type. Although they instructed us in the correct way to do this, using all ten digits, I took an ill-advised shortcut and ended up getting the right speed to pass the exam by using my first fingers and thumb only. If only I'd taken the time to learn the right way, I would have probably doubled my speed by now.

At this time, the war in Korea was claiming a lot of British soldiers. In the last week before our postings were announced, everyone was hoping that they wouldn't be sent to this potentially fatal destination. Imagine my relief when I found that I'd been posted to a small camp of only 100 men in the heart of the Surrey countryside.

Fernhurst was located halfway between Midhurst and Haslemere, and the name of the unit was 12 Field Survey Squadron. On arrival, I was allocated to Headquarters Troop and was suitably content with my surroundings. I couldn't get over how different the place was from the frenzy and chaos of Farnborough. We were billeted in huts that held only a dozen or so men. In the office there was a room for the captain, and in the only other room there was a chief clerk and one other guy besides me. The major in command didn't appear much, and life was very easy and casual. Apart from the morning parades for roll call, there was very little to do in the way of regimented activity.

The only thing I didn't like was that every so often the rotation for guard duty would come my way, which meant night shifts in the guardhouse. We'd be required to patrol the camp every two hours till dawn, and at 4 a.m. it was murder trying to stay awake. For fortification we had metal mugs full of horrible, stewed tea. The trick was to keep a watch out for an unscheduled check by the duty officer, who could appear at any time between midnight and dawn to make sure you were alert. You had to challenge him with "Halt – who goes there?"

We were granted leave on a regular basis for weekends and, as we were so near to London, I really wanted to see the city for the first time. I didn't know anyone who lived there but, through some means or another, I got myself a pen pal with a view to planning a weekend trip. Letters went back and forth between myself and this guy, until a rendezvous was set and I got the train to London.

As arranged, my new pen pal met me at Euston Station. He appeared to be a nice enough guy and took me to his flat in the West End, where I dumped my bag before setting out to enjoy the bright lights of Soho. Girls were uppermost in my mind, and it wasn't long before I was lured into a nightclub by a young lady who promised me a good time. I didn't know it, but it was a clip joint: each time a hostess cuddled up to me at one of the small tables, I was forced to buy her and myself a drink. I didn't drink alcohol, but my glass of fruit juice cost as much as a large whiskey, and she had to be treated to a much more expensive beverage that was probably coloured water. Within fifteen minutes I ran out of money.

I left in a hurry, feeling cheated, and settled for exploring Soho on foot. It cost nothing to see all the bright lights of Piccadilly, the neon, the cinemas and the back alleys. In doorways everywhere, hookers offered their services, but I was much too shy to contemplate their offers and kept walking.

Eventually I took the Tube back to my friend's flat. I looked around his room but saw nowhere for me to sleep. He said, "Oh, it's okay. My bed is big enough for two." Confronted with no other option, I undressed, lay down as close to the wall as I could and fell asleep.

Sometime during the night, I woke up to the feel of hands on my chest and discovered that this guy was rubbing himself against my buttocks. I shot up in bed, lashed out and shook him loose. He said he was just trying to get warm and that he'd thought I wouldn't mind him cuddling up. I firmly told him that he'd got the wrong idea about me, and that he'd better keep his distance.

I thanked him next morning for his hospitality, he apologised for the misunderstanding, and I went back to camp a much wiser person. Despite this incident, it had been terrific to see what London looked and felt like, and I went there several times afterwards.

Back at camp, there wasn't a lot to do for entertainment. As a teetotaller, I was left out of most social occasions, which involved hanging out at the pub across the road getting drunk. Once, at the behest of my barrack-room buddies, I joined them there and tried a glass of local cider. It was a shock to my system; I don't think I even got halfway through the glass before I felt dizzy and had to get out into the fresh air. Drinking was obviously not going to be a part of my agenda – yet.

After that, while my mates were occupied in the pub, I used to keep my ear pinned to the speaker of my radio as I tried to tune in to French radio stations. These were constantly broadcasting jazz and blues. One night, with reception fading in and out, I heard the most powerful boogie record ever and just caught the name of 'Big

Maceo' Merriweather as it ended. It was called 'Chicago Breakdown'. I resolved to get this record one day, as well as anything else Big Maceo had recorded. He was usually backed by Tampa Red on guitar and only recorded for the American Bluebird label, which made the records unobtainable in the UK. To this day, his catalogue of recordings constitutes the most moving and compelling blues and boogie records I've ever known.

When I was at home, I would see my friend Mart Rodger who had various jazz bands in operation; I would sit in with him at gigs. In April 1953 he'd booked himself a gig at Cheadle Hulme Parish Hall and I joined his band for a few tunes on the piano. During the interval, I was struck by the beauty of a dark-haired girl mingling in the crowd. Plucking up courage, I ventured over to her and asked for a dance, even though I could easily have qualified as the clumsiest dancer on the planet. It's a testament to her magnetism that I dared to take her round the dance floor at all, but at least it was a start. I got her address and phone number and permission to call. So began a relationship that lasted for twelve years. Her name was Pamela Heap.

It wasn't long before I found several stumbling blocks to the courtship, mostly to do with her family. Her father, Frank Heap, was a dour and forbidding man who held a high position with the Prudential Insurance Group, so you can imagine what he thought of me – a strange guy who used to live up a tree and about whom rumours abounded of shady goings-on up there. Fortunately, his wife Winifred – who preferred to be called Betty – was much more amenable; she seemed an unlikely match for Frank, although they were devoted to each other.

I got a terrible shock on May 16 when it was announced that the great gypsy guitarist Django Reinhardt had died. Ever since my early childhood I had been constantly exposed to his wonderful music, and my father, of course, was his biggest admirer. I just couldn't believe that such a genius could vanish at the age of forty-three. I shed tears at the thought that his guitar brilliance would be heard no more. His records now seemed all the more precious: I played them over and over as I mourned his passing.

A month later I got a shock of a different kind. It was my understanding that once you got your permanent posting, you were set for the remainder of your service. I'd secured my niche in the office and had a reputation for being a very efficient clerk who took care of all the typing and administrative affairs. Every day I would type up the daily 'Part One Orders', which would list assignments and duties for all, plus the occasional news that some poor sod had been selected from our squadron for a posting to Korea.

The list would come every month from army headquarters, and I would routinely run my finger down the columns to see if our unit was involved. Usually it wasn't – until one day in June, I saw 12 Field Svy Sqn listed with my name next to my destination: Korea.

At first I thought I was seeing things. It couldn't be real – but there was no mistake, and I was the unlucky selection. It gave me chills to have to type my own name on the daily bulletin, although I immediately got a lot of sympathy from my mates. None of us ever expected that any of us would have to go to the war zone.

Once I got over the shock, I applied for two months' leave. These were due to me as a regular soldier if I wasn't going to be able to use the following year's allocation.

As I was finishing up affairs and training someone else to take my place in the office, the news came in that on July 27 an armistice had been signed in Panmunjon, ending the Korean War. This was great news: at least I wasn't likely to die in battle on the other side of the world. Still, there was no escaping the posting, so I packed my bags and duffel bag and went home in July and September to make the most of my remaining time with Pamela. It was ironic that just as I'd found the right girl I should be snatched away from her for a year and a quarter.

While I was at home, I was surprised to get a gold ring from my father with my initials engraved on it. Murray shyly gave it to me when I was at the bungalow one day; it was obviously a very awkward moment for him, as he'd never given me a formal present before. I put it on my little finger, and it has remained there ever since.

★★★

Nothing could have prepared me for the massive size of the troopship *Empire Fowey* when I first saw it docked in Southampton. I'd said my farewells at home, kissed Pamela goodbye and packed for the duration. We were allowed one extra piece of personal, non-army-issue baggage, so I took my four-string guitar.

We set sail on September 2. It was to be a two-month journey to Korea, and our route would take us through the infamous Bay of Biscay where many a seasoned sailor has been known to get seasick. We would then head to Gibraltar through the Mediterranean Sea to Port Said and the Suez Canal, followed by Aden, Colombo, Singapore, Hong Kong and finally Japan. The giant ship pulled out of the harbour and I watched from the deck railings until England was beyond the horizon.

We were allocated our quarters in the lower decks. The bunks were three high and unbelievably close together, with hardly any room to put anything. I had to keep my guitar alongside me in my bunk.

Once we were settled, army discipline and order kicked in and we were given a daily schedule of exercise, fire drills and weapon maintenance. I noticed a message on the bulletin board, asking for anyone who played an instrument to put their name down for possible inclusion in the ship's band. Naturally I lost no time in applying.

By the end of the week, all the musicians had been located; we came with a very strange line-up of instruments. There was a bristly Scottish sergeant major who elected to be the bandleader; considering his rank and ferocious demeanour, nobody challenged his authority or expressed a dislike of his instrument, the accordion. He knew all the standard dance tunes, and in order to hold my position in the band, I had to fake the chords for all the tunes in his repertoire and pretend I knew a lot more than I did.

A drummer held the unit together in the absence of a bass, and an officer called Lieutenant Moon played the alto saxophone. Although he held the most senior rank, he was as intimidated as we were by the sergeant major accordionist.

In addition to the tunes we rehearsed – which kept me away from rifle drill and other unpleasant activities – I put together a solo set of my own to pad out our show. I was singing Lead Belly's 'Backwater Blues', Josh White's 'One Meat Ball' and 'St James Infirmary', and 'I'll Be Ready' by The Spirits Of Rhythm. In our strange way, we all got along despite our differences: the music bonded us, and we enjoyed privileges that our friends down below did not. At the regular ship's dances, we got to wear civilian clothes: I remember the envious looks on the faces of my lower-deck companions as I prepared to mingle with the privileged elite.

My departure for Korea was reported in the *Manchester Evening News* on October 16:

SAPPER JOHN MAYALL, of Cheadle Hulme, sailed for Korea not long ago carrying a heavy kitbag, water bottle, steel helmet, rifle – and a guitar! "Carrying that guitar was more than awkward," he writes to tell me, "but it was worth it." For John played the guitar and sang folk songs, ballads, and blues to the troops and passengers on the ship. In civvy street, 19-year-old John was a keen record collector. Aboard ship he sang the songs of Josh White, Huddie Ledbetter and Big Bill Broonzy – songs remembered from their records.

We went ashore in Aden and I took photos of camels and other sightseeing attractions. The next stop was Colombo in Sri Lanka, where we rode into town in a rickshaw. Traders attempted to pull us into their lairs with promises of dubious attractions. The main event that these guys were soliciting was apparently a woman being sexually mounted by a donkey. I don't know whether this was for real or not, but either way none of us dared to go off with any of these shady entrepreneurs – and in any case, we didn't have the kind of money they were asking for.

At our next stop in Hong Kong, we got off and went for a walk into Kowloon, but by now the attractions and constant bombardment by locals trying to coerce us were getting a bit tedious. We'd been on the ship for weeks and wondered if we were ever actually going to reach Japan and Korea. We relied on these shore trips and were disappointed that we weren't allowed ashore in Singapore for some political reason. Eventually the journey came to an end after eight weeks at sea, and we landed at Kure, Japan.

For an early November day, the weather was surprisingly warm, making my first impression of Japan a pleasant one. Before we bedded down in the transit camp, we were issued with a new wardrobe of clothes that would protect us from the notorious winter temperatures that awaited us in Korea. It seemed that the British had designed a fur-lined, lightweight parka that was so desired on the black market that the Americans would pay anything for one. For good reason: the winters in Korea were deemed so severe that army policy dictated that they couldn't keep you out there for more than one of them.

The following dawn, we assembled in the parade ground and, while all our kitbags (and my guitar) were loaded into trucks, we had to march for most of the day through the countryside to Hara-mura Battle School for a specialised course to prepare us for combat.

As we marched, I fell in love with Japan and its people. It was an amazing revelation to see the farmers and their families knee-deep in water along the tiered paddy fields. The morning mists so resembled traditional watercolour art that the mountains and lowlands barely looked real. The people were clean, polite and proud of their heritage and customs.

On arrival at Hara-mura, we were billeted in tents and began weapon training. It was the first time I got to throw hand grenades and operate a mortar gun. The biggest kick came on the day we used rocket launchers. Now there was a thrill to remember, although it could be lethal if the hardware malfunctioned. On one occasion we heard of an accident on the mortar range: a couple of guys were killed when a shell backfired. Naturally their relatives were notified that they'd bravely given their lives in the course of battle. It wouldn't do to tell the truth in a case like this.

In due course we were dispatched to the dreaded Korea via several small craft that were really not fit to be called ships. On the rough sea they tossed about like corks: the railings were constantly lined with seasick soldiers vomiting over the side. I was one of them, and it took me a couple of days to get over the queasiness.

We docked at Busan late at night. It was freezing cold weather, the kind of cold that pinches your cheeks and cuts through your body like a knife. Imagine the horror of witnessing hundreds of begging children, clamouring for anything we could spare as we marched through their midst. They were starving and wore the scantiest rags: some were barefoot. We were horrified, and although we had been ordered to ignore them, we gave up bars of chocolate and any food we were holding. This was real life at its most painful.

CHAPTER 5

READY TO RIDE:
FIRST STEPS INTO MUSIC

After the beauty of Japan, it was depressing to see the terrain of Korea. How could the two countries look so different? I'd always pictured minefields as flat farmland that had been planted with mines at specific intervals, but here I saw the reality. Hills, streams and any sort of uneven ground had all been mined erratically, and no one had a clue whether the mines were active or not. Taking no chances, the military lined the boundaries with a single strand of barbed wire with a red triangle dangling from it: this meant that anything beyond was potentially dangerous. We were packed onto lorries and driven north beyond Seoul to the 49th parallel, and along that grim ride all we could see were barren hills and brownish green vegetation for miles behind the wire.

At 55 Field Survey Squadron, my posting was to HQ Troop where I would soon be ensconced in a warm wooden building, divided into an office and the captain's quarters. For now, I trudged through snow and ice along an unlit path made of frozen mud to the tent where I would be living. When I opened the tent flap I was met with hostile glances from the dozen or so rugged guys in there. They had had enough of Korea, and weren't ready to put out the welcome mat for some new bloke.

The temperature was in the region of forty below zero: so cold that your piss froze as soon as it hit the ground. There were several latrine pits hacked out of the frozen earth for our usage. The tents each had two stoves, one at each end, with chimney pipes going up through a protective steel panel to keep the metal from setting the tent roof alight. The stove belly was just a steel drum, fed by a constant trickle of gasoline from a jerrycan mounted outside. You weren't allowed to let the stovepipe get red hot at any time, but nobody gave a shit about that and they used to let the gasoline run into the furnace until the pipe would be red hot to within a couple of feet of the tent roof. It was no wonder that a shout of "Fire!" came every once in a while when a tent went up in flames.

It wasn't all bad. Since the Korean armistice, life at the camp had been comparatively free of bullshit. Bulling boots, pressing uniforms, polishing badges and so on had been set aside, and as a result the camaraderie was pretty good once your tent mates got to know you. Each month the longest-serving soldiers were sent home and new blood brought in, so it wasn't long before I felt like one of the ruling sect.

I played guitar and tried to show the other guys what blues was, but they weren't really interested. All they wanted was a song to accompany their beer, which was like lifeblood to everyone I knew. I was regarded as a bit weird because I didn't drink, but as long as I kept them entertained with my strumming, it was no big deal.

My letter writing reached insane proportions as I tried to keep my love affair with Pamela alive. I wrote to her every day when I was out there, but I got far too few from her, and these weren't always of a very encouraging nature. She was now a student at Manchester College of Art and told me that there was another guy there who had been after her for quite a long time. She wasn't sure whether to wait for me, which made me feel powerless and frustrated. One letter I wrote to try to keep her mine was eighty-six pages long.

We had a cinema in camp called the Ka-Mak-San: this was the main source of entertainment, and I took full advantage of it. It was here that I saw the funniest movie ever, *Monsieur Hulot's Holiday*, starring Jacques Tati. It was a French film with so many brilliant sight gags that by the end of the film, my sides hurt from laughing.

I have another memory connected with the cinema, which occurred after a new regime took over and the level of army bureaucracy increased. Suddenly we had full dress parades, rifle inspections and drills, which had never been known before, even in wartime. There was a new RSM who was an absolute tyrant: he would always be on the lookout for someone to bust. Coming out of the cinema one night, he loomed up before me and caught me without a beret. I tried to tell him I worked in the office and couldn't be spared but he paid no attention, putting me on a charge and recruiting two volunteers to quick-march me to the guardhouse.

I was horrified and hoped that the word would get back to my sergeant so that he could put in a good word for me. I was kept in the guardhouse overnight: in the morning, I was relieved to find that my allies had come forward and told the authorities that I was indispensable in the HQ office. I was released unconditionally, but after that you can bet that I always wore my beret, even to go outside the tent for a piss.

Once, we were allowed to visit a US army base. It was a thrill to hear the American accents, see the uniforms and smoke their cigarettes. I went into their canteen and saw a black guy with the name tag 'Gates' quietly picking out some blues on the piano. It was the first time I'd witnessed someone playing in the key of E, and I tried to trade licks and conversation with him. This was difficult: it wasn't until later that I realised he wasn't into friendly conversation because of our different skin colours. I hadn't realised how segregated the races were in America.

In the summer of 1954, I was granted an official seven-day leave in Tokyo. We were driven to an American airbase and boarded a double-decker troop carrier plane; this was the first time I'd ever flown. We strapped ourselves in and took off. It was a horrible ride, and, like any air travel novice, I was worried when my ears went temporarily deaf.

The Tokyo I know today is such a far cry from how it was in 1954 that it's difficult to find the right words. I went into the biggest department store: it was in the same class as Kendals, with the latest fashions and every type of high-end merchandise for sale. It was a big surprise when I went to the toilet and found only a hole in the floor with raised blocks for your feet. Amid all this finery there was not one western toilet to sit down on. This was a shock back then.

Further down the main street I found a musical instrument shop: everything was so cheap that I bought a fantastic electric guitar with a case for 9,500 yen, or about $20. It was a Weldone and had a great action that allowed me to add fifth and sixth strings to my four-string chords. This was the guitar that I later engraved in Mayall style and converted to a nine-string guitar. It appears on the cover of the album *The Blues Alone* and can be heard on many of my recordings from the sixties. This alone was enough to make my trip to Japan worthwhile.

One day there was a day trip to Nagasaki. The atomic bomb had left many areas desolate, but elsewhere there was much construction in progress; the people were clearly trying to put the horrific memories of 1945 behind them, but it was a sobering experience to go there only eight years after the bomb had dropped.

In letters from home, I learned that Philip had built a new treehouse in place of mine, which had blown down soon after I joined the army. It warranted a news story in *Girl Comic*, which devoted half a page to our sister Caroline as its 'Adventure Girl Of The Week': it showed her up the tree in various poses and swinging on the trapeze rope. The article made me more homesick than ever, particularly as I felt my affair with Pamela was hanging by a thread. Her letters were getting fewer, and I was pretty upset by it all.

Sometime in October, when the weather started to get chilly again, I had another seven-day leave due to me. This was termed R&R – short for rest and recuperation – and ours took place in the town of Inchon. We had no duties and could lounge about the camp as we pleased.

At nightfall we could hear the calls of the hookers nearby, advertising their services, and I found it hard not to be curious. One night I followed a couple of guys up there and found various Korean women offering their services. I didn't find them attractive, but because I'd come this far I paid some yen for a hand job.

Don't get excited: this was a pretty awkward event, with me sitting in the grass with flies undone, looking at my limp dick and a strange woman touching it. This was clearly not going to work. The deciding factor was when she brought out a 'chutta muttee' rag: this was pidgin English for 'just a minute'. This revolting bit of cloth was grubby in the extreme, and she was planning to put that round my cock. I got up in a hurry and scuttled back to the camp.

It hit me afterwards how desperately poor the local people had to be to send out their daughters to do this degrading work. My R&R had turned out to be a total failure, but thankfully I was now counting the days to the date in November when I'd be shipped home at last.

At a stop for shore leave in Hong Kong, I bought an off-white jacket which fit me perfectly; it felt as if it had been made to measure. I wore it on the occasions when the new ship's band played on the upper deck for the officers' dances. As we reached the halfway point of the voyage, I celebrated my twenty-first birthday alone. I don't think I was close enough to anyone to bother mentioning it.

Arriving in Southampton, we reported to a transit camp and waited a few days until the paperwork was processed by the authorities. My demob date was March 12, 1955, but having been in Korea for a year, I was due a large chunk of leave before then. I went home just in time for Christmas, and held my breath that the magic of romance would still be as I'd imagined it would be when I met Pamela again.

I shall never forget the moment when we saw each other after the interminable separation. I was anxiously waiting upstairs in my bedroom and my mother was downstairs, ready to open the front door for her. When Pamela appeared in the bedroom doorway, our eyes met and we rushed into each other's arms. All was well; it seemed that our love had stood the test of time. It was the best Christmas anyone could wish for.

As the New Year began, I hardly minded the casual days of army life that followed. I was so near to demob that there was only a minimum of discipline. I was stationed in the office again, and shuffling papers one day I was surprised to find my name in the latest promotions bulletin. I had been made a corporal – and, better still, it was backdated six months, which meant I had a whole pile of back pay to look forward to.

Life was about to change again, and who knew what lay ahead? I recall one vivid moment of doubt and fear about my future. I was on the way to Midhurst in the back of a lorry one dark night when I began to wonder where I'd end up in life. It was a chilling moment, because I had no idea what my life's direction would be. Perhaps this bleak moment was just what I needed.

For all intents and purposes, I was free and out of the army by January 1955, as I applied for my accumulated leave – nearly two months – and I contrived to have it all at once.

A clue about my future career came when I saw a newspaper advertisement that gave an address where you could record an album. As my piano playing had reached a reasonable level, I rang the guy up and went over to his house in the suburbs. He had a piano in the front room, and mike cables ran through to the next room where his recording equipment was set up. He offered a direct-to-acetate disc method, which meant there could be no breaks in the recording, and no corrections afterwards. I sat down at the keys, he shouted "Start!" and I was on my own.

I was nervous, but I did the best I could, playing four pieces of blues and boogie in different keys and tempos. I then took a break while he turned the twelve-inch disc over and began cutting four more songs. The main influences in my solos came from Albert Ammons, Cripple Clarence Lofton and Jimmy Yancey, and although I'd played a lot better when I wasn't under pressure, I was thrilled to have a record that documented my progress. Around forty-five minutes of music were captured, although, because the acetate was the only one of its kind, it could only be played sparingly or it would wear out.

After this, gigs were the next logical step, and I contacted my friend Mart Rodger, who played the clarinet. He was also being demobbed around this time, so we worked up a set of material based on the styles of Slim Gaillard, The Spirits Of Rhythm and other mid-period jazzmen. Somehow we got ourselves a few gigs as a duo

71

called The Dreamland Boys. Our first show took place at the Lancashire Society of Jazz Music on March 5, 1955.

My father Murray was pleased to see me back safe and sound from Korea, and presented me with a gift of Big Bill Broonzy's recently published autobiography, *Big Bill Blues*. He had even had it autographed by Broonzy when the great bluesman was touring in this country. The book was a mine of information. Reading it, I began to feel as if I personally knew the bluesmen about whom Broonzy told anecdotes. It's still one of the only books to document the lives and times of these pioneers of urban blues, and truly entertaining to read.

I was officially demobbed on March 12 and lost no time in getting over to Kendals to reclaim my old job in the display department. Most of my friends were still there and I looked forward to picking up where I'd left off. Unfortunately, I was dealt a blow when the employment office there told me that because I'd signed on as a regular soldier instead of the obligatory two years, they were no longer required to take me back and that there were no vacancies. I was sorely disappointed.

The obvious solution was to enrol at the Regional College of Art in Manchester and study for a degree: this would supposedly qualify me for a career as an artist. The idea was made more attractive by the fact that Pamela was completing her first year there. I made my application and was accepted, and also successfully applied to the council for a college grant, claiming that I was supported by Beryl, a single mother. All was confirmed and I was set to start in September.

Meanwhile, I still needed a job, so I applied to the display department of the second-largest store in Manchester, Lewis's. My references from Kendals got me in. I began work at the end of March and settled in for another easy-going job with pretty good pay. Before I joined the firm, Pamela and I treated ourselves to an extended weekend in London with the help of my best friend in the army, Tony Chambers, who lived in Ruislip. We passed ourselves off to Tony's mother as a young married couple and were given their best bedroom to stay in, with a double bed and the opportunity to sleep overnight together for the first time.

One of my first priorities upon demob was to take a look at what Philip had done with my treehouse. He'd done a great job with the construction, but he too had gone into the army and now it was a deserted structure with an empty interior. I built a bed at the end of the room to accommodate Pamela and me. I added a wardrobe, a table, a couple of chairs, and a recess in the wall to house all my records. There was a sink unit with a tap connected to a water tank mounted on the outside. We had a pressure cooker and electricity for the lights, and a gramophone and radio via extension cables from the main house, anchored securely to various trees. I carpeted the place and papered the walls: it was now such a comfortable place to inhabit that I moved in full-time.

Mart Rodger and I now expanded The Dreamland Boys' line-up, bringing in Nev Taylor on drums, a guy called Dizzy Burton on trumpet, Sue McManus on banjo and a very introverted pianist who didn't say much but was able to plod expertly enough through the changes in our Dixieland jazz repertoire. I have a photograph that shows us posed at our instruments, and in it I'm wearing my splendid white jacket from Hong Kong. I washed it when it became dirty, but it lost its shape and shrank, ending up useless. I was really pissed off at myself for my stupidity. After all, going back to Hong Kong for another one was hardly an option in 1955.

By July, Pamela had finished her first year at art college and had taken a summer job in Blackpool at a boarding house. Obviously I wanted to be with her, so I handed in my notice at Lewis's and travelled to the coast soon after. I found a job at Pablo's Ice Cream Factory and soon became the master of the ice-cream mix. Accommodation was provided on the premises and I had enough time off to continue courting my lady love.

I remember seeing the movie *Blackboard Jungle*, which launched the career of Bill Haley & His Comets. Their song 'Rock Around The Clock' became the spark that separated American youth from their parents' generation. The establishment soon condemned this so-called 'nigger music', but their idiotic views only furthered the growth of rock'n'roll. Artists such as Fats Domino, Chuck Berry and Little Richard broke into the white record market and I was enthralled. A sense of genuine change was in the air, even as far back as 1955.

At one point Pamela and I decided that it was time we got married. We figured out that I would have enough money coming in from my grant to be able to get by, especially as she and I could get part-time jobs to supplement our income. All we needed was permission from her dad.

I will never forget Frank's granite face as I explained my proposal. He let me outline my whole plan of how we'd manage to support ourselves with a modest flat in Manchester. I felt confident that I'd made a sensible and respectable pitch, but he looked me in the eye and told me that he'd allow no daughter of his to marry a person of so little potential. He pointed out that she was under the age of consent, and if we decided to go against his decision and elope, he would disinherit her completely and bar her from the house forever. I left that room a defeated man.

At the beginning of September I began a four-year course at the Regional College of Art, and it was time to grow a beard in keeping with the image of an art student. Beards at this time were a comparative rarity, and on my walks around Manchester I was a constant target for construction workers and their nanny-goat bleats.

When I made the papers again on December 30, in a showcase called 'Solo Spot' about local musicians, I understood the workers' amusement: the photo showed me in threadbare pants and a dreadful haircut. I had cut it myself and had ruthlessly sculpted out two partings with clippers. I was an awful sight. The feature read:

JOHN MAYALL lives up a tree in Acre Lane, Cheadle Hulme. There he has built himself a one roomed home with all mod cons – running water, bed, stove, gramophone and even carpets and wallpaper. Here, as he sways 30 feet above the ground in the branches of the tree, jazzman John practises on his guitar and listens to his large collection of records. Aged 22, he is at the College of Art, where he also plays in the students' band.

To my surprise, this triggered a wave of publicity. Reporters discovered the small column in the local paper and converged on the treehouse. The *Stockport Express* sent a photographer over to illustrate an article that ran in two parts titled 'Life In The Treetops' and 'This Is The House That John Built'. This led to a bigger story in the *Manchester Evening News* headlined 'Their Porch Is A Perch'. The next newspaper to jump on the bandwagon was the national *Daily Herald*. For their story they exaggerated the truth by saying that we were to get married and live up there.

Finally, a tabloid newspaper called *Reveille* sent a team up from London. After a day of posed photos and interviews, they returned to London: the following week we made the front page and a two-page spread inside. The main picture showed Pamela climbing through the trapdoor to blow me a kiss. This irritated our landlord, but fortunately the furore soon died away.

In the spring of 1956, I inadvertently got mixed up in a shady operation which made the papers when the police arrested the two guys responsible. These were drinking buddies of my father's, who concocted a scam to run a football pools lottery; the proceeds supposedly went to an 'institution for the blind'. One of these gentlemen enlisted Murray and me as door-to-door sales pitchers: our job was to sign people up with a membership fee and collect their money every week. Because it sounded like a worthy charity, the people who answered their doors to us didn't mind contributing.

The only snag was that no such blind institution existed: the Royal National Institute for the Blind got wind of it and reported the bogus company to the law. In the subsequent newspaper reports, Murray and I were mentioned: however, we were able to prove our innocence.

I haunted the bookstores of Manchester in my lunch breaks, and there was a shop in All Saints that specialised in American imported magazines. These included *Whisper*, *Flirt*, *Girl Parade* and the forerunner of all tabloid journalism, *Confidential*. In one called *Front Page Detective*, I read the horrific story of the lynching of Emmett Till, a fourteen-year-old African-American boy who had looked at a white woman the wrong way in Mississippi. I wrote the magazine a letter saying how much I loved their publication but that I was having trouble getting it in England. I added that I would love to have a pen pal in the US who would send me copies.

This prompted an amazing response, with a deluge of mail. The local postman required an entire sack to deliver all the packages to our house. Some magazines were rolled up and some were in stacks: I had well over 150 of them. People sent photos and told me about their lives and dreams, evidently excited by the prospect of striking up a correspondence with an English person. It was fascinating to learn so much first-hand personal information from Americans, and months later I had a regular group of pen pals who sent me tons of magazines.

By now my LP collection had grown considerably and I was learning more and more about the bebop movement. I mourned the passing of the movement's greats, such as the young trumpet player Clifford Brown, killed that year in a car accident alongside pianist Richie Powell. I read that Charlie Christian had been one of the most influential pioneers of the electric guitar back in 1941, when Minton's Playhouse hosted Dizzy Gillespie, Thelonious Monk, Don Byas and Kenny Clarke. As my guitar playing progressed I learned a lot of licks from Charlie's live sessions, which were useful when I played live gigs with Mart Rodger.

One memorable night we gathered at the home of my friend Mike Kershaw and set up to play an all-night session in his basement. We had an audience of friends from art college and local jazz fans. The bass player, Nev Matthews, had a wire recorder; he set this primitive recording device in motion and captured hours and hours of our music, which was pretty experimental. In that candle-lit cellar we tuned into our souls, creating our own versions of unlikely tunes such as 'Yes, We Have No Bananas' and 'Sweet Sue'. It felt like magic. Peter Ward was on drums, Mart played clarinet, and Nev was on bass. I hunched over my guitar with half-closed eyes, lost in the moment. These are the sessions that musicians live for.

I wanted a copy of this session, and through an advert in *Vintage Jazz Mart* magazine, I made contact with a guy in Scotland who could make acetates from any source material. We mailed him the wire recordings and I ordered three twelve-inch double-sided discs from him. I made an album to keep them in and painted a moody cover for it, so that it would have the right look to match the music.

The same guy told me that he had a large collection of rare blues 78s, and that he earned extra income by making up LP acetates of these records. He sent me a list of his items and I became one of his regular customers. Through him I built up a great collection of the works of hitherto unavailable blues singers such as Blind Boy Fuller, Barbecue Bob, Furry Lewis and especially Tommy McClennan. He also made me a couple of sampler discs with a whole new catalogue of songs from obscure players like Sloppy Henry, Blind Leroy Garnett and Montana Taylor.

Shortly afterwards, I got together with a few more musicians to form a college group named The Blackfriars Society Jazz Band: we made a record with 'I Wish I Could Shimmy Like My Sister Kate' on one side and a blues on the other. Trumpeter Cephas Howard was the leader: he later became famous as the leader of The Temperance Seven. Roger Woodburn played banjo, I played electric guitar, Peter Ward was the drummer and Ricky Blears was the upright bass player; I don't recall who played trombone.

At one point we went down to London by coach to enter the Annual Varsity Jazz Band Contest. I thought we were the most original of the entrants, but we didn't win – although I received an individual award as 'Guitarist of the Evening', which was gratifying. The soprano sax player from a Cambridge group won the Musician of the Year award: his name was Dick Heckstall-Smith. Who could have guessed that our paths were soon to cross professionally?

In August, I teamed up again with Mart and, with a new rhythm section, we billed ourselves The Hounds Of Sound and played at the Bodega Jazz Club and other minor functions and dances. The material was pretty eclectic, but nevertheless we seemed to be appreciated wherever we performed.

After the summer break, I began my second year of studies and continued my musical partnership with Peter Ward during lunchtime jam sessions. There was a pretty good piano available in the main lecture hall, and sometimes Ricky Blears would bring his bass to propel my boogie-woogie songs to a limited, but enthusiastic, audience.

Later that term I began recording the sessions on my first tape recorder, a three-speed Grundig model that cost quite a bit. This device also enabled me to set up a second-hand record store with a friend from Junior Art School called John Wilkinson. As I now had the Grundig, I figured I didn't really need my records so much, and transferred them to tape so that John and I would have some stock. On Saturdays we were able to use a room above Johnny Roadhouse's Music Store, but it turned out to be more of a social affair than a money-making venture. The downside was that I didn't realise at the time how perishable tape was, and also how much fidelity was lost in the transfer – and so I regretted losing some prized records. I remember ruing the day I got rid of LPs by guitarists Tal Farlow, Bill Harris, Barney Kessel and Howard Roberts.

The same year, Pamela and I decided to marry, and announced our plans to the forbidding Mr Heap – who now had no power to block the union, as Pamela had reached the age of twenty-one a couple of months previously – and set a date. In May we went down to Stockport Registry Office, and with Peter Ward doing the honours as best man, I slipped the wedding ring on Pamela's finger. Returning to her house, Peter set up his drums in the front room, Mart brought his clarinet and I led a jam session on piano.

Pamela wore a casual pale green suit over a black sweater and I was married without a jacket or tie: for us it seemed very natural to be without formal attire. This was reflected in a write-up on the front page of the *Manchester Evening News*, with the headline 'Blue Notes At Sweater Wedding'.

We began our married life by moving out of the treehouse and into a huge one-room flat owned by a man named Rodney Ball. He was a Romany gypsy and an old friend of Grandad's, which was how we got the flat for the low price of one pound ten shillings a week. The drawback was that he was too old or too tired to bother with dealing with the transaction, and left it all to his younger wife, a dragon in human form. From the moment we moved in, she was a constant threat to our happiness. She didn't like anyone living in her property to begin with, and regularly paid unannounced visits to the flat to see what we were up to.

Financially we were able to get by, as I'd got an extra £20 a month as a grant from the council. We weren't living in luxury, though: there was no bath or shower. Next door to us was the public baths, fortunately; otherwise we had to make do with thorough washings at the kitchen sink.

I began looking around for ways to earn extra money with my piano playing and discovered quite a few social clubs run by West Indians and Jamaicans. I began frequenting a place where a guy called Winston had a cool collection of American 45s. This was an excellent introduction to some great electric blues and R&B.

The big new music in the summer of 1957 was rock'n'roll, associated with the emergence of Teddy boys, who regularly made the headlines with numerous incidents of vandalism and mayhem at seaside resorts. Britain seemed profoundly shocked that such juvenile delinquency was becoming widespread and invading our culture.

In America, too, social unrest continued to accelerate. In the south, redneck mayors and sheriffs were seen on TV trying to stamp out rock'n'roll, and radio DJs were leading public rallies and destroying rock records on air. No one could deny the power of Elvis Presley, though, who was captivating America's teenage population with his outrageous gyrations and co-option of black R&B.

We went to Grandad's for Christmas dinner, and in the evening sat around in the front room before a roaring coal fire with a tray of Beryl's home-made mince pies. I plugged in my tape recorder to record our messages to an American pen pal: it still exists today as the only remnant of Grandad's voice.

Four days later, on December 29, our son Gary was born at High Street Hospital. The law didn't allow husbands to be present at births, so I had to keep going down the road for reports on Pamela's progress. It was an incredible feeling to see a living, breathing baby looking so serene and gorgeous in his mother's arms. It truly seemed like a miracle.

We named him Gary Vincent Mayall. We'd chosen his middle name as a dedication to our West Indian friend, Winston; however, his heavy accent had totally thrown me, and I later realised that I had misunderstood his name.

CHAPTER 6

LONG GONE MIDNIGHT: LONDON AND THE FLAMINGO CLUB

Music started to become even more of a presence in my life at this juncture. A turning point was clearly not far away.

In February 1958 I made the title of The Powerhouse Four official, and we began playing gigs in addition to the art college get-togethers. A write-up in the *Manchester Evening News* had this to report on March 1:

RHYTHM AND BLUES BOYS

I met him walking into the Club Rio wearing an orange coloured pullover, flannels and a trilby hat. On his back was strapped a tape recorder and under his arm was a guitar. This was bearded John Mayall, leader of 'John Mayall's Powerhouse Four'. Until just over a year ago John lived up a tree in a house he had built for himself. He furnished this swinging room in the treetops of Cheadle Hulme with everything a jazz fan needs – a gramophone, 500 records, a tape recorder and a guitar.

John is now slightly more conventional – a result of meeting Pam (now his wife). They both went to art school, she to study sculpture, he to train as an art teacher. They live in a two-roomed flat not very far from the college of art. John has decorated the walls of his home with huge paintings of jazzmen. When he's not painting – and even when he is – jazz blares from his gramophone or tape recorder. And young Gary, the Mayalls' seven-week-old baby, sleeps through it all.

It was at the art school that 24-year-old John formed the Powerhouse Four, but now 17-year-old bassist Ricky Blears is the only other art student in the group. The other two musicians are coloured neighbours of John's – Bill Schulz who plays tenor sax and Chick Taylor, 32-year-old drummer. The Four specialise in rhythm and blues, a style that was the forerunner of rock 'n' roll. They play seldom-heard tunes originated by such artists as Big Bill Broonzy, Big Maceo and T-Bone Walker.

"We play our own interpretations of these artists' tunes," John says. "The rest of our material – about half of our repertoire – is original." John sings with the Four. He also plays piano, guitar and harmonica with them. He may soon be playing trumpet – he has been practising it at home. Although formed only a month ago, the group has already had a string of dates in Manchester and district. Last Sunday the boys played in Liverpool.

The article mentions the trumpet, which I had taught myself with a self-devised chart of finger positions. I bought a couple of second-hand instruments, one brass and the other in tarnished silver. Inspired by Dizzy Gillespie, I sawed through the silver one's connectors and bent the bell up at an angle of forty-five degrees.

Adding a mute so that I wouldn't arouse the ire of the neighbours, I made a huge chart out of poster board and stuck it up on the wall of the flat. On it, I illustrated which of the three valves had to be pressed down in order to find the right notes. This diagram went all through the octaves and I managed to achieve the right sounds. At the top of the placard was a bold header proclaiming 'The John Mayall Sure-Fire Trumpet Method'!

At the end of June I got another write-up in the paper following an incident of great importance to me. As part of a European blues tour, Brownie McGhee and Sonny Terry played a concert in Manchester and I got to go backstage afterwards and meet them. Somehow I got Brownie to agree to a social visit at our flat after the show. I think my friend Mike Kershaw had a car, and we promised Mr McGhee that he wouldn't be taken too far from the Milbank Hotel where they were staying. I suppose he came with us to break the monotony of the road and as a way to avoid going back to a room with nothing but a bed and four walls to look forward to.

Once he arrived we put the kettle on; he brought out his guitar and, for the next three hours or so, entertained us with songs and stories. For me this was magic beyond the scope of any dream, having collected and almost worn out so many of his 78s. I suggested that I record him but right away he refused, saying that he didn't want his music to get into the wrong hands. I didn't blame him as I knew how many bluesmen over the years had been ripped off by record companies. Throughout the entire late-night gathering, baby Gary stood spellbound with his little face peeping over the bars of the crib, taking it all in without interruption.

During the summer break I got to see one of my all-time idols in concert at the Free Trade Hall. The bandleader Chris Barber sponsored a visit from Muddy Waters to play a set in the midst of one of his own shows. Muddy not only came prepared to tear things up on his own, but he brought the singer and pianist Otis Spann along as his accompanist. This, of course, was magic for any boogie blues piano player worth his salt: here was someone who was a legend in his own right.

I had never even seen a photograph of Otis before he stepped on stage and effortlessly poured out the heaviest Delta blues on the Steinway grand. I couldn't believe that he was mostly rolling out this great music in the keys of E and A, which are generally considered difficult keys for pianists. The concert was electrifying in more ways than one: Muddy was playing through an amplifier, which apparently was not what the critics were expecting.

The next day the reviewers were up in arms about this choice, evidently expecting him to stay forever in acoustic guitar mode. As usual they were a bit behind: perhaps they hadn't been following what was happening on Chicago's South Side, where soon-to-be classics such as 'Hoochie Coochie Man', 'I Just Wanna Make Love To You' and 'I'm Ready' were being recorded.

Just as I was rejoicing in having heard these guys live, we got the word that Big Bill Broonzy had died from cancer on August 14 – a huge loss to blues lovers worldwide. As I never got to see him, it made me treasure his autographed autobiography even more.

By now, Gary was getting big enough to be strapped safely onto the seat I'd made on the rear of my tandem, so I occasionally took him for a ride back to Cheadle Hulme to see Grandad and Beryl. While Grandad doted on him and played with us up in the paddock – where he'd recently made a hideaway hut out of the lumber from the downed treehouse – my mother was going through a rather strange period and seemed not to want to see her grandson. I found out later that this had to do with a very unreliable relationship with a Mr Halstead, her then employer. He professed to be madly in love with her and yet wouldn't follow through with his promise to divorce his wife.

After Christmas, Pamela discovered that she was pregnant again. We were excited to know that we'd be expanding the family in the New Year, but it meant that Mrs Ball's flat would no longer be big enough to contain us. Something had to be done, and of all people it was Mr Heap – who had by now accepted us as a married couple, and was delighted to have a grandson – who solved the problem. He owned a semi-detached house in Fallowfield, currently occupied by a little old lady who was always more trouble than she was worth when it came to prompt paying of the rent. It took months to get her to vacate, but eventually we were able to bid goodbye – and good riddance – to the omnipotent Mrs Ball.

Mr Heap sold us the Fallowfield house for the ludicrously low price of £1,000, and when we moved in, it felt like heaven on earth to have so much space. It had two bedrooms upstairs and a front and rear room downstairs with a kitchen, a coal house, upstairs bathroom and a spare room next to our bay-windowed front bedroom.

Elsewhere, too, life was improving: I completed my degree, gaining the academic title of John Mayall DA Manc., which stood for Diploma of Associateship. I had studied photography in my final year, which helped me gain access to the Free Trade Hall for jazz concerts. The promoters would let me in the back door to meet and photograph the visiting Americans. Through my camera lens I got to meet a veritable who's who of stars – Oscar Peterson, Roy Eldridge, Sonny Stitt, Herb Ellis, Ray Brown, Ella Fitzgerald, Junior Mance, Willie Dixon, Memphis Slim and the entire Duke Ellington Orchestra among them. I truly felt like I belonged in their world.

On August 10, Pamela gave birth to another healthy, robust son. We named him Jason and gave him the middle name of Walter after his godfather Wally Houser, a good friend of Pamela's and someone I came to know well through his excellent saxophone playing; it was

Wally who first turned me on to the music of Cannonball Adderley. As soon as we were back home in Beverley Road, Gary became a very proud older brother; he was constantly checking out baby Jason to see what he was up to, which was mainly sleeping and being fed.

Soon after Jason was born, I was accepted as a junior typographer at a firm called Wilson Advertising. I was given a desk in a studio run by Tony Perrin, who was a real taskmaster; nevertheless, he taught me all I know about typography today. He was such a meticulous fanatic for detail that I would go back to my desk time and time again, adjusting gaps between letters, sometimes by only a hair's width. Most studio chiefs would have let these fine details go, but thanks to Tony I became a master of the razor blade and rubber cement.

The only time I was given a project of my own was to design a logo for a new company that sold frozen poultry. I ended up with a profile of a fat turkey and emblazoned lettering reading 'Polpak'. I never heard of this company again.

Outside the design department, I frequently had to liaise with the copy department; one of the copywriters employed there at the time was Jack Rosenthal, who later became famous as a TV dramatist. He was one of the earliest scriptwriters on the great British soap opera *Coronation Street*, which we watched once we had rented our first television set in 1960. At that time, I expect nobody imagined that it would still be running into the twenty-first century.

Every so often, an American jazz or blues package would come to the Free Trade Hall. I will never forget the thrill of witnessing my first gospel group. As The Clara Ward Singers came on stage, I was sitting near the front, taking photographs. When the shutter clicked, I felt a bond with the emotional make-up of black America. The voices blended and soared, and the naked passion of their harmonies moved me greatly. I remember developing my pictures and seeing the faces in close-up emerging from the developing tray. The images gave me a ghostly feeling: I could almost see into the segregated lives of the five singers.

I felt the impact of the Delta world when I heard the pianist Memphis Slim effortlessly conjuring up a lifetime of hardship in the rural south. His big black hands rolled and crashed through majestic clusters of notes. *This* was the blues.

When Slim was on tour with Willie Dixon, I got to meet them backstage after the show. Slim seemed rather unapproachable, perhaps a little resentful that it had to be white foreigners who were recognising his music. Years later, he became one of the first black bluesmen to follow in the footsteps of many a jazz artiste, leaving America to live in Europe, where race relations were better.

Dixon was quite the opposite: a huge, genial man who was more than willing to spend time talking to his admirers. As well as writing some of the best-known blues songs in the world, he was also an astute businessman. During his lifetime he made the most of his position as producer and became a major force behind the Chess recordings in Chicago. When I met and photographed these guys, I knew I'd been close to greatness.

Back home, I was inspired to get out my guitar and compose a few blues songs. One was called 'I Cried Last Night', a soulful mid-tempo blues, and the other was a tongue-in-cheek slow blues titled 'I Wanna Be A Star On Television'. I had a line in there that ran: 'I want a thousand pounds a week salary and a car.' Both of those were beyond comprehension at the time. It seems so strange now.

With all this music being played at home, it was no wonder that young Gary began to tap his feet and nod to the music around him. One day I plugged a mike into my recorder, got out my guitar and played a fast boogie in the style of Lightnin' Hopkins, a strong influence in my musical direction. I called it 'Boogie Gary' and structured it so that in the breaks I could coax the three-year-old lad into saying the word 'boogie'. After a while he got into the rhythm of it and came in on time. I'm glad I still have a rough tape of that moment.

Life in Beverley Road seemed to settle into a comfortable routine, until one day Pamela realised that she was pregnant again. We'd been intending to have a third child, and this seemed to perk up our relationship. Without knowing it, we had ended up in a slight rut again, going to the movies occasionally and entertaining my jazz friends at weekends.

Pamela was still a creative artist, and at one point she had attracted the attention of a bearded gentleman down the road who shared the same interests. He definitely had a thing for her that transcended painting and sculpture, and he was frequently seen at our house having cups of tea and planning trips to art exhibitions. Needless to say, I didn't care for his company too much and eventually he stopped coming around.

On April 14, 1961, our daughter Tracey Ann Mayall came into our world. Pamela was very weak afterwards: it hadn't been an easy birth, and she needed to be looked after for quite some time. Somehow we all made the adjustment to the new family member, while major changes were afoot in my musical career, such as it was at the time.

In the summer, I got wind of a part-time job opening at a youth club in Wythenshawe. I was required to be available a couple of evenings a week in a classroom where budding musicians could gather and play. After a slow start, one or two guys filtered in to see what it was all about, and among them was a drummer called Hughie Flint. He had a terrific feel and he swung simply but relentlessly. I got the same feeling from playing with him that I always had with Peter Ward, and we also found that we had a liking for the same modern jazz musicians. There was also a pianist named Roy Hilton and a tenor saxophonist called Chris Logue, and Ricky Blears came along sometimes with his upright bass.

Talk flowed freely, with names traded back and forth – Miles, Coltrane, Bird, Clifford Brown, Dizzy Gillespie – and in such amateur company I felt confident enough to start bringing my bent-up trumpet to make flurries of random notes. Hey, I thought, if Ornette Coleman could get away with it, why couldn't I?

At the weekends, we got together to check out Manchester's jazz club scene. Pamela's good friend Wally Houser was the first to tell Hughie and me about a great player from London who had an uncanny likeness to Cannonball Adderley. Wally was raving about him, having seen him a few times in London. One night at the Clarendon Hotel, where modern jazz flourished, we got to see for ourselves what he could do. This fellow's name was Graham Bond – and he was sensational.

We saw so many visiting London jazz players at this club. These included Tubby Hayes, tenor sax duo Jimmy and Alan Skidmore, pianist Brian Auger, drummer Phil Seamen, trumpeter Ian Carr and the amazing team of drummer Ginger Baker and bassist Jack Bruce. The first time I saw Jack and Ginger, they'd teamed up with tenor man Dick Heckstall-Smith and were ripping furiously through a repertoire of jazz standards and blues originals. Jack was playing upright bass with a ferocity I'd never seen before. He blew me away.

Having discovered a record shop in London that specialised in American import records, and armed with information on new releases from the monthly *Downbeat* magazine, I was aware of new albums before my friends had even heard of them. The LPs at 37/6d were priced at double the British equivalent, but for me it was worth it to feel those beautiful thick cardboard sleeves bearing the magic designs of Riverside, Prestige and Blue Note.

Fortunately, Pamela was very understanding: she and the three children somehow slept through the night, undisturbed by our gatherings downstairs as we reverently soaked up the new sounds of The Adderley Brothers, Wes Montgomery, Horace Silver, Jimmy Smith, Art Blakey, Clifford Brown and Johnny Griffin.

Around this time a new kind of music was born: soul. Organ groups abounded, and funky pianists such as Gene Harris, Les McCann and Wynton Kelly spearheaded the movement. Sax players like Stanley Turrentine, Lou Donaldson, Roland Kirk and Hank Mobley kept us glued to the speakers and inspired us when we congregated later at the Wythenshawe Youth Club jam sessions. It was a wonderful time.

This whole period was incredibly inspiring for me. More and more opportunities to see visiting American jazz stars came along. I count myself lucky that I got to see many of these groups at the height of their fame. I saw Art Blakey & The Jazz Messengers two nights in a row at the Free Trade Hall, with the classic line-up of Jymie Merritt on bass, Wayne Shorter on tenor, Lee Morgan on trumpet and Bobby Timmons on piano.

Another classic line-up that I was fortunate to see at exactly the right time was the combination of Miles Davis with John Coltrane on tenor and soprano saxes, McCoy Tyner on piano, Ron Carter on bass and Elvin Jones on drums. I have to confess that it wasn't nearly as exciting to me as the Art Blakey concerts. There was a warmth and humour about Blakey's show that was totally missing from Miles's internalised presentation. He never said a word to the audience or his band members all evening!

I also got to see Ella Fitzgerald and Thelonious Monk as a double bill, and when Duke Ellington came to town I met many of his famous sidemen backstage – Johnny Hodges, Ben Webster, Cat Anderson, Russell Procope, Paul Gonsalves and trombonist Buster Cooper, who years later I employed as one of my sidemen on a gig. Then there was the Jazz At The Philharmonic package that featured Oscar Peterson, Ray Brown, Herb Ellis and Gus Johnson, plus featured players such as Dizzy, Roy Eldridge and Sonny Stitt.

While I was going to jazz concerts and running my all-night listening sessions, a new music was stirring in London coffee houses. Folk music was enjoying a vogue across the Atlantic, spearheaded by the twenty-year-old Bob Dylan, who opened in Greenwich Village that September. This movement was reflected in England as singer Alexis Korner and harmonica player Cyril Davies began building an audience for their brand of music, which combined traditional folk with Chicago-style urban blues. These two guys were credited with the birth of the British blues phenomenon, although they didn't know it at the time.

And then there was the small matter of The Beatles… Not far from my home town, the seeds were being sown for a musical and cultural revolution. This ragtag bunch of musicians from Liverpool began a regular engagement at a Hamburg strip club in August 1962. Who could possibly have forecast where their music would go?

The Rolling Stones also enter my story at this point, albeit tangentially. Alexis Korner had begun playing live dates at the Ealing R&B Club earlier that year – essentially the basement of a little pub that was willing to give him a shot at bringing in more customers. In order to publicise the opening, the press were invited to come down and see what was going on. The purist blues critics hated it when Alexis brought in guitar amplifiers and went electric, but while their laughter was loud and derisive, it was not enough to stem the rising tide of blues fans who were beginning to catch on.

Among those fans were Mick Jagger, Keith Richard (later Richards) and Brian Jones, as well as Paul Jones of Manfred Mann. On the opening night, the line-up featured Alexis and Cyril alongside Dick Heckstall-Smith, pianist Andy Webb and future Stones drummer Charlie Watts. When Alexis Korner's Blues Incorporated secured a Thursday-night slot at the Marquee Club on Wardour Street, the writing was on the wall for the jazz band movement.

As I read *Melody Maker*'s weekly columns about the Marquee and the now infamous Flamingo and All-Nighter clubs, I began to yearn for the bright lights in the south. Alexis himself was the catalyst that gave me the impetus I needed.

This occurred when his band began branching out of London. I remember the red-letter day when they were booked to play at the Bodega Club in Manchester. Needless to say, my friends and I were more than impressed. What a sound Alexis had – and what a strong and varied repertoire, which went beyond the usual Chicago blues bag. I went home buzzing with ideas and ambitions.

It so happened that a friend of Roy's called Jack Massarik, a sax player who had been to a few of my late-night Saturday listening sessions, was also at Alexis's gig with his pal John Rowlands, a jazz trumpeter. After the show John said to Jack, "It's just jazz that they're doing. We could do that! All we need is a singer and we'll be away. Do you know anyone?"

Jack replied, "Yes, I think I do. There's this guy with a great record collection whose house we go to. He plays, and he knows a fair bit about the blues stuff."

The next thing I knew, Jack brought John over for a chat about the idea: I was definitely interested. I knew I could bring in Hughie, and if I played the piano, I could get Ray Cummings on guitar. We'd use Ricky Blears on bass. I don't remember who suggested the band name, but we decided to call ourselves Blues Syndicate.

I phoned Paddy McKiernan, who ran the Bodega. He had been one of the judges at the college contest back in 1956 where I'd first met Dick Heckstall-Smith. I somehow persuaded Paddy to let us open for Alexis Korner when he next came up to Manchester. Money wasn't a factor: we'd have done it for nothing, just to get the exposure. We didn't have a specific date: it was simply agreed that Blues Syndicate would get the call in due course.

For rehearsals, John booked an upstairs room over a pub near Oxford Road; it had a slightly shop-worn upright piano on a large stage. Jack remembers that I showed up with a guitar, a tape recorder and a big black book with words and chords for about eighty songs. By the evening's end we had enough material to fill an hour-long set, and probably more. I simultaneously felt very inspired and completely intimidated by the thought of playing such a high-profile gig.

Thanks to John's contacts and determination, we were able to secure some warm-up gigs and got to the point where we were sounding pretty professional, or so it seemed to us. Pianos were generally unreliable or nonexistent, so I got enough money together to buy my first electric keyboard. It was made by Hohner and called a Cembalet. With its clavinet-type tone and optional slow vibrato, it was well suited to the blues songs. In addition, we didn't always have a bass player, and so we started to rely on my left hand for the basslines.

I was writing songs by now and including them in our set list, such as 'Twist All Night' and a tribute to Mose Allison called 'Blues For Mose'. I had also improved enough on a ten-hole harmonica to be able to feature the instrument on Chicago blues numbers such as Muddy Waters' 'Soon Forgotten', 'Long Distance Call' and 'Hoochie Coochie Man'.

As we played, I was keeping up with developments in the music scene. In October, another great blues package came to the Free Trade Hall. This was my first contact with John Lee Hooker, who was regarded as a man of mystery and dark secrets. I reacquainted myself with Brownie McGhee and Sonny Terry, who remembered the night he visited our house. T-Bone Walker was a consummate showman on stage, playing the guitar behind his back and with his teeth. Willie Dixon was paired again with Memphis Slim; the other performers were blues belter Helen Humes, harmonica player Shakey Jake and drummer Jump Jackson. This concert was yet another inspiration to me: it was time to do something decisive about my career.

By December, there was a buzz going round about Liverpool's contribution to the British music scene, particularly from The Beatles. If you turned on the radio over Christmas, you never had to wait long before their first single 'Love Me Do' would come on. During the next year their meteoric rise to the top of the pop world was marked by hit after hit. It was the beginning of what was later to be known as the British Invasion.

It's important to remember that until The Beatles broke into the American market, British music was barely noticed in the States. Their impact made the Americans take note of what was going on over here. Most relevantly for my story, The Beatles paved the way for the next influential wave to hit America – England's take on the blues.

Early in 1963, the promised gig at the Bodega, opening up for Blues Incorporated, finally materialised. By now Charlie Watts had left the band to join The Rolling Stones; he was replaced by the popular young drummer Ginger Baker, who was highly respected in jazz circles. Ginger had a dynamic style that was heavily influenced by the great jazz drummer Phil Seamen. He and Jack Bruce ignited the whole band with their fiery chops, creating a veritable tornado of rhythm. Finally, Johnny Parker, who had made an impression on me with his boogie-woogie piano on Humphrey Lyttelton's 'Bad Penny Blues' a few years before, played piano.

Organist Cyril Davies and singer Long John Baldry had also left Alexis's band, replaced by the organist, singer and saxophonist Graham Bond and a good-looking black American serviceman called Ronnie Jones. Ronnie was the best modern blues singer on the British scene, with a style based on that of Bobby 'Blue' Bland. When he got on the mike and sang 'Stormy Monday', I got the chills.

This was the best band that Alexis Korner ever put together, and it was a shame that it didn't remain together long enough to be recorded. All that is left today is a memory of how they tore it up that night – and my band and I were a part of it all.

After the show, I talked to Alexis about coming to London to try to break into the music business. He was extremely encouraging – a complete gentleman who didn't mind sharing his after-hours time with anyone interested in the blues. He told me that there were certainly doors he could open for me in London. He was happy to introduce me to the Flamingo audiences by inviting my band to open for him at his regular Thursday-night residency, and he would even make enquiries about a Friday and Saturday booking on the blues circuit.

Later, we all went out for a curry. It's difficult to describe what I felt like in the company of these great musicians. They were all so much larger than life than anyone I knew. Ginger Baker's every adjective was 'fucking'. Jack Bruce was a fiery Scot wired on uppers and full of loud laughter. Dick and Graham would discuss the merits of Charlie Parker and Coleman Hawkins, with Johnny Parker the quiet listener. At the table of the Indian restaurant that we'd taken over, Alexis presided over us all – and somehow held it all together.

Before Alexis loaded everyone into their cramped van, he gave me his address and phone number in Bayswater and disappeared into the night with his motley crew. I couldn't get over the fact that he was going to drive that van all the way back to London.

The very next day, I announced to the members of Blues Syndicate: "That's it! I'm going to London to be a professional musician. Anyone who wants to move down there with me is in, and if you choose to stay here, you're out!"

There was no going back after that, but hardly any of them wanted to join me in London, so that seemed likely to be the end of Blues Syndicate. Hughie Flint had a job that he wasn't ready to leave; John Rowlands felt he'd be lost amid the jazz elite of London; and Ray Cummings felt too settled to contemplate an uprooting.

Jack Massarik was up for it, though. His family lived in London and he was studying there for a university degree. So then there were two…

I lost no time in calling Alexis Korner. This wonderful man returned my call with the news that he'd actually set up a date for me and Blues Syndicate to open for him at the Flamingo in a couple of weeks. Not only that, but he had set up a second gig for us at a small pub called the Wooden Bridge in Guildford the same weekend.

Although a permanent move south was not going to happen for the band, the guys were keen to do these two shows – and before we had time to digest it all, we were heading down to the big city in John Rowland's van. I can't recall where we spent the nights, as we certainly couldn't afford hotels, but I do remember the excitement we felt at being in London and seeing at first-hand what the famed Flamingo Club was like.

It was a great deal seedier than I'd expected. The smell of spilled drinks, cigarette smoke and disinfectant filled the air, and the floors were sticky with chewing gum residue that had resisted decades of cleaning. I met the owner, the legendary Rik Gunnell, late on the Friday and found him rather imposing and a little scary. His broken nose and weathered features spoke volumes about the lifestyle of a nightclub owner: he was on speaking terms with the Kray brothers, the feared rulers of London's gangland empire.

Rik loved to brag about his club. I learned a few amusing things about his operation there and then. As he told me, "No way could we get a licence to serve liquor, so we'd open up thirty cases of Coke and spike them with a splash of Scotch. We used to start off very reasonable, with one-third Scotch to two-thirds Coke, but eventually we got greedy, and by the end it'd be just a splash or two of Scotch on top. By then nobody gave a fuck: they were too wasted on pills and the heat in the club to notice. Of course, we had our drinks the other way round – just a splash of Coke to go with the straight Scotch!"

Hammond organist Georgie Fame was the reigning king of the Flamingo Club. He'd previously played piano in Billy Fury's Blue Flames until December 1961, when Billy put a new group together and Georgie inherited The Blue Flames. He landed a residency at the Flamingo, expanded his quartet to include horns, and became the first person in London to use a Hammond organ. By the end of 1963, he and the guys were playing as many as forty gigs a month. Georgie had even recorded his first live album at the club.

The show we did with Alexis was accepted fairly well, although I detected a certain cautiousness in the applause: the clientele were evidently accustomed to the smooth sophistication of Georgie and The Blue Flames. Despite R&B being the Flamingo's dominant sound, Rik seemed open to booking me with a new band whenever I got one together.

I was beginning to feel as if I belonged in this strange new world.

CHAPTER 7

PLAN YOUR REVOLUTION: BIRTH OF THE BLUESBREAKERS

The night after our debut, we drove out to the Wooden Bridge in Guildford, where there was a lot less pressure on us. After a terrific session where we played at our best, I picked up a flyer that listed all the coming attractions. For the modest sum of five shillings you could look forward to seeing The Mann-Hugg Blues Brothers, Cyril Davies' All-Stars and The Rolling Stones.

After this groundbreaking weekend, I returned home with major decisions to face. The main consideration was my family's financial stability. We'd worked so hard to get a house of our own, and then invested so much time customising it to our lifestyle, that it seemed drastic to consider giving it up and moving to London.

I have to stress here that if Pamela hadn't been so supportive and understanding, none of this would have happened. I would undoubtedly have withered away in obscurity in the commercial art industry of Manchester. As it happened, she had enough belief in me to encourage me to give it a shot.

The plan was that I should go down to London on my own and, while testing the waters in the music scene, secure a job in advertising. This would enable me to make the transition from one reliable salary to another. My good friend Peter Ward had got a very high-paying position in advertising in London after moving up the executive ladder, and he was the man to open doors for me in that area.

Peter duly made a list of studios where he thought I should try to get a job in typographic design. I wrote them letters of introduction and set up interviews, which was also where Peter came in handy. He used to come to Manchester at weekends to see his folks, driving a crazy three-wheel German bubble car made by Heinkel. It was designed for a single person: you entered it by raising the glass top like a lid and climbing in like a racing car driver. Peter would pick me up late on Sunday night, and, with a bit of effort, I somehow squeezed inside along with his laundry and my portfolio for a perilous all-night drive down the motorway, dwarfed by every other vehicle on the road.

I told my employers the Cartwrights that I would be leaving them soon and moving to London: they kindly gave me a bit of time off to find a new job. I trekked around London for days, with exaggerated references and my portfolio on my back, until my search paid off. I met with the manager of an advertising company, and was accepted. I must have had a good gift of the gab: the salary exceeded what I was making in Manchester.

To give you an idea of how quickly things changed back then, I'd no sooner become the biggest fan of Alexis Korner's Blues Incorporated than that line-up split, before their music could even be captured on record. I was worried that the impetus of the British blues movement would suffer, but as history has shown, this was far from the case. Graham Bond, Jack Bruce, Ginger Baker and Dick Heckstall-Smith branched off to become The Graham Bond Organisation, while Alexis rebounded quickly, replacing them with Art Themen, Chris Thompson and Phil Seamen. Ronnie Jones continued to belt out his Bobby 'Blue' Bland-style vocals, impressing me time after time.

As Blues Syndicate was also no longer together, I had to come up with a name for my new band. I recall sitting down with a long list of names, all starting with the word 'Blues'. There were about thirty combinations, with pairings such as Blues Bombers, Blues Kings, Blues Shakers, Blues Conquerors, Blues Buddies, Blues Belters and so on. Among them was Bluesbreakers, which I settled for after much thought. I figured it was as good a name as any.

As to who would be in the band, I needed all the help I could get. Alexis was my only contact, so I went to see him in February 1963 at his basement flat in Moscow Road. I was completely star-struck: I still remember the thrill of seeing my musical idols casually dropping by to see Alexis and his wife Bobby. It was obvious that his flat was the hub of the British blues movement; I felt so privileged to be hanging out with the likes of Dick Heckstall-Smith, Jack Bruce and Johnny Parker. In addition to the musicians present, it turned out that the renowned jazz writer Charles Fox lived in the apartment upstairs. I was indeed in fine company.

Alexis suggested I hook up with a guitar player named Davey Graham, who was highly recommended, having had some success with a single called 'Angi'. After I phoned Davey, he and I got together and found that we had enough in common to decide to give it a go. Crucially, the enthusiasm was there.

For our first official gig under the name of John Mayall & The Bluesbreakers, we had a ramshackle line-up. The first bass player was Mike Sealey, who didn't last more than a couple of gigs, and there was a procession of awkward would-be drummers. Our honking sax player's choice of notes left me with mouth agape.

It was all tremendously nerve-racking: I've never felt more as if I were aboard a sinking ship, as I laboured through those early gigs at the Flamingo. Furthermore, the music was so alien to the club's signature sound that the audience became hostile. It was hard to ignore the derision of the regulars. In response to my announcement, "We'd like to do one more song," a loud West Indian voice from the crowd yelled, "No more, man, no more!"

Over by the door Rik Gunnell was heard telling his confused regulars: "We've got this weird guy on now, with a squeaky harmonica round his neck. I don't know what the fuck it's all about, but don't worry, Georgie'll be on soon. Sounds fucking horrible, but the kid's got guts!"

It was a relief to go back home to Manchester for the weekend and play with Blues Syndicate at the Rex Ballroom in Wilmslow. If only those guys had been willing to move to London! But I was determined to make things work, so Davey and I moved into a flat together. Musically, he and I were an odd match. I loved listening to him play his instrumental pieces, influenced by roots music from India, Morocco and jazzmen such as my much-revered Horace Silver. Davey was a larger-than-life character who had lived hard and fast and had travelled the world extensively. He'd become an occasional heroin user, and told tales of lost loves and experiences on the streets of Morocco.

Davey and I often played gigs as a duo. Our most notable was at a very posh event that the famous bandleader Johnny Dankworth had arranged. Here we found ourselves dressed like poor relations at a black tie and ballgown affair in honour of Princess Margaret. In our blue jeans and sweaters we felt very much out of place as we shook hands with royalty. I remember thinking that the princess was much shorter than I'd imagined – but she was very courteous as we went off to our section of the ball and launched into renderings of Lead Belly tunes. For this, we earned an appropriately princely sum of ten pounds. That took care of the rent that week.

With The Bluesbreakers' Thursday-night residency in place, the search for the right musicians continued. It became apparent that Davey's acoustic guitar wasn't working out and we parted company professionally, although we remained compatible flatmates. There was little time for auditions as such, so whoever showed up after a quick phone call took the bandstand that night.

At one gig, the great Alan Skidmore agreed to play. It was a shambles. I wasn't prepared for an avant-garde jazz soloist to be thrown into the mix, and our styles just didn't gel. We were fast losing hold of the Flamingo gig; Rik was even talking about letting us go because we were aggravating his punters.

Still, English audiences were definitely becoming attracted to jazz and blues. By now, The Rolling Stones had become all the rage at their regular gig at the Station Hotel in Richmond. We stopped by one night on our way home and I got to meet Mick and Brian while they were packing up their amps. They were very keen to talk about blues and I was pleased to make their acquaintance at last. They were already being hailed as the latest rebels poised to claim the south of England from the north, which was ruled by The Beatles.

By March, the Stones had secured a regular Sunday-afternoon residency in the Ken Colyer Club off Shaftesbury Avenue, and I went to see them play there for the first time. The low-ceilinged room was totally packed. The Stones' dress and long hair were an obvious statement of provocation; this appealed directly to the new generation, who were discovering the exhilaration of electric rock'n'roll. It was great to hear what people had been raving about. The Stones were already being marketed as a pop group with a future, in the hands of the young impresario Andrew Loog Oldham.

Over the rest of the year, their profile rose rapidly as the brash Mr Oldham took over their management, relegated their pianist Ian Stewart to road manager and got them exposure on TV shows such as *Thank Your Lucky Stars* and the first *Ready Steady Go!* They soon signed a record deal and their first single, 'Come On', was everywhere.

My search for a stable band continued. I saw Cyril Davies play a few times at the Marquee; usually his opening act was The Andy Wren Trio. I was impressed with Wren's guitarist, Jimmy Page, and offered him a job with The Bluesbreakers. He said he wasn't interested in joining a touring band, though, as he was earning a pretty good living as a studio musician.

Cyril's bass player, Cliff Barton, suggested that I try an eighteen-year-old bass-playing friend of his who had just left school and taken on a job in the tax office in Ealing. His name was John McVie, and he had just started to take bass guitar lessons from Cliff. I remember going to his parents' house and asking him to join The Bluesbreakers. John was keen, but I had to convince his folks that I was a respectable family man and had no plans to drag their son into a life of depravity in Soho.

I will never forget our first rehearsal at a pub in Acton, and the look of total bewilderment on John's face as he asked me, "What's a twelve-bar in C?" I lent him a few blues albums and all became clear...

An acquaintance from Manchester, Sammie Prosser, did a few gigs on guitar with us, followed by Bernie Watson, previously of Cyril Davies' All-Stars. Bernie was a very strange little guy whose chief interest in life was to become a second Segovia. He professed nothing but disdain for anything other than classical music, but he was such a perfectionist that he had technical mastery over any kind of guitar playing. It was quite incredible: when you listened to him play the blues, he did it with such emotion and finesse that you'd swear that it was his forte.

I hired Bernie, prepared to tolerate his odd stage behaviour because he played so beautifully. However, he refused to get involved with the audience and preferred to hide in the back corner, seated on a chair with his back to everyone. It was difficult for me to communicate signals and cues, but for the first time the music that came out was what I'd envisioned, so I put up with it – especially once our regular gigs got back on track and audiences began to accept us.

As for drummers, we ended up with a guy named Keith Robertson, who was very keen but had two drawbacks. One was that he tended to slow the tempo down on most tunes, making me feel like I was wading through mud; the other was his lack of personal hygiene. I had decided that we should have a band uniform consisting of black trousers, red shirt and black Naugahyde waistcoats. From the day that Keith was issued with his outfit, the shirt was never washed; consequently, long rides in the cramped interior of our van became difficult to bear.

The Bluesbreakers finally came together as a band on July 16 when I persuaded my old pal Peter Ward to join on drums. All through art college, he'd been the perfect match for me; it was as if we could read each other's minds. He'd previously been reluctant to take on the gig since he had moved to London, as he was climbing rapidly up the ladder in the advertising world. I guess because we mainly worked the London area during the week, he could still show up for his day job – just as I did.

The Twisted Wheel in Manchester was a historic venue for us. It opened on September 28 and featured The Graham Bond Quartet with Jack Bruce, Ginger Baker and Dick Heckstall-Smith. Spencer Davis opened the show as a solo act. The club was a huge success and I had the honour of playing the following weekend.

Despite the Bodega putting on a heavy rival bill – Cyril Davies' All-Stars with The Velvelettes and Long John Baldry – the Wheel was packed with mods, R&B fanatics and pillheads knocking back their 'blueys' or 'purple hearts'. At dawn everyone would tumble outside in a daze and hang around the cafes till buses and trains started running. We didn't get much sleep, as we would have to load the van and head down to the next gig.

That summer, Pamela, the kids and I moved into a large house at 17 Southbrook Road in Lee Green, at a price that we could afford after she'd sold the Beverley Road house. Peter lived in nearby Blackheath, so after our gigs, our van driver Tony had to drop him and me off first before swinging back to south-west London to take Bernie and John home. These journeys took more out of us than the gigs themselves.

Soon Tony's van began to feel the strains of the road and I had to buy a new one. I couldn't afford a brand-new vehicle, so Rik Gunnell talked me into buying Georgie Fame's clapped-out Thames van. It had accumulated countless miles on the clock, and it had no windows, but it was still a step up from Tony's van.

I set to work to convert it into a passenger and equipment combo. Out came the plywood and two-by-fours, and I partitioned off the back to hold our amps and drums before lining the remainder with two rows of bench seats. Even though I thought this the most comfortable solution, everyone else gravitated to the front, where they could see where we were going.

On occasional overnight stays in Manchester, I wasn't the most popular bandleader, because I gave John and Bernie the choice of kipping on couches at my father's bungalow or staying in the van. Peter would stay at his parents' house and I'd get to stay at my mother's, and I felt bad about that, but hotels were simply not an option with the income I was pulling in. London gigs earned us only between £15 and £25 a night, with an occasional £35 or £40 for out-of-town dates.

Things were slowly looking up, though. In November, Manfred Mann – who was a neighbour a few houses down along Southbrook Road – offered me the opening spot at one of his gigs at the

Marquee. Manfred had originally led The Mann-Hugg Blues Brothers, but when he and Mike Hugg parted company that May, Manfred began his move into the more lucrative world of pop music. Paul Jones became his frontman and they soared to the top with the singles 'Why Should We Not?', 'Cock-A-Hoop', '5-4-3-2-1' and 'Do Wah Diddy Diddy'. The opportunity to play on the same bill as his band was invaluable.

I met and heard The Spencer Davis Group for the first time when they came down to play the Flamingo; I was knocked out. Their singer, Steve Winwood, was amazing and we soon became friends, with plenty in common when it came to mutual musical influences. Towards the end of the year another pivotal club, the Scene, opened up in Soho's Ham Yard and quickly became a centre for a mod clientele. Live bands, mostly booked by the Gunnell Agency, appeared at the weekends, while the weekdays were hosted by an ebullient DJ called Guy Stevens.

Guy was connected to record company people, and in particular to Chris Blackwell of Island Records, as well as to Pete Meaden and Ian Samwell, who were launching the ultimate mod group, The High Numbers – soon to be renamed The Who. Through Guy and Ian, I began to build a profile: eventually they were able to pave the way for me to a record deal with the Decca label.

Another group to impress me that year were The Animals. They came down from Newcastle in December to play the Scene, and there was such a lot of hype about them that I had to go and see them play. They were a tight, powerful unit fronted by singer Eric Burdon. The other musicians were Hilton Valentine on guitar, John Steel on drums, Chas Chandler on bass guitar and singer Alan Price on keyboards. I met up with them that night; they were immediately planning to move to London.

Their last show before they relocated to London was on December 30, 1963, backing the great Sonny Boy Williamson in Newcastle. I found big Chas to be a most affable and approachable young man; his charm later stood him in good stead when he discovered Jimi Hendrix performing in a small New York club and persuaded him to come to Britain, where he thought Jimi would be more appreciated. He wasn't kidding!

As for Sonny Boy, he had been craftily attached to The Yardbirds by their manager Giorgio Gomelsky in the hopes that it would lend his boys a bit more credibility in the blues department. To that end he had them record a live album at his Crawdaddy Club, backing the master. Upon his return to the States, Sonny Boy was quoted as saying: "Those English boys want to play the blues real bad, and that's how they play – real bad."

I first heard the magic of Sonny Boy's harmonica on a Chess LP I bought in 1957. This contained the track 'Don't Start Me Talkin'', on which he was backed by Otis Spann, Muddy Waters, Jimmy Rogers, Willie Dixon and Fred Below. If there was ever an all-star session, that had to be it. I was hooked, to the point where I tried to adopt his style and tone on my own harmonicas. British Pye International released a single of 'Help Me' coupled with 'Bye Bye Bird', two songs that were seldom absent from my early club performances.

I saw the man for the first time when he appeared in concert with the American Folk Blues Festival. I couldn't believe the sounds he coaxed from his instrument. He fell for Europe in a big way, finding ways to get around visa restrictions and play the aforementioned gig with The Animals, as well as with Spencer Davis and The Yardbirds.

After The Bluesbreakers and I backed him on several London gigs, I remember him showing me a twelve-hole harp in the key of A. This was a key that was unobtainable in any catalogue or store; he told me that Hohner had made it especially for him. As he was going to Hohner's office the next day, Sonny Boy said I could come along with him. On the way there, sitting in the back of the taxi, he and I pulled out our big C harps and began to trade off. He would play a phrase and I tried to replicate what I'd heard.

I thought I was doing a pretty good job, but was somewhat crushed to be interrupted by his gruff, impatient voice yelling, "No, no, no. That's not right. You'll never be a harp player, man – because I'm the best there is!"

At the year's end we had our first family Christmas in our new home. Most of the family activity took place in the kitchen, which now housed a magnificent ornate harmonium that Pamela had picked up for next to nothing. The room above the den was a living room and playroom, and it was here that we had the television. Like most people, I remember when the programme we were watching was interrupted to announce the shocking news of President Kennedy's assassination. It felt like the end of enlightened leadership: we were stunned.

Another shock came on January 7, 1964, when Cyril Davies died at the age of only thirty-one, having ignored doctors' advice about cutting back on his drinking. He was a pretty obstinate guy and saw himself as a hard-living bluesman, like many of his idols, which made everyone on the scene even more surprised at the suddenness of his death from endocarditis. At our age, most of us musicians hadn't yet given a thought to our mortality. Long John Baldry later took over Cyril's band, and renamed it The Hoochie Coochie Men.

A benefit for Cyril was set for the night of January 28 at the Flamingo. It was going to be the biggest all-star line-up that London had ever seen, and I recorded the whole affair on my reel-to-reel tape recorder. I was second on the bill, following Jimmy Powell & The Five Dimensions, and I started the tape rolling when I went on. Unfortunately, the quality of my recorded set was highly imbalanced as I was using one of my mikes as my PA vocal. Ah well, it didn't matter.

Up next were Georgie Fame & The Blue Flames, and then Long John, who announced that a friend of his would like to come and sing a couple of numbers. This turned out to be none other than Rod Stewart, who at the time was totally unknown outside Birmingham, where he sang with a semi-pro group called The Dimensions. He sang 'Ain't That Loving You Baby', and I thought he had great potential, even though he tended to sing a little sharp.

Alexis Korner was next in line. All sorts of rumours had abounded about who would show up after midnight; the Stones were mentioned, but didn't materialise, although The Animals did arrive and played with their usual sweat and gusto. Next came The Yardbirds and Sonny Boy Williamson.

The Yardbirds' guitar player sounded good, although he hovered modestly in the background for most of the time. I was told that his name was Eric Clapton.

Sonny Boy was red-eyed and weaving around the stage after a long day on the bottle, and his set was loose, to say the least. Standing at the mike, he left long gaps between the tunes while he hunted for the right kind of harp. "What the devil did I do with that thing?" he mumbled in frustration as he searched the pockets of his two-tone harlequin suit.

Drunk and incapable as he frequently was, Sonny Boy still had superb command of his harp; I was in wonder at his sounds. He made it all seem so easy, even when he stuck the harp up his nose or played it inside his mouth without using his hands.

As this wondrous night grooved on, Graham Bond, Ginger Baker, Jack Bruce and Dick Heckstall-Smith set up and played until 4 a.m. I was in danger of running out of tape, but the event was nearly over. The last act ended up playing to a very sparse audience, nodding off in the seats. It was Dave Davani & The D-Men, featuring a singer called Beryl. After the previous excitement, they seemed somehow out of place – but someone had to play on until dawn. I imagine quite a few sleep-deprived punters reported groggily to work that morning.

The Bluesbreakers were working pretty steadily by then, with several regular weekly bookings. We'd do the Marquee on Monday nights, the Ealing Jazz Club on Saturdays and the Flamingo at the weekend, which might include four shows. Other regular spots were Dick Jordan's Klooks Kleek, the Scene, and the Ricky-Ticks of Guildford and Windsor, as well as trips up north to the Twisted Wheel and the Place.

However, in February, Peter Ward decided to leave; our increasing workload was conflicting with his advertising career. He hated to go, and I was just as daunted by the prospect of finding a replacement. I don't recall exactly how I came up with a new guy, but the very next night Martin Hart took over the drums for a

Saturday night show in Brentwood, Chertsey on Sunday and the Marquee on Monday.

In the meantime, Ian Samwell had organised the deal for us with Decca Records, and we reported to a studio in Portland Place to record for the first time. It was all very exciting; we lugged our gear up several flights of stairs and set up to record 'Crawling Up A Hill', my signature tune.

I learned a lesson that day, and it's been a guideline in my recording career ever since. Don't do more than two or three takes! I'm not kidding when I tell you that we did about forty takes and each one was successively stiffer and more frantic. I've never been comfortable listening to this record, because it all sounds so desperate.

We recorded the B-side, 'Mr James', much more quickly. This song was my tribute to the great bluesman Elmore James, who had died in May the previous year. When I listen to it today, I can see myself huddled over the keyboard with my harmonica harness strapped on, playing the blues while Bernie Watson weaved a beautiful guitar solo into the song.

By now, we were up to an average of thirty shows per month, which meant that I was able to announce that we were officially turning pro. From now on I would be paying the guys a salary of £20 a week, which felt like a landmark step. I began to make a reasonable amount of money too. After paying the band, instalments on the van and taking care of my family, I usually had enough to carry over in case of a short week when there wasn't as much money coming in.

Although Martin Hart was doing a solid job as my drummer, I began to think more and more about my Manchester friend Hughie Flint. Apart from Peter Ward, Hughie was the only other drummer I'd ever worked with who dovetailed perfectly with me, and I wanted to give him another shot. I rang him and offered him the gig, which he accepted; he only needed a couple of weeks to quit his day job and move to London. Martin was sorry to have to give up the gig, but understood that this was the way it had to be.

No sooner was I celebrating my reunion with Hughie than Bernie quit! I had only a week's warning and there was barely time to get a new guitarist on board. John Gilbey took over for a while, but I didn't feel he was quite right for the band, and through an advert in *Melody Maker*, I located Roger Dean. Roger's main interest was in country and western music: he was more familiar with Buddy Holly and Johnny Cash than Muddy Waters and Lightnin' Hopkins. He was a very accomplished technician, though, and a nice bloke who was ready to have a go.

R&B still hadn't caught on with the BBC or Radio Luxembourg, whose radio shows barely hinted at our world. The Beatles still led the popular music pack, along with Gerry & The Pacemakers, The Swinging Blue Jeans, Lulu, The Dave Clark Five, The Kinks, Dusty Springfield and Sandie Shaw. The nearest we got to being represented was by The Rolling Stones, who belted their way to the top of the charts with a version of Buddy Holly's 'Not Fade Away'.

Things improved when two pirate radio stations appeared and began to challenge the BBC's monopoly of the airwaves. Because they were broadcasting from ships offshore, they were able to operate without the usual licences, and rapidly became the new champions of music broadcasting. Radio Caroline and Radio London still played the same lame fodder for the masses, but one of the latter station's DJs, John Peel, managed to bring his personal taste to the listeners with a late programme called 'London After Midnight' and later 'The Perfumed Garden'. He later became a staunch Mayall fan.

On May 8, the 'Crawling Up A Hill' single was released and I eagerly awaited my first reviews. When the music papers came out, I was dismayed that the reviewers seemed more interested in the fact that I used to live in a tree than in the actual music. It didn't help that I was overshadowed by another Decca artiste, a flashy extrovert called P. J. Proby. His abominable single 'Hold Me' was released on the same day as mine, and my persona was no match for his. Proby was a moody, American Elvis wannabe, posturing in skin-tight black leather pants, a loose shirt and a ponytail with a flowing black ribbon. He looked like one of the Three Musketeers. It was no wonder that 'Crawling Up A Hill' got buried. Still, my regular following were happy that I'd finally got a record out.

Rik Gunnell had an option that month to book John Lee Hooker for a night at the Flamingo: he came to me to ask who John Lee was, and if I'd heard of him! With the chance to be John Lee's backing group for a month, I eagerly filled Rik in on a bit of blues history and assured him that the show would be a success. Rik did the deal with the infamous Don Arden, a notorious British booking agent and manager. The show was scheduled for June 1 at the Flamingo, with The Bluesbreakers in support.

In anticipation, I wrote a song called 'John Lee' to be performed as an introduction to him after we'd played our forty-five-minute opening set. It was a thrill to look forward to playing with him, but my excitement was crushed the week before the show, when Grandad died on May 28. He'd been doing some routine gardening when he fell and complained of pains in his chest. He was taken to Stepping Hill Hospital where he died of a massive stroke. He was eighty-seven years old.

My mother took it particularly hard. Grandad had been such a family figurehead to us all, and it was hard to accept that he wasn't with us any more. Due to the imminent month of bookings with John Lee Hooker, I was unable to go to the funeral: I remember an empty, sad space in my heart as we prepared for the shows.

CHAPTER 8

YOU MUST BE CRAZY: "LONDON'S NEWEST RAVING R&B SENSATION!"

On the opening night, the line of punters stretched all around the block. This was Rik Gunnell's reaction:

"I came by about six o'clock and thought, who the fuck are all these people? They were a great hairy lot with duffel coats and beards – definitely not the usual we got in the club. Ninety per cent of our usual clientele were American servicemen and prostitutes, and the other 10 per cent got in by mistake. Then it registered that they'd come from all over the country to see John Lee Hooker. I couldn't believe it.

"It was a pound to get in, which was robbery back then, but we just stood at the bottom of the stairs grabbing notes. Things were a lot looser then, and guys could be bribed – police, or whoever. You'd never get away nowadays with the things we got up to back then. The place was licensed for 322 people or something, and suddenly we had about 1,200 packed in. The crush was unbelievable! The air conditioning consisted of six fans, which were totally useless: after two hours of being open, the floors were so slick you were sliding. Sweat was falling from the ceiling like it was raining inside.

"We had an emergency exit, but it was a farce! It was always bolted with chains around it. About two in the morning some guys wanted to come in that way. Tony, the guy on the door, said, 'It's a pound to get in.' The guy said, 'But we were pushed out of this door! We've got cloakroom tickets here.' It turned out that the chains had broken and all these bewildered people had been squeezed out of the emergency exit. Tony said, 'Sorry sir, it's still a pound,' so these poor bastards had to pay to come back in and get their coats. It was a great night, although I never heard a note!"

The Cheynes were the opening act, led by pianist Peter Bardens; the drummer was a tall, skinny youth named Mick Fleetwood. Rik had also booked Zoot Money's Big Roll Band, whose guitarist at that time was Andy Summers; he later found international fame with The Police.

We finally met John Lee Hooker in the cramped excuse for a band room, where Coca-Cola crates were stacked to the ceiling. They had one chair for John Lee back there; I think it was a bit of a culture shock for him.

Rik once described the band room as "a tiny little fucking space at the side of the stage". He added: "Sometimes there'd be people crammed in there, with guys shooting up and birds stripping off. On crowded nights, you couldn't get out to the toilets without ducking across the bandstand, so people used to piss on the amps or up against the wall. We always had a rat in there, because the sewage pipes used to come out from the Chinese restaurant next door. We used to hurl things at it. In that room you had to be smashed out of your fucking brain – but Mayall would be sipping a pint of milk in the corner!"

Mr Hooker could hardly help comparing this facility with the spacious band rooms and first-class travel that he'd become accustomed to, but he was happy to see such an amazing turnout. We talked and prepared ourselves for an evening of blues of indeterminate structure. Between the choruses you could be looking at nine bars, or thirteen bars, or something in between; the secret was to stay on your toes and change chords as best you could.

We went on stage, performed our usual material and then brought John Lee on. He plugged in his guitar and adjusted the mike, and we were off. The audience went wild, even though the heat was so intense that condensation from the ceiling was dripping constantly on their heads. I'm sure most of them couldn't actually see him at all.

The next day we checked the music papers for reviews. *Melody Maker*'s Max Jones gave us a good write-up, but when the purist John Broven got his typewriter out for a report in *Blues Unlimited*, he tore us to pieces, complaining about having an organ as part of John

Lee's backing band and it being too pop-oriented. As Broven saw it, The Cheynes and I added up to two hours of synthetic rubbish.

John Lee was an easy guy to work with, although we didn't see much of him during the daytime during that month of shows. We travelled to the gigs in the usual way in the van, while he was transported by chauffeured car from London to wherever the gig was. He had quite a few grumbles; the main thing that bothered him was English food. He was used to being able to go out any time of day or night and grab a burger, while we had no fast food places. Even the fish and chip shops were open for only a few hours, six days a week. There were only two TV channels, and by the time we'd get home after a show, broadcasting would be finished for the night. I also remember him being freaked out when fights broke out at two shows in Newcastle, which I thought was strange − surely he'd seen a ton of fights in his long career back home?

These problems aside, once John Lee got out his guitar and opened his mouth to sing, he was in his element; listening to him, we were transported to a different plane. I hung on every nuance and learned so much in a short time about vocal dynamics.

We were booked to play with John Lee until July 5, after which we had a full calendar of dates of our own. The popularity of the tour called for extra Hooker dates, but I declined, mainly because we'd been earning too little money as a double bill. I recently dug out the contract for a show in Nottingham, where the total fee for both of us was £50!

The Groundhogs backed John Lee for the subsequent dates; I know their guitarist Tony McPhee hadn't been happy that we were originally chosen to do the tour. He now got the chance to hang with John Lee on a regular basis. I think John preferred their accompaniment, as it happens, because they were more rooted in traditional blues than I was. He even took to travelling in The Groundhogs' van rather than being chauffeured in a private car.

Because Rik was our agent, we were paid correctly for the John Lee Hooker tour. However, I later learned that Don Arden royally screwed John Lee, who said that he got nothing except a list of expenses of hotels, meals, chauffeur wages, car rental, commissions and God knows what else. An absolute disgrace.

Shortly afterwards, Alexis Korner opened up a new club: it didn't last more than a couple of weeks after the opening night – but it was a hell of an opening. The billing boldly advertised Alexis Korner's Blues Incorporated featuring Ronnie Jones and Phil Seamen, plus The Johnny Parker Trio.

Lower down the list, I was advertised as "London's newest raving R&B sensation, the Roland Kirk of the R&B world, playing three instruments – John Mayell [sic] And His Fabulous Bluesbreakers, plus Mr Excitement, Sensational Singer Sammie Prosser!"

Sammie, who had recently returned from the drug culture of San Francisco's Haight-Ashbury, had asked me to get him a solo spot. It was a long night with set changes: during one of the breaks, I took a couple of harmonicas into the toilet and composed the instrumental 'Blues City Shakedown'.

During the month of July, The Beatles' film *A Hard Day's Night* was a big hit; their songs just kept on coming. They were the sound of that summer. Meanwhile, The Bluesbreakers and I racked up thirty shows, culminating with the Ricky-Tick in Windsor, where we backed Sonny Boy Williamson for a full set for the first and only time.

Sonny Boy gigged almost constantly in England and Europe that year, but his body couldn't cope with the amounts of hard liquor he was consuming day after day. He apparently had a feeling that he wasn't going to last much longer and headed back to the States, where he died on March 24, 1965.

At this time I was composing songs and recording them on my reel-to-reel at home, and wanted to shop them around. Rik's girlfriend Jeannie Lincoln owned a demo studio and we went there one afternoon to make proper-quality demos; the studio was tiny, but the engineer was very helpful and did a good job. His name was Eddie Kramer, and he later became famous for his work with Jimi Hendrix, Led Zeppelin, David Bowie, Kiss and many other huge-selling bands.

One song was later picked up and released by Tony Sheridan as 'I Gotta Travel All Over'; another, a ballad called 'Something', was later recorded by Georgie Fame. I thought his uptempo version destroyed the whole meaning of the song.

The summer nights were filled with shows, mostly in and around the London area. Mike Vernon, a house producer for Decca, persuaded the label to record us for a live album. One of our regular venues was Klooks Kleek, which happened to be next door to Decca's studios; we ran the cables out of the studio skylight, across the roof and through the window into the club.

The recording took place on November 7. As we played, Mike Vernon phoned through to the studio engineer Gus Dudgeon – who later became well-known as a producer with Elton John – to tell him to roll the tape. I was very nervous, and played and sang rather too frantically throughout the two sets, but the sound quality on the finished mix was great.

I was thrilled to have an album of my own ready for release. With a cover designed by Peter Ward and me, and liner notes by Alexis Korner, the album was titled *John Mayall Plays John Mayall: Live At Klooks Kleek*. It was released on March 26, 1965.

Early in January, I got a shot at backing another of my American blues heroes, T-Bone Walker, who was famous as an early practitioner of the electric guitar as well as for his hit song 'Stormy Monday'. He was a lot more outgoing than the intense John Lee Hooker and performed crowd-pleasing stunts such as playing the guitar behind his back and over his head.

This was followed by a recording session for my song 'Crocodile Walk', which Decca wanted to use to promote the Klooks Kleek live album. At the same session I recorded two possible B-sides, Little Walter's 'My Baby Is Sweeter' and the instrumental 'Blues City Shakedown'. The latter got the vote, partly because I wasn't happy with Roger's guitar solos. They were tolerable on stage because they were transient, but on record, the fact that he wasn't a natural blues player was obvious.

I began looking for a new guitar player, and soon found one. His name was Eric Clapton.

I'd run into Eric a few times with The Yardbirds. The group had released a live album backing Sonny Boy Williamson, and another live album, *Five Live Yardbirds*, was doing fairly well, but Eric wasn't happy. He felt that the band knew very little about the blues, and he was getting sick not only of their desire to be pop stars, but of their managers Giorgio Gomelsky and Hamish Grimes, who were dead set on pushing them as the next Rolling Stones. It was perhaps a little unfair to dismiss them in such a cursory manner; even though they had blues numbers dominating their repertoire, they obviously had their eyes open for acceptance among followers of the British charts.

The last straw for Eric came when The Yardbirds released a single called 'For Your Love', which didn't feature guitar playing. Instead, it emphasised an uncredited Brian Auger on harpsichord, plus bongos and Beatles-style harmonies. Eric, who knew full well that he was the only star of the band as far as The Yardbirds' audiences were concerned, was pissed off that the band should even consider a single that had no guitar on it.

The single did feature Eric on its B-side, with an instrumental called 'Got To Hurry', but it was credited to O. Rasputin, Giorgio Gomelsky's nickname. It was unfair that Gomelsky should get the credit and the royalties for the song, and although the single shot up the charts and made The Yardbirds a bona fide pop group overnight, Eric quit on March 13. It hadn't helped that Gomelsky had sent out a barrack-room memo of rules and regulations about being on time, with the band members fined for minor infractions.

'Got To Hurry' was incredible. When I heard it, I felt a surge of excitement and my imagination kicked into overdrive. It was a killer track that conveyed the power and emotion of great blues guitarists like Freddie King; I could almost feel Eric talking to me through his guitar solos. I knew I had to ask this guy to join The Bluesbreakers. If he only wanted to play the blues, we would give him the perfect opportunity.

I got in touch with Eric's grandmother Rose, who got a message through to him; having left The Yardbirds, he was now doing odd jobs on building sites. He called me and asked, "What about the guitarist you've already got?" I explained that I had to make a choice between keeping on a musician who was conscientious and a pleasure to work with, or putting artistic integrity first. Eric told me over the phone that he would consider the offer, and we arranged a meeting at Southbrook Road to sort it out.

I remember this young fellow in a tan raincoat coming on foot towards the house; once he'd come inside and we'd begun talking about the music, he said yes. Afterwards, I played 'Got To Hurry' for John and Hughie, and told them that Eric was going to join us. They were excited, although, like me, they knew it would be difficult to tell Roger the bad news. It would be my first real test as a bandleader.

Roger took the news calmly, however. I think that he must have had some inkling about it from the general vibe in the band. Gentleman that he was, he said he understood my reasons. We played our last gigs together and parted as friends.

Before Roger left the band, a French TV station asked me to do a curious promotional film for 'Crocodile Walk', to which I mimed as I played the Hammond organ at the Flamingo. The shoot was nerve-racking in the extreme, because they brought in a live crocodile and set it on top of the organ. Understandably, I found it hard to look at the camera – or indeed remember the words.

Four days after the release of the single, Eric Clapton officially became a Bluesbreaker. As our new guitar player was still living in Oxford, with occasional trips back to the Claptons' family home in Ripley, there seemed no reliable way to have him in the band other than to offer him a room in our house. There was a small spare room at the top of the stairs with a window facing the back garden, and it wasn't being used for much other than storage, so we put a bed in there for him.

On the day of the move, Pamela, the three children and I drove out to Ripley to meet Rose and assure her that Eric was going to be looked after respectably. Even though Ripley and Lee Green weren't far apart, he and Rose were reluctant to say goodbye to each other, but we loaded up his possessions and were on our way.

At first, Eric kept himself to himself. We didn't see much of him, although we could hear him constantly practising his guitar. His first gig with us took place at one of our regular clubs on April 6, with no rehearsal or soundcheck. I'd played him tapes of our repertoire, which was enough to get us started.

Initially, we all found Eric difficult to get close to. He was moody, quiet and aloof – but at the same time, there was something about him that made you want to be his friend. Fortunately, within three or four days it felt as if he'd always been in the band. It was clearly a relief to him to be able to play freely within the loose structure of our shows. He evidently still felt some rancour towards his old band; as The Yardbirds climbed rapidly to the top of the charts and also broke through in America, he had very little praise for the group or their music.

Our profile escalated after Eric joined us, and it wasn't long before we played on *Ready Steady Go!* and *BBC Saturday Club*, tapes of which are still floating around. We were still performing 'Crawling Up A Hill', 'Crocodile Walk' and other tracks from the *Klooks Kleek* LP, but as a feature for Eric, we started to do Freddie King's classic 'Hideaway'. This song went on to become a tradition for Bluesbreakers lead guitarists.

At the end of April it was announced that Bob Dylan was to come over for a tour. No one was more surprised than I when word came through the office that, of all the people in the English music industry, Bob wanted to meet me. Apparently, my 'Crawling Up A Hill' single had taken his fancy.

I felt very honoured when I went over to the Savoy Hotel to meet him. As I entered the Dylan party's assigned suites, an all-American cast of characters greeted me – Bob, his manager Albert Grossman and his wife, the producer Tom Wilson, and also the folk singer Joan Baez, who had come along for the ride. The room was filled with American accents; it was as if I'd jumped across the Atlantic Ocean.

Over everyone's shoulder was the movie camera of documentarian D. A. Pennebaker. He shot fly-on-the-wall style for most of the tour; the resulting footage later became the film *Don't Look Back*.

I sat between Bob and Joan in a car that drove us up to his first show in Sheffield on April 30, and listened to their anecdotes as Pennebaker's camera rolled. At the shows he performed in England, it was a shock for audiences to see that Bob was playing electric guitar. His strictly 'folk' image was tarnished, and mixed reactions came from the punters.

Bob played eight shows in England; during that time I was his contact for any other people he wished to meet. Bob asked me to get Marianne Faithfull's number, as he fancied her.

"Is she dateable, John?" he asked.

"You'll have to sort that one out yourself!" I laughed.

I believe Bob and Marianne arranged some sort of tryst before he and his entourage headed back to New York. A few weeks later, she married the artist John Dunbar.

Shortly afterwards, we were asked to back the American bluesman John Hammond for a show at the Flamingo. John's father was the famous blues and jazz researcher and impresario John Hammond Senior, who had been responsible for the 'From Spirituals To Swing' concerts at New York's Carnegie Hall in 1938 and 1939 – shows that would have featured Robert Johnson, but for his untimely death.

The Bluesbreakers were now beginning to attract a lot of attention. Thanks to Eric, there was a marked increase in the prevalence of girls at every show, which was new to us. As a married man I wasn't inclined to stray, although a groupie did once pounce on me as I stood at the side of the stage. Wrapping her arms around me, she kissed me passionately. Perhaps I'd finally made it as a sex symbol?

The incident inspired me to write the song 'I'm Your Witchdoctor', which became the first single that Eric played on. A chance came in June to record this song for Andrew Loog Oldham's new Immediate label. I think it was because the producer, Jimmy Page, admired Eric's guitar so much that we got the gig. After we recorded the 'Witchdoctor' track, we did a new blues of mine as the B-side. This was 'Telephone Blues', which I used to showcase Eric's guitar prowess. It was magnificent, and still one of Eric's best solos in my opinion.

My Manchester band The Blues Syndicate in 1962 before trying to put together a new line-up of strangers in London, although Hughie Flint eventually moved south to join me. They are Hughie, sax player Jack Massarik, trumpeter John Rowlands and my art college pal Ray Cummings on guitar.

Pretending to play tambourine next to my redecorated pedal organ in the first flat that my wife, Pamela, and I shared in Manchester.

A rare sixties poster from a London club that we played frequently. Not my idea to be called Johnny but the poster shows that The Rolling Stones had to start somewhere too.

Posing for my first press photo with harmonica harness strapped on tightly. John McVie is playing bass behind me. RB/REDFERNS

A typical funny portrait of me pretending to be asleep in a plywood box. This was taken at the all-night gig at the Flamingo in 1966. MIRRORPIX

A very nice day at the beach with Pamela and our three children, Jason, Tracey and Gary, before he changed his name to Gaz.

Another family grouping that now includes our adopted son, Ben. MIRRORPIX

One of the very rare group photos, taken on a London street in 1966. (L–r) Drummer Hughie Flint, Eric Clapton and bassist John McVie. You can see how none of us took this too seriously. TCD/PROD.DB/ALAMY

A special concert in Europe showcased the talents of (l–r) Carl Wayne, Stevie Winwood, Jimi Hendrix, myself and Eric Burdon. PICTURE ALLIANCE/PHOTOSHOT

I was very proud of my long hair and lots of beads in this 1968 press photograph. IVAN KEEMAN/REDFERNS

We are now a six-piece band and were only months away from our first trip to the USA in 1968. Drummer Keef Hartley and saxophone-wiz Dick Heckstall-Smith look to the sky as I pose with sax player Chris Mercer, bassist Keith Tillman and guitarist Mick Taylor. IVAN KEEMAN/REDFERNS

Proudly showing off my Los Angeles tan in my first home in Laurel Canyon in 1968. GEMS/REDFERNS

I had a special leather belt that held all twelve of my harmonicas in their different keys.
MICHAEL OCHS ARCHIVES/GETTY IMAGES

A nice shot of me playing the harp at a summer festival in 1969. I was very proud of my new hat.

Now a permanent fixture in Laurel Canyon, I happily pose for a press shot surrounded by my various Western style collections. CHRIS WALTER/WIREIMAGE

Another casual shot of me in the California sunshine, 1972.
CHRIS WALTER/WIREIMAGE

After my Laurel Canyon home tragically burnt to the ground, I'm seen here trying to find anything to salvage from the disaster that claimed twenty-four other homes. It didn't deter me from building again on the same site.

'I'm Your Witchdoctor' was one of the first songs to feature guitar feedback, a sound pioneered by The Who; in the bridge, Eric leaned his instrument towards the amp and achieved a succession of wailing sounds. Talking of The Who, in June we played the Uxbridge Blues And Folk Festival, where they were the headliners. On the bill with us were Long John Baldry and The Spencer Davis Group. This was the only time I heard The Who live, and although Eric rated Keith Moon as a great drummer, I had a hard time with Moon's erratic timekeeping. He certainly captured everyone's attention, though – he flailed away at the kit like a madman.

Eric could be a little hard to work with at times. For example, he refused to use feedback when we played 'Witchdoctor' live; he stood there, staring defiantly at me, as the song fell apart with an empty space in the middle. His moods were always changing and his behaviour was unpredictable. One day he'd be your best friend in the world, and the next day he and Hughie would gang up on me, complaining about having to travel in the windowless van.

He was also becoming unreliable when it came to being picked up in the van at Charing Cross Station. I knew that he was spending time with famous rock musicians; sometimes I wondered if playing with The Bluesbreakers had become a chore for him. Then again, on some nights he played with incredibly deep emotion. He was like a man possessed. At those moments I knew there was no other guitarist in the world to match him.

When Eric was in a good mood, though, he was great company. He particularly enjoyed practical jokes and pranks. One night, we were at a petrol station and a woman popped her head through the van window. She asked us what our group was called, and Eric told her we were The Death Rats. She backed away in horror. Remember, it was 1965.

As the summer passed, Eric was often late for gigs, and sometimes didn't show up at all. We could sense something brewing well before he came to me to say he was leaving the band. His plan was to trek across Europe with friends, stopping anywhere they felt like and playing music. I'd seen it coming, but it still hit me hard; I knew of no guitar player who came close to Eric's genius, and we had a full calendar of gigs lined up.

My solution was to audition new guitarists on stage at those gigs. There was quite a succession of candidates for the job; during August I went through four or five guys a week. Eventually I settled on a nice young man named Geoff Krivit; he wasn't a great soloist, but he was a good rhythm player and I felt as though I could breathe easily again. However, once Eric was gone, a large percentage of my audience vanished with him, which was rather upsetting.

By August I'd had enough; I needed a vacation, so Pamela and I rented a caravan in Devon and we went down there for a family holiday. Although there wasn't much in the way of hot weather, we made the most of the scenery and the beach. I also did a bit of filming, and although the film is now lost, I still remember a shot of Pamela turning towards me, caught unawares. Her affectionate look was to haunt me when our marriage later came to an end, but at the time there was no hint of the break-up to come.

In fact, she and I were seriously planning to have a fourth child. This time around, Pamela didn't feel like another nine months of carrying a baby, and so we decided on adoption. As we investigated the procedure, we were told that the most in-demand babies were white girls, closely followed by white boys. Right at the bottom of the list, and the hardest to place with adoptive families, were black boys. We decided to apply to adopt a child in this category, and began the paperwork when we got back from our holiday.

Back in London, I got very friendly with Steve Winwood. One night, after a Spencer Davis gig in south London, he came back to our house for an all-night jam session which I recorded on my reel-to-reel. He had recently discovered the powers of the Hammond organ, and the fact that I had one was more than enough to coax him round. We took turns switching from guitar to organ as the tape rolled. It was such a special night for both of us.

Two years later, when the producer Mike Vernon was gathering together a variety of tracks from different musicians to put on a Decca compilation album called *Raw Blues*, I selected a piece of our session and had John McVie and Aynsley Dunbar overdub bass and drums onto the track. I called it 'Long Night'.

October was a dramatic month for The Bluesbreakers. Our 'Witchdoctor' single was released to good reviews, albeit moderate sales, but unfortunately I had to sack my bassist John McVie for drunken behaviour. Although he'd joined the band as an innocent eighteen-year-old with no apparent vices, he'd been seduced by being on the road and spending too many nights at the decadent Flamingo, where Scotch and Coke flowed endlessly. He'd soon discovered a taste for vodka, and over the course of the previous year, he'd been drinking more and more.

Eventually the booze began to interfere with John's performance: towards the end he would sometimes be so drunk that he had to be steered to his place on stage. Once the show started, it was anybody's guess what John would get up to, including falling backwards onto his amp. One night he ran off stage in the middle of a song and came back swinging on the curtains.

I pride myself on a reasonable tolerance for high jinks, but this was going too far. On top of this, we always had a long drive home to deal with. Our driver Tony would drop everyone off at their homes, and if you were the last one, the journey seemed to last forever. Hughie and I lived in Lee Green in south-east London, while John had to go to Ealing in the west. By the time he got home, he often had to be literally carried in, as he'd passed out from his booze intake. John eventually sobered up for good in 1987, and we're friends to this day, but back in 1965 he was impossible to deal with.

With poor old John out of the picture, I approached Jack Bruce, whose bass playing had enthralled me since the Graham Bond jazz days. He was available because the internal strife and fireworks that typified the relationship with him and Ginger Baker had made him quit The Graham Bond Organisation for good. As a canny Scot, he wasn't too thrilled at the £20-a-week wages that I was paying, but he needed the work and signed on. Jack's amazing playing really kicked the band up several notches; we now had another guy with the skills to feature as a soloist, in his case on a six-string Fender Bass VI guitar.

John Lee Hooker was now back in England for a second club tour. Once again he was backed by The Groundhogs, featuring the excellent slide playing of Tony McPhee, who had recently declined my offer to take Eric's place in The Bluesbreakers. The Groundhogs had another engagement on October 12, and so we got to back John Lee for a show in Nottingham.

It's amazing to see the typewritten contract that I have framed at home. It states that for an evening's performance at the Dungeon Club, we were paid only 50 per cent of the door. However, we played two full sets from The Bluesbreakers and another one, lasting thirty minutes, with John Lee Hooker!

The next night we were playing the Flamingo, and a young guy with black curly hair and a strong East End accent stood at the front of the stage while we played. In the interval, he began to pester me about letting him play guitar with The Bluesbreakers.

"I've been to a lot of your gigs," he said, "and I heard you were still trying people out — so I was hoping you'd let me have a go. If you're going to have auditions, you should really hear everybody! I'm not saying I can do what Eric does, but I've got my own style, and I think I'm as good as some of the guys you've been using."

There was something about this young man's self-confidence and persistence that I couldn't ignore, so I invited him to our house to see what he could do. He said he was mainly a blues guitarist, but was currently learning the bass and playing in a local group. Plugging an electric Harmony Meteor guitar into my amp, he played through some of the current repertoire, including 'Stepping Out' and some Freddie King stuff.

To my ears, his playing was a revelation. He played the blues with the purest tone I'd heard since Eric left. The young man's name was Peter Green, and he was later to become a bona fide blues legend with Fleetwood Mac. Geoff Krivit was told the bad news and Peter took the stand with us on November 24. The old sound, spirit and intensity of The Bluesbreakers were back.

In the meantime, Eric and his motley crew — appropriately calling themselves The Glands — had set off to conquer Europe in a second-hand bus. They didn't pick up any work until they got to

Greece, where they fell foul of a shady club owner who hired them as a backing band for some local singer. As the story goes, it wasn't long before the owner recognised Eric's talent – and when the boys decided it was time to move on, Eric became a hostage. The club owner locked up all their equipment and forced Eric to stay on; he eventually escaped through a window.

Now, I had told Eric that when he'd had enough of his adventures, his place in The Bluesbreakers would be there waiting for him when he returned. After all, I reminded him, I was running one of the very few remaining blues bands of note that hadn't enjoyed a hit record or 'gone commercial'.

You'll understand, then, that when Eric got back to London, it all got rather tricky. I had just given the gig to Peter Green, one of the finest blues guitarists of his generation, only to have his predecessor return before Peter had barely settled in. It was the worst possible dilemma for me, because Eric wanted to take me up on my promise to have him back.

In the end, Peter got to play with us for only two or three gigs. He was very upset to lose his job, and we didn't part on good terms. His last show was at the Mojo Club in Sheffield, run by Peter Stringfellow, later the epitome of the London nightclub owner.

On December 1, Eric was back on The Bluesbreakers' bandstand. He and Jack Bruce locked together instantly; boy, did we cook now. Hughie was in heaven, blending in with Jack's jazz licks, and the searing blues of Eric's guitar took us to new heights. It was a night of mutual admiration all around – and it felt great.

Now Eric was back with us, a surge of extra punters showed up at the gigs. He seemed to revel in the acclaim some nights and resent it on others. There was a rumour that graffiti on a south London wall was proclaiming 'Clapton Is God' – and he had mixed feelings about that. He also began to experiment with unusual stage gear.

We had previously worn seersucker jackets, slimline ties and button-down shirts in the mode favoured by Georgie Fame and his Flamingo Club successor, Zoot Money. However, after The Who's influence and the Carnaby Street wave grew, Eric began showing up in very eclectic garb. He used to regularly dress up in Victorian military jackets, for example.

The oddest outfit he wore was at the Club A'Gogo in Newcastle, where he wore a full-length priest's robe complete with white dog collar. This didn't really seem appropriate for Newcastle audiences, who were always such a hard-drinking, rowdy crowd, but there was no questioning Eric's incredible guitar prowess. With his eyes closed, facing up to the heavens, it seemed as if he was undergoing a religious experience. Perhaps the priestly gear was appropriate after all.

He could still be unreliable, unfortunately. On one occasion we waited at the usual Charing Cross meeting place, but Eric didn't show up, so we went on without him. We drove up to the show in Hatfield feeling pissed off and let down, and wondering how to make it through the sets. Of course, Jack's elaborate bass playing was a big help, and he also sang his vocal and harmonica feature 'Train Time', which helped fill the first session.

During the interval a young lad who couldn't have been much older than sixteen or seventeen came backstage to ask if he could sit in for the second set. He said he'd brought his guitar with him and that he knew our stuff from hearing us at the Flamingo. With nothing to lose, we said yes – and his playing was terrific.

This was my first meeting with Mick Taylor, the future Rolling Stone. By the end of the set I was determined to get his phone number – but he vanished as mysteriously as he'd appeared.

Things were moving fast, and we were then asked to record another single for Immediate. I wrote a song called 'On Top Of The World', a song designed specifically to move us forward. Jack and Eric played energetically on the session, and Jack also sang backup harmonies on the hook lines. Again, Eric displayed his feedback skills, supplying a sustained wail that moved from one note to another without a break. It sounded fantastic. For some reason we didn't get to do a B-side, and although we were booked to come in later and do one, a line-up change was about to complicate things.

You will recall the frown on Jack's face when I told him what the wages would be... Well, unknown to me, none other than Manfred

Mann had decided that he wanted to have Jack in his band – and with the chart-busting singles that his band had enjoyed, he could afford to pay him anything he liked without denting his budget. The first we heard of this was when we read in *Melody Maker* that Jack had signed up as Manfred's new bass player.

Eric and I were both incensed that Jack hadn't let us know about this first. We even felt bitter enough about it to sit down and write a slow blues together called 'Double Crossing Time', with the lyric 'double crossing Mann' spelling it out. This, we decided, would be the perfect B-side for the Immediate single. Not only did it express our disdain for Jack's betrayal of loyalty, but it would showcase Eric's guitar on a down-and-dirty blues.

As Jack had already gone, I got hold of a bassist named John Bradley to play on the song. It was a killer track, so we were disappointed when Immediate decided they didn't want to release it after all. I held on to the master recording, as they weren't going to use it.

When it came to finding a permanent replacement for Jack, my only option was to approach John McVie and see if he was ready to be a good boy. He said he'd appreciate another chance and that he was ready to rejoin. Eric always had a soft spot for John, so he was welcomed back into The Bluesbreakers.

We were a close-knit unit on and off stage. Many were the hours we spent in the van going home when the three of us would act out all the dialogue we could remember from *The Caretaker*, the Harold Pinter play that we loved so much. "Don't come it with me." "That Scotch git." "I'd have cracked my head on that pavement..." – all great lines delivered by Donald Pleasence.

Once John rejoined the band, things went smoothly and I hoped that there would be no more personnel dramas for a while, at least until the end of 1965. I wasn't to know that more upheaval was on its way, and that it would land on me like a ton of bricks.

On December 26, we were booked to play at Eel Pie Island, but Eric didn't show up. There was nothing else to do but go on and play as a trio, and I was pretty pissed off. However, I soon brightened up when I saw a beautiful, long-haired blonde standing by the entrance, looking as if she was waiting for someone. I went over to talk to her, and was instantly smitten. Christine, as she was called, turned out to be one of Eric's many girlfriends, and she was just as annoyed as I was that he hadn't shown up.

After the show, the promoter said that he was having a party at his flat, which was just the other side of the Eel Pie bridge. I was captivated by Christine and asked her to come along too. We talked, and after some hours of heartfelt conversation, we melted into each other's arms.

It was almost painful to return home. My mind was in turmoil.

The following night, after an unsuccessful attempt at making love to Pamela, I rolled over on my back and lay next to her, side by side in the darkness.

"What's wrong?" she asked.

I plucked up the courage to say what needed to be said.

"I've met someone, Pamela, and I don't think I can stay married to you any more."

She was silent for a while, and then asked, "Have you slept with her?"

"No, but I want to," I replied. "I don't want to be unfaithful to you, though. I don't know how we can go on."

It was a terrible night. It seemed inconceivable that this was happening.

When daylight arrived, Pamela told me that she couldn't have me around in this situation, and suggested I move in with Christine for a week so that I could make up my mind about what I wanted to do.

I called Christine and told her what was happening. She gave me her address and the next time Tony came for me in the van, I packed some things and left Southbrook Road.

I duly spent the week with Christine in her basement flat and we consummated our affair. It was liberating and exciting – and at the same time very strange – to make love to someone other than the woman I'd known for twelve years. On the other hand, it wasn't all roses: there were a few quarrels about me being a married man and how such men 'always go back to their wives'.

I felt torn between the two options, but came to the conclusion that temptations were out there and, now that I had experienced them, I would never have the same relationship with Pamela again. There would be other women, even if Christine wasn't the one.

It was strange and sad to be away from the children; I'll never know what the kids were told about my absence. I suppose Gary, being the oldest, would have been the most curious; he certainly took it the hardest when I made the tough decision to leave for good.

CHAPTER 9

FULL SPEED AHEAD: UPHEAVALS AND BLUE NOTES

Unsurprisingly, the first four months of 1966 were complete upheaval.

Some of the time I was staying with Christine, and at other times I was at home, trying to sort things out. This wasn't made easier by the fact that I was pretty transient at the time, often moving from place to place and staying at friends' houses or flats while they were away. Even worse, Christine's demands for exclusivity were causing us to have constant arguments. I began to realise that this relationship wasn't actually what I wanted.

Still, I couldn't bring myself to return to married life, and I had to tell Pamela that I was leaving her. She was devastated. As I began to take stock of my records and books in the front room, I overheard her breaking down as she called her mother to tell her the sad news. It seemed unreal.

My professional life gave my world some much-needed solidity. Mike Vernon was campaigning with Decca to give me another record deal; this was timely, as we were drawing huge audiences in the clubs since Eric Clapton had rejoined us. When the deal was offered, Mike brought Eric and me together to record a couple of tracks for his Purdah label before I signed on the dotted line. He wanted to capture the raw sounds heard on the early Chicago blues recordings, and set us up with a single mike, a piano and my voice.

The two songs that emerged were, I'm pleased to say, British blues classics. I sang 'Lonely Years', a song about the break-up of my marriage, and a piano boogie duet called 'Bernard Jenkins', an in-joke and a reference to Donald Pleasence's character in the 1963 film of Harold Pinter's *The Caretaker*. I still listen to the record today and marvel at how closely Eric and I blended so seamlessly with our ideas and emotions. Only one take was needed to say it all. Mike was able to release the single on Purdah very quickly and then Decca came through with their deal.

Shortly afterwards, Champion Jack Dupree came over to England for a club tour and Mike secured the studio so that Jack could make an album backed by British musicians. Of course, Eric and I were first on the list, and both of us soloed on a few tracks. I think this was the first time that I met Keef Hartley, the drummer of The Artwoods. Art Wood himself was the frontman, and his younger brother was Ronnie Wood, who played a mean lead guitar and who later enjoyed a stellar career with Faces and The Rolling Stones.

On March 30, Eric turned twenty-one and we held a lavish birthday party for him. It was a fairly wild event, with a lot of wine and spirits imbibed by Eric's friends; many of the high jinks were captured on my movie camera. One of Eric's best pals, the poet Ted Milton, collapsed with drunken laughter at the sight of Eric lurching around in a rented gorilla suit. Pete Brown, who later wrote a lot of material for Eric's future band Cream, also showed up.

In April, I began to look for a flat. As Bayswater was Alexis Korner's territory and I was familiar with the neighbourhood, I soon found a place on the top floor of 56 Porchester Road. My affair with Christine didn't die easily; for over a year we continued to see each other, on and off. She could never accept that it was over. If I had another girlfriend – and there were a few of them – she would fly into jealous rages and rant at me on the phone or bang on my door in the night. There was very little peace.

It felt like being in the movie *Fatal Attraction*; once she even broke into the flat and threw furniture about, as well as emptying a box of cornflakes all over the floor. We did have some highs as well as lows, though – and our tumultuous affair was the inspiration for songs of mine such as 'Little Girl', 'Key To Love', 'Have You Heard', 'Leaping Christine' and more.

These songs were committed to tape when we went into Decca Studios to record the *Blues Breakers With Eric Clapton* LP – note that the title used 'Blues' and 'Breakers' in two separate words, unlike the name of the band. I had decided that as Eric was such a focal point of the band, he should get the credit in a big way for the sound of the tracks. We took our regular road gear into the studio; I recall that the engineer, Gus Dudgeon, was horrified that Eric was intending to play through his Marshall amp at full volume. This simply wasn't the acceptable way to do things in 1966. However, Eric stood his ground, refusing to turn his amp down. Mike Vernon had to mediate in order for us to start.

The whole album took three days to record and was all done on a four-track board. Gus did a great job of capturing everything. He put the drums and bass on one track, organ on the second, guitar on the third and vocals on the final track. After that he combined the tracks into one, freeing up three open tracks for overdubbed guitar solos, more vocals and horn combinations.

I wanted a tenor sax solo to lead off 'Have You Heard' and I chose Alan Skidmore to play it, because his earthy tone in the Johnny Griffin mould had really impressed me at a jazz gig back in Manchester. When he came in and played the solo, it was a lot busier than I wanted, and a bit too jazzy, but it was still impressive, so we kept the only take he recorded. From there, Eric came up with an incredible solo that approached the intensity of the best of his live performances.

The album included songs that we'd been playing since before Eric joined the band; some of them even went back to the Manchester days, such as Mose Allison's 'Parchman Farm' and Ray Charles' 'What'd I Say'. I played the twelve-hole harmonica that Sonny Boy Williamson had given me on 'Another Man', a song that I'd adapted from an Alan Lomax prison field holler. This had haunted me when I heard it on the documentary LP *Blues In The Mississippi Night*, recorded back in 1942.

The songs that Eric introduced to our regular repertoire were the instrumentals 'Stepping Out' and Freddy King's classic 'Hideaway', plus Otis Rush's 'All Your Love'. My contributions were three songs, all of which concerned Christine and the course of our affair. After we'd done all the tracks, Eric came to me and asked my permission to sing Robert Johnson's 'Ramblin' On My Mind', although he only wanted to try it if no one else was around at the session except me on piano. It was the first time he'd sung on tape, and he was a little hesitant – but with encouragement from Mike Vernon and myself, he hid behind a screen and it was brilliant. Before that, he'd never let on that he could sing.

We finished the album, and I'm proud to say that a classic was born. The only thing left to do was have a photo taken for the front cover, which I designed and hand-lettered. I remember that none of us felt in a very good mood when we were driven round London, looking for a site where we could be photographed. It would have been better if the photographer had previously sought out a suitable location. Eventually we saw a vacant lot and pulled up to it. We found somewhere to sit, with a graffitied wall behind us.

Eric had brought a copy of *The Beano* with him, and made a point of showing his lack of interest in the shoot by not looking up from the pages, even though the photographer was trying to get us to smile and look at the camera. A lot of supposedly hidden meaning has been ascribed to this over the years, but it was purely by chance that Eric brought the comic, just for something to read in the van. The LP inevitably became referred to as *The Beano Album*!

It was roughly two months before the album was released. In the interim, the usual flow of gigs continued, with a couple of memorably dramatic moments. One night, when we played in Wolverhampton at a big, echo-laden town hall, Ginger Baker happened to be there. He had played an earlier gig that day with Graham Bond and thought he'd come and check out Eric's guitar playing; he had never paid too much attention to Eric before. Of course, he wanted to sit in on drums, and we let him do so, but his style of playing was pretty outlandish and didn't fit with The Bluesbreakers' material. It was difficult to sing and play with his barrage going on behind us.

However, Ginger was totally fired up by the intensity of Eric's playing; this, it later emerged, was the night when the idea of forming a supergroup first came into Ginger's head. All he had to do was tempt Eric away from my band and reunite with his sometime arch-enemy Jack Bruce.

As these machinations began to take place, I had some wonderful news in my personal life. Although Pamela and I were no longer living together, we still felt the same way about adopting a child. Our application was going through, which involved visits from various agency people who wanted to check out the family home. Pamela would ring me up when one of them was coming over and I'd hop on the train to keep up the appearance of us still living together.

The procedure took six months or so, and one day we were notified that a boy was available. He was three months old and the child of a West Indian mother and an African medical student. Thus, in the middle of June, we became the adoptive parents of a gorgeous little boy whom we named Benedict (Ben) Mayall.

Back in the band, I began to feel more and more uneasy. Eric appeared to be distant and distracted, and yet again he would show up late for gigs or not at all. Before long a short piece appeared in *Melody Maker*, announcing that a new supergroup was being formed under the management of Robert Stigwood. It was named Cream and the personnel were Ginger Baker, Jack Bruce and Eric Clapton.

I was angry. This had all taken place without a word to me from Eric. It emerged that the trio had been secretly rehearsing a complete repertoire at Jack's flat, and had even gone into the studio to record a single.

Eric officially left The Bluesbreakers on July 16, and I was once again without a guitar player. Immediately I thought of Peter Green; I hoped that Peter would be willing to put aside what had happened when Eric took his place the previous year. I called him and made an offer, but he was reluctant to commit. Perhaps he thought I deserved to sweat a bit, and he was also torn between two offers. The first came from me and gave him a chance to play the blues with complete freedom to add his own ideas, although I wasn't offering much money. The other was to join Eric Burdon's New

Animals and fulfil a dream by going to America and meeting his blues heroes. Musically, however, he wouldn't be quite as free. To his credit, he chose to rejoin The Bluesbreakers, and I heaved a sigh of relief.

Less than a week after Eric left, the *Blues Breakers* album hit the streets and began to climb the British charts, much to the mystification of the powers that be at Decca. From that point on, they knew better than to interfere with anything that Mike Vernon presented to them. Their philosophy was: "We don't understand this blues stuff, but it seems to sell – so we'd best not ask questions!"

As we played around the country that summer, it rapidly became a drag that Peter had to put up with endless comparisons to Eric. Punters came to the shows, demanding "Where's Eric?" and "Who's the new guy?" These questions made Peter determined to prove his own worth. This was never more evident than when he played with savage genius on the first recording he did with us – covers of Otis Rush's 'So Many Roads' and Johnny 'Guitar' Watson's 'Looking Back'. He thought afterwards that he'd overplayed, but personally I loved the aggressive ferocity of every lick. The record really helped to connect Peter with the fans.

Peter and I became great pals; we shared the same fervour for the music. When the flat below me in Porchester Road became vacant, he moved in, which was very convenient because we could get together at any time, listen to music and put ideas down on tape. He once asked me how songwriting came about. I suggested that he start with a lick or melody from one of his favourite blues records. The most important song to come out of that advice was his amazing 'Black Magic Woman', where he took a riff from Otis Rush's 'All Your Love' and built on it. The lyrics were dedicated to the love of his life, Sandra Elsdon.

Around this time, Hughie started to show signs of withdrawal. He seemed very depressed, as though he had other things besides music on his mind. I noticed that he would sit in the band rooms, or on the long drives, and get stuck into books on Zen Buddhism. Eventually his moods began to affect his playing, and with great reluctance and sadness I asked him to leave.

133

I had heard that Mickey Waller was the top drummer around, so we used him for a while. However, I needed a heavier beat, which is how Aynsley Dunbar came along. As I remember, he met us at a show at the Fishmonger's Arms in Wood Green and I asked him to sit in. At the end of the night I hired him, and he became the next Bluesbreakers drummer.

Aynsley's input was immediately felt; he was a really powerful rock drummer and his drive really kicked us up the arse. He was also more of a showman than other drummers we'd had, and when the subject of drum solos came up he was all for it. He became a real crowd-pleaser.

At the same time, John McVie's alcohol intake had increased again, and once more I had to sack him for being out of control. He was replaced briefly by a guy called Steve Usher, but then promised to behave and got his job back – talk about a revolving door. John was the most solid blues bass player when he put everything into it. He and Peter Green were close musical partners right from the start, which was to be a factor in the later birth of Fleetwood Mac. Do you see a pattern emerging…?

My tumultuous affair with Christine continued off and on and was still inspiring me to write songs. One night I arranged to meet her at a flat in Kensington, where she was staying at the time. She didn't show up and it started to rain. I took shelter under a tree in the nearby park and composed the lyrics to a song that we subsequently recorded called 'Sitting In The Rain'. It was almost all acoustic; I played rhythm guitar along with Peter's subtle, scintillating lead. Aynsley was a little dismayed to hear that I didn't want him to play his drum kit. Instead, I asked him to tap out the rhythm on the back of one of my guitars.

For the B-side I gave Peter the opportunity to write and record his own slow blues. We recorded it one late night after a drive from a gig up north; the track was 'Out Of Reach'. It was Peter's first record as a singer and we recorded it in a single take. Talking of long drives, in October we hired a new driver named John 'Speedy' Keen, who had previously been one-third of the group Thunderclap Newman. Speedy was an incredible guy, with a wealth of anecdotes.

He sat behind the wheel and seemed to have an unstoppable flow of hilarious adventures to regale us with in his broad cockney accent; the journeys were like attending a comedy show.

The same month, we recorded the *A Hard Road* album in a short space of time. I preferred it to the Clapton LP as I felt it possessed more subtlety and a greater variety of moods, even though most of the songs I wrote for it referred in one way or another to the Christine affair. I'd tried to get her motivated into doing something for herself, instead of relying on me for constant support, and put this message into the song 'Top Of The Hill'. I was on an optimistic path with 'Hit The Highway' but in a darker mood with 'Living Alone' – and in 'Another Kinda Love', I referred to Christine's suggestion of a threesome with a girlfriend of hers. I accepted, but she backed out.

A month later Mike Vernon was putting together the aforementioned budget LP *Raw Blues*, to be made up of various odd tracks that he could round up from musicians he knew. My contribution was to bring my nine-string guitar into the studio and sing the highest notes of my career on 'Burn Out Your Blind Eyes'. Afterwards, I sat down at the piano and was just about to start an uptempo boogie-woogie when the door opened and a milkman dropped off a crate of bottles. This led to the title of the piece, 'Milkman Strut' – and we left the sound of the crate on the finished mix. On this LP I also found a home for a part of the Southbrook Road jam session between Steve Winwood and myself. John and Aynsley played along with the track, 'Long Night'.

One night we were booked at a modern, disco-type club which was all glass and mirrors. It was hardly the type of venue we would normally come across, and before we did our set we witnessed a flamboyant singer from Wales, dressed ready for Las Vegas in tight pants and a ruffled shirt front, belting out Little Richard songs. This was Tom Jones, who was just getting his start in London.

On the same night I met a quiet, diminutive girl called Sunny. I fell hard for her and we began to see each other regularly. She even moved in with me for a while, although our love affair didn't survive me being invited up to her parents' home in Carlisle for the weekend. Her father happened to be a chief inspector of police, and quite a formidable person to win over.

Disaster struck during the after-dinner pleasantries, when I happened to make a reference to having served in Korea. There was a sudden silence as the chief inspector worked out how old I was. When he realised that I was nearly thirty-five years old, this man told me in no uncertain terms that I must leave the next morning. The idea of a boyfriend who was almost twice the age of their precious girl was way too much for them. Dinner was over, and so was I!

Back in London, the biggest musical news of the month was the arrival of Jimi Hendrix. For weeks now Chas Chandler, who had left The Animals and was now in a managerial position with Mike Jeffreys, had been telling everyone about this amazing guitarist he'd seen in New York. He was so good, raved Chas, that he planned to bring him to England and make a star of him.

We took all this with a pinch of salt until the day came when Jimi was ready to make his London debut. He'd been in the UK for a while, rehearsing with Noel Redding on bass and Mitch Mitchell (late of Georgie Fame's band) on drums, and they had been styled in the latest Carnaby Street garb. Their show on November 25 at the Bag O'Nails club was more than a revelation. I was only glad that I wasn't a lead guitarist, because all the hotshots – Eric, Jimmy Page, Jeff Beck, Pete Townshend and so on – were in a state of shock.

As the world now knows what Jimi sounds like, you can only imagine what it must have been like to hear a guitarist of that intensity and originality for the first time. He did a few of these private members' clubs – the Scene, the Cromwellian, the Scotch of St James among them – and once the buzz got around, the top rock guitarists had to rethink their positions in the hierarchy. Jimi genuinely changed the course of rock'n'roll.

The American bluesman Paul Butterfield also brought his band over for a short tour that year. I caught them at the Marquee, and while I really liked Paul's singing and harmonica playing, I didn't care for his guitarist Mike Bloomfield, who had been touted as a serious contender for Eric Clapton's throne. I just didn't see it –

even today, I'm still in the minority. I rather preferred Elvin Bishop, Butterfield's second guitarist, who played some good slide solos.

Mike Vernon was eager to make the most of Paul's visit and tried to arrange a deal for Paul and me to record together. His record company, Elektra, would only consent to the union if the contract stipulated that the record would be released in the USA. That was good enough for us, so we prepared to record an EP with two tracks featuring Paul's vocal and two more with mine. The line-up was John McVie, Peter Green and Aynsley Dunbar, and we did the four songs in a single afternoon in December. Paul sang 'Little By Little' and backup vocals on 'Riding On The L And N', while I did Jimmie Lee Robinson's 'All My Life' and one of my own songs, 'Eagle Eye'. I still see copies of that EP in collectors' hands at gigs.

There was a bit of excitement at the start of 1967, as Rik Gunnell had arranged a short tour of Scandinavia for us. It would be the first time I'd been outside the country, with the exception of my Korean posting. After arranging passports and visas, we set off one wintry morning for the ferry, with Speedy driving our van. We were all in good spirits and looking forward to playing for a foreign audience.

That very week, Sweden had switched to driving on the right-hand side of the road. This had thrown many motorists into confusion and there were collisions all over the place as we headed out of Gothenburg on the snowy road to Örebro. Once we cleared the city we were in an empty white world, and when we stopped at the side of the road for a pee, I saw in the distance a deserted little hut. Ever watchful for souvenirs, I tramped through the snow towards the hut and came across an old cast-iron stove. It was all rusted up, but it had a great-looking door with the manufacturer's name, Husqvarna, on it. Later, when cleaned up and varnished, it made a great wall decoration.

It wasn't long before the Swedish tour started to unravel, simply because the van was being asked to perform beyond its limits. It was an old crate to start with, and the bad weather didn't help the engine, which began making strange and ominous noises as it struggled east. Örebro was an empty little town, with no signs of activity in the streets except a few farmers staring at us as if we were from another planet. What on earth were we doing here, and where were we to expect blues fans to come from, we asked ourselves?

However, as darkness closed in, a few hairy blues fans emerged at the hall where we played. They gave us a mixed reception, which was hardly a very encouraging start to our overseas venture. I've driven past Örebro many times in recent years, and nowadays it looks like any other large town, but I still can't shake the image of how it felt back on that cold winter day. I don't remember much about the rest of the tour, although I do recall that the Swedes' reaction to our music was very academic – even stone-faced.

After this tour, and especially when we were accompanying the visiting American bluesman Eddie Boyd, I began to sense strong negative vibes from Peter about our collective volume. At the same time, I was becoming impatient with Aynsley's extravagant drumming. Night after night, it seemed that his drum solos got longer and longer, and the rest of us had nothing to do but stand around and wait for the barrage to end. I felt that this line-up had run its course – and there would have to be changes once again.

Peter had been listening to and hanging out with the drummer Mick Fleetwood, who was still playing with The Cheynes. He suggested that we hire Mick, because of his simpler, more basic approach to rhythm. Mick hadn't been playing professionally nearly as long as Aynsley, but he seemed to be the right choice and so I made him the offer. Mick was taken aback at the invitation, evidently wondering whether he could match Aynsley's command of the kit. In fact, he thought we were mad to consider him – but it was an offer he was happy to accept.

As usual, I had the tough job of giving Aynsley the bad news – and his face fell. We'd been getting along well socially, and he was truly an expert musician, which must have made this even more of a shock. He took it rather badly.

"I'm afraid we've decided to recruit a new drummer," I told him.

"What?" he replied sharply.

"We're going to find someone whose style suits our music better."

"What's wrong with my style, John?"

"You're overplaying too often, unfortunately," I explained.

"No I'm bloody not!" he spat.

But he got the message, and left. I think there was more than a hint of revenge when he later formed his own group with Tommy Eyre on organ, John Moorshead on guitar, Alex Dmochowski on bass and the eccentric Mancunian Victor Brox on vocals, trumpet and assorted instruments, and named the band Retaliation. What else could the name imply?

With Aynsley's reputation and determination, he didn't have too much trouble lining up work. After the dust had settled, he chose me to produce his first album. This was a first for me, and something that I enjoyed as an outside project.

With Peter now feeling a little happier, he began to assert himself more in the band and took more control of the material we were playing. Over at Decca, Mike wanted us to come up with another single and we chose Otis Rush's 'Double Trouble' as the A-side. I sometimes had a hard time deciphering lyrics from blues records, and in this case it wasn't until years later that I found my version of the lyrics differed from the original!

For the B-side, I laid on a heavy, Chicago-style piano while Peter tore it up on slide guitar for Elmore James's 'It Hurts Me Too': this song bore a strong resemblance to 'Big Maceo' Merriweather's earlier classic 'Worried Life Blues'.

The blues was enveloping me now; the question was only where I should go with it.

CHAPTER 10

MOVING ON:
HEADED FOR AMERICA

In May, Mike Vernon came up to me with another proposition. Decca wanted him to produce some blues albums cheaply, for their budget offshoot label Ace Of Clubs. They didn't want to spend much money on the packages, so Mike asked if I would record an album's worth of original songs, with me as a solo artist, playing as many instruments as I could manage.

Songwriting inspiration came easily, as my personal life was barrelling along at a fast pace and I had more than a few stories to tell. It took years for me to get over the feelings of guilt over leaving Pamela and the kids, and these feelings formed the themes of 'Burn Out Your Blind Eyes' and 'Don't Kick Me'.

Mike and I recorded the album, *The Blues Alone*, pretty much in one day. It included two songs about an ex-girlfriend; 'Broken Wings' referred to how she'd once been raped and subsequently lost all faith in relationships. When I think about it now, I had planned to be the one to save her and love her, but the affair didn't last. It didn't help that I caught the clap from her, which was a total surprise for both of us. My later song, 'Stand Back Baby', said it all. I felt rather daring about coming out in the open with that one, but that's what the blues is supposed to be all about – putting it all on the line.

'Down The Line' was about another previous girlfriend whose father, a farmer, wasn't keen on her staying out late with The

Bluesbreakers. Dropping her home in the van one night, we saw her father emerge in a rage from the farmhouse holding a shotgun. We revved up the motor and got the hell out of there.

Another song, 'Cancelling Out', was a catalogue of romantic disasters. One verse was inspired by an occasion when I picked up a girl at a gig and brought her back to the flat. Before any romance could occur, she locked herself in the bathroom to prepare. I had a shock when she emerged. Gone was all her make-up, as were her false eyelashes, and her hair was up in curlers. She might as well have been wearing a tea cosy on her head.

Christine was still cropping up every now and then, and not always in a rage. 'No More Tears' was about one night when we talked by the fire and I tried to give her some consolation and sympathy. 'Sonny Boy Blow' was a tribute to the memory of the great Sonny Boy Williamson, who had died in 1965 and remained one of my true influences on harmonica. There'll never be another like him.

Three songs were inspired by my new lover, Marsha Hunt, who I'd recently met through our mutual acquaintance, Alexis Korner. My songs were 'Marsha's Mood', 'Brand New Start' and 'Brown Sugar'. She was a black American from Boston, and she and I enjoyed living together as she developed her own singing career. In 1967, when her visa was due to run out, she needed to get married in order to become a legal resident of England. She had a friend, Mike Ratledge of the band Soft Machine, who volunteered to help out, so on April 15, Marsha and I took a cab to meet him at the registry office.

The ceremony was carried out swiftly and legally, and when the registrar said, "You may kiss the bride," Mike did so, with me acting as best man. Then we were out the door, and after a handshake, off he went one way while Marsha and I got a cab back to the flat in time for lunch. Funnily enough, long after Marsha and I broke up and she began seeing Mick Jagger, Mick wrote his own song for her, also called 'Brown Sugar'; it became way more famous than mine.

The recording of *The Blues Alone* was a lot of fun, because I got to play everything except the drums. I gave them a shot for the songs that required them, but it was beyond me, so I called upon Keef Hartley to help me out. As I've mentioned, Keef was the drummer for The Artwoods, and we'd met while playing together on the Champion Jack Dupree sessions.

The album came out great, and I learned a lot about what I could and couldn't do instrumentally. I played harmonica, piano, organ, lead guitar, rhythm guitar and bass guitar. Radio Caroline DJ John Peel wrote some flattering, amusing liner notes, and although the album was released in mono on the low-budget Ace Of Clubs label in the UK, it was released on a major label in the States.

Back on the road, things were getting out of hand thanks to an excess of alcohol in the bloodstreams of Mr McVie and our merry drummer, Mick Fleetwood. My rhythm section seemed to be treating the gigs like one big party. Although I don't remember what the final straw was, Mick got the bullet after he'd been with us almost exactly six weeks. Somehow John managed to escape the axe this time around.

As I'd just worked with Keef Hartley on the *Blues Alone* project, he was my next choice to take over the drums. With his great sense of humour and positive attitude, he and I had a rapport that lasted for years into the future. The change in personnel didn't sit as well with Peter, though; after Mick left, Peter began to look more downcast, as night after night we tried to recapture the previous glories. I could sense that, with his heart no longer in it, he would be the next one to quit the band.

Shortly afterwards, Peter and John decided to take off on a trip to Chicago, hoping to immerse themselves in blues culture and absorb all they could in the way of inspiration. I think they had visions of moving out there permanently, until they realised that the amount of red tape, visas and permits would sink the idea – and so they abandoned the project. This left Peter frustrated about the direction of his career, and he seemed to feel more than ever that it was time to move on and form his own band.

In June, the inevitable happened. He resigned.

"I'm sorry, John," he said sadly. "I hope we can still be friends?"

"Don't worry," I told him. "We're still flatmates, after all."

With gigs still to show up for, I had to think quickly. I realised that this was my chance not simply to replace a guitar player but to do something bigger with the band. By now I had enough money coming in to expand the line-up with horn players. We were due to make another album for Mike Vernon at Decca, so here was my opportunity to escalate my public campaign for further recognition of the blues in the British media. Even in 1967, the music papers were still lagging behind when it came to covering the scene.

For the new album, I planned to record songs by those heroes of mine who were a little less known than greats such as Muddy Waters or B. B. King. I chose songs previously covered by Albert King ('Oh, Pretty Woman'), Eddie Kirkland, Buddy Guy ('My Time After Awhile'), Little Joe Blue ('Me And My Woman') and Otis Rush.

Above all I chose to honour J. B. Lenoir, one of my true idols, whose premature death on April 29 had stirred me to write a memorial anthem in his name. His death had merited so little attention that I felt that more people should be aware of his tremendous stature. I noticed a one-paragraph news item in *Melody Maker* at the beginning of May, which reported that he'd been killed in a car accident in Illinois. However, I later found out that although he had indeed been in a minor car crash, his death came three weeks later as a result of internal injuries that had been diagnosed incorrectly. Although it is hard to believe, he was apparently sent home from hospital and subsequently died from internal bleeding.

I was in tears when I discovered these facts. I could hardly believe that someone so vital was not with us any more. It was even sadder to me that the last and only time I'd met him, we'd discussed making a studio album, with him using myself and The Bluesbreakers as his backing band. Now that this dream was over, all I could do was to put my feelings about him into song.

The first order of business was to get a new guitar player. I thought that the young Mick Taylor, who I'd remembered for his remarkable takeover at Hatfield on the no-show Eric night, would be the perfect choice. The problem was where to find him. I needed horns too, so I put an ad in *Melody Maker* for musicians to join an established blues band. I got many, many calls straight away and I swiftly realised that I wouldn't have the patience to set up formal auditions for everyone. I took down a few numbers and asked a couple of guitarists to come round to the flat to be heard.

Among them was Robin Trower, who had been proposed to me in such great secrecy by his mother that I thought I was about to witness the second coming of Christ. Unfortunately, his mother had extolled his genius to such an extent that he couldn't possibly live up to it. He was a nice guy with a good technique, but I knew he didn't have the right feel for the blues. We shook hands and I wished him luck. Ultimately he didn't do too badly though, did he?

As luck would have it, Mick Taylor himself then came out of the woodwork – and I told him he'd got the job right away. Chris Mercer also arrived, recommended by someone I knew, and accepted the role of tenor player. Instead of trumpet, I decided I needed a baritone sax man, taking my cue from the horn section of Georgie Fame's Blue Flames. I didn't receive too many applications for the job, though, and was running out of time when the doorbell rang.

I peered out of the window and from three floors up I saw a blonde, bearded gentleman dressed in an antique military jacket and holding a large black case. As I studied him from above, he appeared to me as though he'd just returned from the Battle of Trafalgar! The only criterion I'd required from prior applicants was that they knew about the blues – and in all cases up to now, they had failed to deliver. This guy on the street didn't look like a jazzer, so I shouted down to ask him who his favourite bluesman was. When he replied "Elmore James!" I shouted back, "Okay, you've got the job. Who are you?"

He was Rip Kant, a quiet, sombre-looking character whose playing chops were a bit on the rudimentary side – but he knew and loved the blues, and that was good enough for me. I also thought we should have a rhythm guitarist in the new Bluesbreakers, and, indeed, for the first week of shows we did have one – Terry Edmonds, a regular at the Flamingo. However, it soon became apparent that we didn't need the extra instrument and, after some brief get-togethers, we were back on track again with our usual line-up plus horns. The audiences were delighted with the new direction, and I was having a great time directing the traffic, so to speak, handing out solos for Mick, Chris and Rip on songs where they would be the featured soloists.

Meanwhile, Peter Green was lying low and figuring out his new direction. He'd approached Mick Fleetwood and John McVie about forming a new band, and while Mick was up for it, John didn't want to commit just yet to leaving the financial security of The Bluesbreakers. Instead, bassist Bob Brunning was going to join Peter's new venture, as was guitarist Jeremy Spencer, an Elmore James fanatic who could play and sing the blues of his hero note for note and very effectively. He was also a good rock'n'roller when he belted it out on piano.

We went in to Decca to record the album on July 11. The guys were a bit taken aback at how fast I urged them on. We played at a breakneck pace, with barely time to hear the playbacks, and rarely being allowed to do the track again. My cries of "Next!" rang out many times during the session, which lasted only eleven hours, but it was enough time for us to record high-quality takes on all the songs for the album, titled *Crusade*.

The band were in a bit of a daze when I finally called it quits, but we did justice in a rough and spontaneous way to all the tunes. Sure, some of them could have been a little tighter, and the solos might have benefited from extra studio time, but when Mike Vernon, Gus Dudgeon and I polished off the mix the following day, the songs sounded great.

I wrote three songs for this LP: 'Streamline', inspired by the music of Junior Parker; the slow blues 'Tears In My Eyes', about lost love; and the aforementioned 'The Death Of J. B. Lenoir'. Rip was the featured soloist on the last one, and he came up with a brilliant solo on baritone sax that perfectly captured the sadness that I felt inside.

We had Decca line up a location photography shoot for the album cover, whose layout and artwork I designed. I also painted and made up banners nailed to poles, which we brandished on an old bomb site. Their theme, made clear by statements such as 'The blues needs your support', was that the British public were missing out on the music of some great American bluesmen.

We had one of those rare British summers when the sun actually came out, which gave me an eccentric but effective idea of working on my suntan while travelling. The van had a roof rack, so I built a six-foot-long platform out of plywood and affixed eighteen-inch-high walls around the edges. This enabled me to climb up on the van roof, lie down in my underwear and sunbathe en route to gigs. The walls prevented me from being seen by other motorists. Everyone used to laugh at this rather dangerous idea, but it sure worked!

I soon bought a new van, which had enough room for me to build a double bed behind the rear row of seats. As soon as we hit the road I'd get under the covers and go to sleep. This bed was soon to play an important part in my ever-fluctuating love life.

For some time, Rip had been going on about his girlfriend, to whom he was supposedly engaged. One day he asked if it would be okay to bring her to a gig up north, a journey of six or seven hours. Everyone was curious, as we'd heard so much about her, so we said we'd make room – and so began a drama that I can never forget.

Her name was Rosalind and she was only eighteen or nineteen years old. As soon as the van pulled up at the curb to let her and Rip come aboard, she and I made instant eye contact; it was electric. I couldn't stop staring at her, and every time she turned around on that drive, I felt as if there was something serious going on between us – something that excluded Rip.

We played the show, and during the waiting around at the hall I got to talk to her quite a bit. With every passing minute, we both felt a mutual attraction growing between us. An hour into the journey home, all of a sudden her arm came over the back of her van seat towards me and her fingers met mine. Her conspiratorial squeeze was enough to confirm that we shared the same desires.

Suddenly I saw and heard Rosalind telling Rip that she was going to move to my bed in the back of the van. This happened so quickly that it stunned all of us; there was an uncomfortable silence from the troops, most of all from a shaken Rip, who simply sat there without a word of protest. Rosalind cuddled up to me under the covers and our bodies were glued together for the rest of the trip home.

The two of us were left alone when the others got out for food and petrol at the Blue Boar; only then were we free to talk about what was happening. She told me that she wasn't engaged to Rip, and that she was less interested in their relationship than he was. This was a chance for her to end it.

From then on, we were in love, and we quickly started making plans to live together. Needless to say, things between Rip and myself were difficult. His resentment over my betrayal was quite understandable. Furthermore, his sax playing wasn't adding much to the band, and under the circumstances it soon became obvious that I was going to have to be the bad guy again and fire him.

This seemed pretty brutal under the circumstances, but I called him up and tried my best to let him have it legitimately. Naturally, I knew I'd been a total heel. Sorry, Rip.

Dick Heckstall-Smith had recently left the disintegrated Graham Bond Organisation, so I gave him a call, offering him the sax position in the band. Dick and I had known each other for ages, since we were contestants in the Varsity Jazz Band Contest after I came out of the army. He was surprised to receive my offer, and wondered whether he wouldn't be too avant-garde to fit in with my more traditional sound. I assured him that the partnership would work – and one thing was for sure, he would be a spectacle, as a wild soloist with a Roland Kirk stance, playing tenor and soprano saxes at the same time. Dick's first Bluesbreakers gig was at the Fishmonger's Arms, with no rehearsal or preparation. He simply joined in with Chris and delivered fresh energy to the horn section.

There weren't many more gigs to do before we broke up for the annual summer holiday towards the end of August. Rosalind and I made plans to go to Spain for a camping adventure with John McVie and Mick Taylor. All we had to do was fly to Malaga, take the bus up the Mediterranean coast to Marbella and pitch our tent on or near the beach. It sounded like a simple plan, but we hadn't reckoned on the ruthless vigilance of the Spanish police patrols.

We could tell that Spain was still under General Franco's dictatorship as soon as we cleared customs. The four of us got on the bus and rode to Marbella, only to find that, alongside the tourists, it was full of police officers in threatening uniforms, looking for an excuse to arrest anyone looking vaguely disreputable. Sleeping bags and backpacks were definitely not welcome, and there seemed nowhere to camp out. We decided we'd rather try our luck in Ceuta, on the Moroccan border, so we got back on the bus and boarded the ship that ferried people across the Strait of Gibraltar.

On deck, we met a little guy who wanted to make our acquaintance for reasons we couldn't quite fathom. He invited us to his house and said that we could camp on the beach at the bottom of the cliff below the property. Although this sounded too good to be true, we accepted. It was getting dark as Rosalind and I pitched our tent on the sands of the beautiful little bay. John and Mick wanted to move on and head south towards Morocco, and when my sweetheart and I woke up, they had gone.

As we parted the tent flaps, we were set upon by swarms of the biggest flies you ever saw: huge black insects that wouldn't leave us alone. I headed for the water to escape their attentions and was having a great time swimming in the clear waters until I stepped on a sea urchin and limped out with several needles in my foot.

Flies weren't the only marauders: large numbers of small children gathered from all over to come and stare at us. They kept on at us to give them some money, but once we'd given one kid a coin they all wanted one. As we tried to move away, the mob followed. It was clearly time to move on, and under their scrutiny we broke camp, headed up the cliff path to the main road and hitched a ride back to the ferry.

We docked once more in Gibraltar and caught the bus to Marbella, resolving to try again. This time, we made a point of being less conspicuous and enjoyed the beach, the sun and the sea. When the sun went down, we hid round the back of the rocks; I slept on top of the highest one, which acted as a lookout post.

It was hard to relax under these conditions, so we headed back down the coast to the small town of Estepona, which we'd passed on our way. It had a nice beach and a gazebo-like structure on the sands that was used as a bandstand, I suppose. This was in such a position that if you were underneath it you couldn't be seen by the police – and so it was our secret hideout for a few more nights.

Back home, the Windsor Jazz And Blues Festival in September marked the debut of Fleetwood Mac. They sounded good, and it was great to see Peter leading his own band and being able to do his own thing, although I was less keen on the songs devoted to Jeremy Spencer's Elmore James impressions. Also at the festival – all for an admission price of fifteen shillings – were Denny Laine, P. P. Arnold, The Alan Bown Set, Pentangle, Chicken Shack with Christine Perfect, Jeff Beck and Cream. It was the strongest line-up ever, and a victory for our brand of British blues rock.

My family was there – Gary in a top hat and furry hippie vest, Jason similarly attired and Tracey snapped by the official photographer as she and I were testing out the grand piano on stage. The same guy took a photo of me with Rosalind; I had the print blown up and framed on my wall. Our affair was documented permanently in a song I later recorded called 'Picture On The Wall', recorded as a single and backed by a song written for another one of my short-lived loves, 'Jenny'.

Both songs were conceived as a return to the *Blues Alone* format, and I did both tracks playing keyboards and guitars and rhythm tapping by myself. I had Peter Green come along to play some heartbreaking acoustic slide guitar on 'Picture': I still get chills of sadness today when I hear either of those songs.

Rosalind and I were together for a few more months, but, as often happens with passionate love affairs, we burned each other out and she moved out of the flat to go her own way. It was mainly my fault because I was feeling hemmed in and needed space. It was a sad parting.

Decca was now asking for another single. I thought this time I'd have a sure-fire hit with a song called 'Suspicions', which we recorded on September 14 and 15. It was the first time that Dick was the featured soloist, on an extended part two B-side with Mick taking the solo on the shorter A-side. I had horn parts scored for several session musicians, who were to build up the groove, hitting higher and higher trumpet notes into the final fade-out. I thought we had a winner – but it quickly sank like a stone, like all my other singles.

'Suspicions' was also John McVie's swansong. He had been waiting to see what would happen to Fleetwood Mac before he was ready to swap jobs, and now that it looked as if Peter was well on his way after a successful debut at the Windsor Festival, he left me to take over from Bob Brunning. The 'Fleetwood' and the 'Mac' of the band name were now complete.

John's replacement was Paul Williams, who I'd known for a long time as the bassist and vocalist with Zoot Money's Big Roll Band. He was known to be a bit of a nutter – on several occasions at the Flamingo Club's all-nighters I'd seen him climb up onto Zoot's organ and play lying down – so I had a few doubts about how long he'd last in The Bluesbreakers.

In October I bought a new reel-to-reel tape recorder with a view to documenting all our gigs. My idea was to put together a double album of live stuff, illustrating life on the road, documentary style. I wanted to include not only music, but also interviews and backstage eavesdropping – anything that was amusing or that would capture the feel of the road.

By December, I had recorded over sixty hours of tape, as we were working consistently all over the place, including gigs in Scandinavia and Holland. Choosing material was a huge job, and it was difficult to pick out the most unusual incidents. Some I remember were from shows like the one at the Club A'Gogo in Newcastle, where a fight broke out in the audience and Paul got set upon. In flew our road manager Mick Lawford to the rescue – and in the melee, his wig got dislodged, much to our amazement, as we'd never seen his bald pate before. Minor scratches resulted in me improvising a song called 'Blood On The Night'.

My recordings also included a slow blues in B flat, recorded one late night at the Speakeasy, when Jimi Hendrix came on stage and took over Mick's guitar. Unfortunately, only a brief moment was recorded, as we weren't allowed to acknowledge Jimi's performance for contractual reasons. It's tantalising to hear him play, with the volume turned down to almost nothing.

By the time the tapes were done, Paul had left the band and Keith Tillman was brought in at short notice. He was another great character who enjoyed playing pranks on people. He would offer unsuspecting musicians – usually ones with no talent – a recording contract with a fictitious record label called Puff Adder Records. I was usually around to record the charades.

While we were at a gig in Schiedam in Holland, my hand-carved guitar was stolen. I was most upset. It's an awful feeling to have that happen, let alone on the road when you need the instrument every night. By some miracle, I got it back a few days later, after putting an appeal in a local rock newspaper. All the blues fans in Holland were instantly alerted and on the lookout. They found the thief, who anonymously returned it, and we picked it up just before we left the country.

When we were in Denmark, I took a fancy to Mick Lawford's girlfriend. He had been seeing her on and off for some time, but their affair was on the wane. I asked his permission to chat her up and he said to go ahead. I took him at his word and began to make my interest known. She and I got on great, and one night after an early show in Copenhagen, I left the band's hotel for the night and set off into uncharted territory on the train to her house. I made it back next day in time to move on, but I got the feeling that Mick wasn't too thrilled that I'd actually gone through with the deal.

The Bluesbreakers were moving forward, but too slowly for my liking – in particular when it came to America. Towards the end of 1967, I started to get aggravated that a lot of my friends in major bands were crossing the Atlantic and doing well. I got the bug that Rik Gunnell, as my agent, seemed to be doing nothing for his 10 per cent commission except sit back and line up the same old gigs. It was time for things to change.

My first move was to go and see the fearsome Peter Grant, soon to be Led Zeppelin's manager. He had a lot of US contacts, but on talking with him I didn't get the feeling that he was too into the idea of managing me – so I went to Robert Stigwood, who had brought the Bee Gees and Cream to the international limelight.

He said, "John, I'll manage you as long as you can get away from Rik Gunnell without too much bad blood."

"That's good," I replied. "What percentage would you want?"

"I want 15 per cent as my management commission."

I considered this. Fifteen per cent for a manager of Stigwood's calibre wasn't too bad.

"...and I want another 10 per cent as your agent," he added.

"But that makes a quarter of my gross earnings!" I replied, surprised.

He shrugged and said, "That's my offer."

If I remember correctly, I think Stigwood also wanted a slice of my future record earnings. Obviously I wasn't going to go this route, but it was all I needed to go back to Rik and tell him what his rival had offered. I said I'd finally sign a management deal with him if he could beat that offer – and more importantly, guarantee me a tour of the USA.

My negotiations paid off. Rik wasn't about to let Stigwood snatch his artiste away, and we settled on a total of 20 per cent commission. Finally he got off his arse and made some calls, and within a couple of weeks he'd miraculously come through with dates in New York, Detroit, Los Angeles and San Francisco, all due to commence in the first week of January 1968.

The band and I were over the moon with excitement, and we began doing the paperwork for work permits, making many trips to the US embassy. Seeing the American flag in the lobby and talking to people with American accents was almost impossible to believe! Everything seemed to take so long, though, and we were worried right up to the time of departure that we wouldn't get our visas granted and passports stamped.

At last, on a cold drizzly day, we found ourselves at Heathrow. Bad weather in the form of impenetrable fog intervened and the plane was rescheduled several times, until it was apparent we wouldn't make it to New York in time for our first gig on January 8. When we finally got airborne, there were further complications at the other end. New York City was all but snowed under, in the worst ice storm in memory, and the club couldn't open anyway.

After clearing customs, we stood on the kerb outside JFK Airport, waiting for someone to meet us – but within minutes of setting my bags down and turning my back on them, an unseen thief had stolen them. I was devastated. My camera, all my harmonicas in the special gun-belt holster, and all my leather stage clothes were gone. After a fruitless attempt to report the theft to the police – who shook their heads apathetically – a guy from London Records called Lenny Meisel got us into limousines, and off we went to the ramshackle Hotel Earle in Washington Square.

I had been warned that the expenses on any American tour were astronomical. In fact, the received wisdom was that no band – at least, no band at our level – ever came back to England with anything more than a hefty debt. I was determined to defeat the paradigm at any cost, however, which was why I'd booked this run-down hotel as our place of residence for two weeks.

Early on January 9, we checked into three rooms at the rate of $8 a night each. I had a shared room with my mate Keef, Mick shared with Dick, and Chris roomed with Keith. It wasn't the cleanest of places, but – thankfully – it did have an elevator to get us up to our rooms on the twenty-fourth floor. The Cafe Au Go Go was only a short walk away, and somehow the task ahead didn't look quite so daunting once dawn came.

Phone calls were made to our American agent, Jack Bart, and Lenny and I went over to his office to meet him. I had a hidden tape recorder capturing all the dialogue. I'll always remember Jack yelling constantly at his assistant Dick Allen, who eventually rose to the position of Chuck Berry's manager.

"Dick! Hey Dick!" he shouted.

"What?" replied Dick.

"You'll get harmonicas at Manny's. Dick, get 'em at Manny's. Go to *Manny's*, Dick!"

I loved New York. Walking through the snowy streets of the city, with skyscrapers towering on either side of the avenues, I realised how different it was from the sights and sounds of London. There was a palpable sense of excitement and adventure in the air – which even transcended the seediness of our cockroach-ridden hotel.

Soon enough, it was time to check out the club, and I was delighted to see that there were lines around the block. It was freezing outside, but inside we found a warm and eager audience waiting for us. Ticket sales had been so great that we were booked to play three sets a night. Opening up for us was Blood, Sweat & Tears, who were very supportive; they made us feel great to be in New York, as did Steve Miller, who was there for the first few shows.

Afterwards, we came face to face with groupies for the first time. This was a new phenomenon for us, and not something we were expecting as a blues band – but there they were, decked in all their finery. I remember there being quite a few feathers and flimsy dresses. We didn't have to do anything to attract their attention; they simply made their selection from our ranks after we'd played our show.

Although I was flattered by the opportunities to acquire some new bedmates, I didn't fancy any of the girls – even though they were considered leading ladies among their profession – and didn't do the deed. As a bonus, three or four of them had come from San Francisco and offered the band the use of their houses there for when we played our end-of-tour shows.

In the daytime, we explored the Village; the huge selections of food at most fast-food restaurants and delis such as Nedick's amazed us. One day, Lenny Meisel took me up to the offices of London Records, where I met the company bosses. The chief was Walt Maguire, who came across as a family man rather than a record executive – although his larger-than-life second-in-command, Herb Goldfarb, made up for that, dominating any given topic of conversation, even though he knew nothing about the blues.

I was beginning to get the feel of New York and the American way of life – and I liked it.

Lenny took the time to walk me around the Village, and it was at a record shop opposite the Cafe Au Go Go called Village Oldies that I first met Kansas J. Canzus, a lanky hippie from Hutchinson, Kansas who'd changed his name from Billy Porter to that of his home state.

The government wouldn't allow him to have 'Kansas' for both his first and last name, hence the unique spelling of the latter.

Mick and I spent a lot of time hanging out at the Cafe Au Go Go with him and Bleecker Bob, the owner. Kansas also worked for Frank Zappa, and through him I was able to visit Frank, his girlfriend (and future wife) Gail, and Pamela Zarubica, also known as Suzy Creamcheese, at their house on Christopher Street. They were fascinating people, and I was beginning to feel that I belonged among them.

CHAPTER 11

GOOD TIME BOOGIE: TAKING GIANT STEPS

Over at the Cafe Au Go Go, all our shows were sell-outs; we had a great couple of weeks there before flying off to Detroit for a one-nighter at the Grande Ballroom. It was quite a contrast to be playing in such a big place, which had huge light shows projected on the screens behind the stage. It was packed with hippies; we were introduced to the audience by a wild guy with an eight-foot boa constrictor writhing around his body.

After Detroit, we were booked to play a week at Los Angeles' famous Whisky A Go Go on the Sunset Strip. Leaving the ice-cold January weather behind in Michigan, we landed in LA in a comfortable twenty-two degrees; I'll never forget the magical sight of the lights of the metropolis, spread out below me like a giant cobweb, as I looked out of the plane window.

After clearing customs we were met by London Records' West Coast representative Gerry Hoff, whose casual, droll manner was a stark contrast to the sharp edges of the people we'd met on the East Coast. Not only were we greeted like royalty by Gerry, but there were two great-looking girls with flowers for me with him, offering to take me into town. Nothing like this had ever happened to me before.

And so began my love affair with Los Angeles... The girls sat next to me in their red open-top sports car and took me to the Tropicana Motel on Santa Monica Boulevard. As this was still a budget tour, and we would be there for a week, we were allocated two rooms, each just large enough to accommodate us comfortably. With the balmy weather and the shimmering swimming pool, it felt like heaven compared with the cold climates from which we'd just escaped.

We weren't due to play until the following night, but we couldn't wait to see Sunset Boulevard and the action that we'd previously seen only in movies. This felt like the big time!

The Whisky's owner, Elmer Valentine, who had made our booking for the week, escorted us into the club – and heads turned as we walked in. We were ushered to a booth in the back corner, where three or four girls were holding spaces for us.

I was instantly drawn to a striking woman named Salli, and the attraction appeared to work both ways. There was no returning to the hotel for me that night; I was spirited away by Salli to her apartment on Fountain Avenue, where we spent the night entwined. This was life in Hollywood, folks.

The following evening, we opened to a packed house; the audience were already shouting requests for songs from the new album, *Crusade*. 'Oh, Pretty Woman' was one of their favourites, but anything that Mick Taylor played raised the roof. Girls were lining up for his attention as he played those blues with eyes closed, weaving his magic among the flashing, psychedelic light-show projections trained on the walls behind us by Frank Zappa's art director, Calvin Schenkel.

The sold-out show was such a success, and Elmer was so impressed with us English lads, that he made the offer to move us to the famous Chateau Marmont hotel at his own expense. This suited the guys nicely, as they'd get their own rooms – but believe it or not, Mick and I decided to stay where we were. It was less fancy, more convenient and more modern than the Chateau, and we had great food going on at Duke's famous coffee shop down the steps from the pool level.

We were never short of company from this moment on; the phone kept ringing with people wanting to meet us. Keith Tillman had hooked up with a girl called Linda Francis, one of the dancers at the Whisky, who drove him wherever he needed to go during the day.

These girls were groupies, but let me explain how I regard that term, which carries a stigma that I feel is a bit unworthy. These were beautiful days; we were experiencing America's rich, open rock'n'roll world, and the ladies who came forth to greet us and make us feel like visiting royalty were most welcome. Their motives may have differed from case to case, but we were always grateful for their friendship. I did once write a put-down of their lifestyle on my 1971 album *Back To The Roots*, titled 'Groupie Girl' – but I was referring only to those who were only interested in conquering a rock star and notching him up on her bedpost. The girls we knew were not like this.

The music-business people we met were interesting, too. Through Pam Zarubica I got to meet John Judnich, Lenny Bruce's sound engineer and friend – and the last person to see Lenny alive on the night of his fatal overdose in 1966. As a Lenny Bruce freak, it was a thrill for me to meet John and spend time together at the house where Lenny died, up near the top of Sunset Plaza Drive in Laurel Canyon. John had inherited all of Lenny's recorded tapes and had managed to secure them before the vultures closed in; apparently a few businessmen were involved, and Lenny's mother Sally was also trying to get hold of them. In John's room I saw these boxes of reel-to-reel tapes – most of them unmarked – and later on he gave me full access to them.

I enjoyed Salli's company so much that I made arrangements to fly her up to San Francisco, where we were to play the Fillmore. Unfortunately, when we arrived there, her personality changed quite unexpectedly. Instead of the carefree girl who I thought I knew, she became shut down and sullen; it seemed to be related to her relationship to members of Jefferson Airplane, one of whom may have been her ex-boyfriend. Our plan had been to move into that band's communal house, but we took separate rooms; the affair was over.

I didn't feel too comfortable around the house, so I spent most of my time in the city. One day I went down to Haight-Ashbury to check out the hippie scene, which was an eye-opener for me; so many people there seemed to be high on something, but I wasn't used to being around the drug culture. To this day, I've never even taken a puff of a joint, and I've never had the desire to do so. Still, I thought the scene was very mellow and friendly. Flowers and good vibes abounded everywhere, and there were posters and flyers in the head shops and on the walls announcing the forthcoming shows, headlined by none other than Jimi Hendrix, with us and Albert King completing the bill for a three-day run on the first three days of February.

We already knew Jimi well, but we were in awe at meeting Albert for the first time as he had long been a hero of ours. At the show, we went to his dressing room and told him how much his music meant to us. He was overwhelmed by playing at a place such as this before a huge audience of predominantly white kids – a totally new experience for him. The shows were great, and the audiences went nuts each night.

The following weekend, we were the headline act above The Loading Zone; fewer people were there, but we were well received. We had an unexpected surprise one night when Little Joe Blue showed up and sang 'Me And My Woman' with us. He'd heard about us recording his song on the *Crusade* album and was delighted to meet us and sit in.

On the evening of February 11, we trudged onto the plane back to London. There was a feeling of sadness that our American experience was over, and as we flew through the night towards the regular grind of English gigs that was awaiting us, my thoughts were doing overtime. Did I really want to live out my career in grey England?

We didn't get back to London until seven o'clock the following morning, and we were too late to get it together for a show that had been booked at Cooks Ferry Inn in Edmonton. I guess Rik Gunnell had misjudged our return flight information. It didn't seem to be a big deal for him to put one of his other regulars in there instead, but when I showed up at his office the next day to tell him I'd returned home with $2,000 – about $15,000 in today's currency – stuffed in my boots, he thought it was a very big deal indeed. He was overwhelmed with amazement.

Let me explain why. At this point in the history of touring bands, I was unique in that I'd not only not lost money on the road but had actually come home with a profit. This was literally unheard of, given our modest tour income and the high cost of living in America. Rik couldn't wait to get on the phone and tell everyone he knew about "that fucking John Mayall" being an example to all the other bands he was sending to the USA.

The gigs we did over the next three weeks were within striking distance of London and included a show at the Royal Albert Hall. I made some changes to the crew, replacing our roadie Col Smith with Kansas J. Canzus, who'd decided to come back to England with us; this left Mick Lawford and Bernie Boyle as senior roadies. Mick did the driving of the personnel van and Bernie took over the managerial side of things, collecting the money, doing the accounts and advancing the shows.

We also switched bass players. Keith Tillman was planning to quit, as he wanted to try to get a small record label underway and was fed up with playing one-nighters. I talked to Alexis Korner to see if he had any recommendations for bassists; he happened to know of a talented fifteen-year-old kid who hadn't been playing long but was already very accomplished. His name was Andy Fraser, later a very famous songwriter in his own right.

Andy showed up at the Wooden Bridge, Guildford on February 25 with a miniature bass guitar and took over from Keith, who played the first set. He did very well indeed, and was obviously our new Bluesbreaker. The next day I also added a trumpeter violinist, Henry Lowther, because I wanted to expand the horn section to create a broader sound. I had envisaged a new solo spot for the violin, but I must confess that I wasn't too impressed with his command of the instrument. Violins can be painfully screechy in the wrong hands, and so I encouraged Henry to stick to trumpet solos, which were excellent.

While we'd been away in America, the single 'Jenny', backed with 'Picture On The Wall', had been released, but it didn't meet with much commercial success, despite Peter Green's understated slide guitar work on the B-side. Also that month, both volumes of *The Diary Of A Band* were released – although they didn't perform well either.

On the upside, in February I was voted Number One Blues Artist in Britain – over Georgie Fame, Alexis Korner, Long John Baldry and Eric Clapton! – in *Melody Maker*'s annual jazz poll. This was my first and only victory in a poll of this kind; I assume it helped bring in a few extra punters at the gigs that followed. These included the aforementioned prestigious performance at the Royal Albert Hall, which was a first for us, complete with friends and families fighting to get backstage passes out of the management.

There was too much echo on stage at the Albert Hall, and it was difficult to get a tight sound after being so used to the acoustics of clubs on our regular circuit. Still, Andy fitted in nicely; he and Keef had a great rapport. They worked up a little off-stage routine that had us all in fits. Andy would sit on Keef's knee and pose as a ventriloquist's dummy. "Gimme a gottle of geer!" Keef would mime out of the corner of his mouth.

After a brief Scandinavian tour, there was a notable incident at the Queens Ballroom in Wolverhampton. The venue was barring people who were without ties, were wearing jeans, or had long hair – an unthinkably outmoded approach in 1968. I stated that I would not play under those conditions; the crowd outside began chanting "Mayall, Mayall, Mayall!" Only after the intervention of police with dogs could the crowd be dispersed.

One article in a Wolverhampton newspaper reported that a young man went all the way home to get a tie, but when he returned he was still refused admission because his hair was too long. The reporter noted: "One other point: Mayall has long hair, wears jeans and I've never seen him with a tie. It seems unfair that he can be booked to make money for the Ballroom when people who dress the same way are treated as louts and troublemakers."

A venue spokesman said that if I'd been a member of the audience, they wouldn't have let me in either. This was completely against my principles and I refused to play, forfeiting that night's income as a result.

By now Decca was calling for a new album – possibly because they wanted to make the most of my heightened profile as a *Melody Maker* poll-winner – and so I began to think of ways to make it special. I wanted to try putting together a so-called concept album – a suite of songs that would tell a story, track by track. Side one would be one piece of music, with the tracks segueing into each other, and side two would be made up of related happenings in my life at this point.

The subject wasn't hard to come up with, as I was experiencing feelings of sadness and guilt about the break-up of my marriage with Pamela. I started with a poem titled 'Bare Wires', which summed up the theme of the album to come.

Before I could go much further, however, I realised that the rhythm section of Keef Hartley and Andy Fraser wasn't going to be technically advanced enough for what I had in mind – and, sadly, I concluded that there would have to be another break-up, planning the last Bluesbreakers gig for April 21. This was particularly upsetting for me because of the great friendship I had with Keef, and I dreaded making that telephone call.

Funnily enough, I needn't have worried. On Keef's first solo album, *Halfbreed*, released in 1969, he asked me if we could recreate the phone call as an introduction to the first song. He called it 'Sacked (Introducing Hearts And Flowers)' and it featured me saying, "Hi Keef, it's John. How are you today? I'm afraid I've got some bad news…"

Through Dick Heckstall-Smith's associations in the jazz field, I wanted Jon Hiseman as my next drummer. Jon was probably the most advanced jazz drummer in Britain at the time, and when I asked him to join the band, he expressed the concern that his style would be far too complex for a blues band. However, he agreed to give it a go, although this was a little hard on Keef as they had had a friendly rivalry going on for some time. Jon suggested a friend of his, Tony Reeves, for the job of bass player, and he too accepted the gig. The horn section would continue unchanged and Mick would remain as my guitar-slinger.

In March and April we had a continuous run of shows up and down the country, including our first visit to Scotland. It was a big deal to cross the border; we'd heard that the Scots hated English bands and would give them a really hard time. However, they took to us and the gigs were great, with the only notable incident the theft of my recording microphone, which was plugged into a recorder off to the side of the stage. I was pretty pissed off. Thirty-two years later, the thief contacted me via my website, saying that the mike was one of his most prized possessions. It didn't seem to occur to him that I might want it back!

Keef and Andy's last gig came on April 21 in Erdington, near Birmingham. Keef and I had often talked about the tradition among railwaymen that they would receive a gold watch for long service – and in keeping with this idea, I bought him a gold pocket watch with the inscription "To the one and only Keef from John and The Bluesbreakers. April 21st 1968". I gave it to him at the end of the show, although I don't know whether the audience thought I was serious.

Andy Fraser was teaming up with a few guys who wanted to form a new blues rock group. The ever-helpful Alexis Korner had put him in touch with Mike Vernon, who knew of a guitarist named Paul Kossoff. Together, Andy and Paul went to a local club and met up with drummer Simon Kirke and singer Paul Rodgers. A few knockabouts later, they realised there was an exciting bond between them – and another piece of rock history fell into place. The name of the new band was Free.

Meanwhile, the *Bare Wires* album was progressing. For the first track, we asked Pamela's permission to borrow her antique pump organ, and – in two sections – we lugged it from Lee Green to the studio and back. The pitch was slightly off, and I remember that Gus Dudgeon had to do something fancy with the tape speed to match it up with the tuning of the tracks that would follow.

The album's themes included my confusion about being married and yet driven by wanderlust ('Where Did I Belong'), the decision I made to leave home ('I Started Walking'), finding a new freedom in my daily life ('Open Up A New Door') and sex ('Fire'). The last of these featured a recording I'd made of me making love to a girl on the last Scandinavian tour. Perhaps this sounds a little odd, but I brought it into the studio and played it to Jon, asking him to get behind the drums and play a free-form solo to match the accelerating rhythms on the tape. He was flabbergasted, but promised to give it a shot. He did magnificently.

The next piece was an ultra-slow blues in double time that expressed my sadness at leaving Pamela ('I Know Now'). This led into the final track of the suite, on which I sang that I'd made my decisions and now I'd have to live with them ('Look In The Mirror'). To close this off with a dramatic statement, we inserted the sound of a mirror breaking into a thousand fragments – which was exactly how I felt my life had gone.

For the songs on side two, I drew on the experiences of my new love life. At a show in Swansea University one night, I met a beautiful girl called Caroline and hoped that we would meet again. Although I wrote long, loving letters to her, we never did – but I wrote 'I'm A Stranger' for her. 'No Reply' was about unreturned phone calls from prospective lovers, as was 'Killing Time'. Also on the album was an instrumental showcase for Mick titled 'Hartley Quits', which came from a *Melody Maker* headline. In response, Tony Reeves jokingly threatened to write a song called 'Hiseman Joins'.

At the end of May we appeared as part of a two-night all-star package concert in Zurich, Switzerland. This was an amazing event to which we flew on a private chartered plane, accompanied by The Move, Steve Winwood & Traffic, Eric Burdon & The Animals, and Jimi Hendrix. During my part of the concert the next day, someone snatched my cigarette case from the top of my organ; I briefly stopped the show until the light-fingered punter returned it. I was clearly very serious about my smokes in those days.

Our tenor player, Chris Mercer, wrote about the Swiss trip in our newsletter for the fans, saying: "This tour was something of a landmark for us, as it was the first pop tour The Bluesbreakers have ever done. When we got to Zurich, the fans waiting at the airport were disappointed as we were all taken to a far corner of the airfield and disgorged through a mobile customs coach into cars. The

Bluesbreakers immediately claimed a huge twelve-seater Chevy Impala, which we had for the whole three days."

He went on: "After the usual fiasco of a press conference we went to the gig, which turned out to be in a huge cycle racing stadium. The stage was about twenty-five feet high and we managed to set up in the far corner. After the local groups had finished, we were the first group on. The first night went down a storm for us, but poor Traffic had the misfortune to be on when the large crowd decided to have a go at the fuzz at the front and side of the stage, and a great punch-up ensued.

"However, on the second night it was our turn and we played more or less to ourselves, as the crowd was engrossed in watching the police beat up members of the audience determined to scale the stage. By the time Traffic came on, the chairs were being broken up and the stage became a mass of flying projectiles. This wasn't a reflection on Traffic, who were great, but just a night out for the Swiss who had never had a concert like this before. We were surprised to find a strong contingent of fans out there. Bluesbreakers fans look the same the world over, you can always recognise them."

Chris ended up with a note of gratitude towards Kansas, who was returning to the States to work for Frank Zappa. He returns to the story before long, as you'll see.

By the summer of 1968, the band was on a creative high that seemed to be limitless. We were doing unheard-of things like setting tempos and keys before going into totally improvised pieces which went in several directions. We also gave Jon a drum solo in a slow blues; nothing was beyond him. I used to stand by the kit, fascinated by the ease with which he could build such complex patterns.

In June we toured Europe, and while we were there, Decca released *Bare Wires*. The reviews were very favourable, especially an article in *Melody Maker* by Chris Welch, which was positively glowing. He praised in particular my skill in putting together music that incorporated all his favourite British jazz musicians, but in a blues setting.

As ever, the good times couldn't last. The sheer calibre of the current Bluesbreakers line-up meant that there were seven soloists in the band. Every night became a jam session in which all categories and styles of music came to the fore. As the singer, I would only get a look-in from time to time, which wasn't what I wanted, and so I decided to refine the band as a quartet, keeping Mick Taylor and recruiting a new bassist, Steve Thompson. Jon Hiseman agreed to stay on for a while, but he was planning a new band, Colosseum, which would also feature Dick Heckstall-Smith.

By July, I'd had enough of the constant pace of the road and the dismal British weather, and I arranged to go to Los Angeles to see if it still held the magic that I remembered from the January tour. I had also promised Pamela, long before we split up, that I would take her on a trip to either America or Japan. The circumstances of our relationship were different now, of course, but she had friends who she intended to visit in LA; we agreed that after we arrived, we wouldn't cross paths again until the journey home.

In Los Angeles we were met by Gerry Hoff, who had invited us to stay at his house. It was slightly awkward because he wasn't aware that Pamela and I didn't live together, and was expecting us to share a double bed in their spare room. We duly made some phone calls; Frank Zappa was our first connection, and he invited us to visit his place at 2401 Laurel Canyon Boulevard. From there, Pamela went to stay with Frank's photographer friend Andee Cohen – and that was that. Later, she told me what a great time she'd had, hanging out with Andee's friends and meeting up with the actors Jack Nicholson and Ted Markland out in Palm Desert.

At Frank's log cabin, Pam Zarubica made it obvious that she was interested in me; I had to break it to her that I wasn't keen. She took it in good spirit; our friendship continued and she drove me around the local sights in her Volkswagen Beetle.

I enjoyed my brief stay at the log cabin. It seemed to be a constant magnet for all sorts of bizarre characters, such as The Mothers Of Invention, Calvin Schenkel and an insanely eccentric group of girls called The GTOs. There was Miss Christine, who lived at the house and made most of the group's clothes; she was anorexic and very hyper. Then there was Miss Pamela, the cute, shy-acting blonde one who became known later as the super-groupie Pamela Des Barres;

Miss Mercy, with raccoon-like eye make-up; and three or four others. Needless to say, they made quite a spectacle when they went out together to clubs and concerts. Frank recorded their conversations and songs and made an album from them.

It was great to be around Frank, who was at the centre of all this social whirl. When he and I were alone, we went through his rock and blues records and shared a lot of information about some of the artists. He had a 45rpm single by the duo Don & Dewey, one of whom was Don 'Sugarcane' Harris, who played the most searing raw violin. It blew me away.

The remainder of the trip was an education, for sure. I moved from Frank's house to stay with the band Canned Heat, who had a rented home near the Strip. I met no fewer than three beautiful women, all of whom stole my heart. There was Roxanne, who gave me a dose of gonorrhoea, which prevented me from sleeping with another girl, Catherine James, and there was Connie, who I asked to visit me in London – but when she did, there was a distance between us, and she soon returned to the USA.

Music kept me sane through all these affairs of the heart. The new Bluesbreakers quartet stepped on stage at the Marquee on August 13 and we instantly meshed. We were all delighted, although Jon soon departed to form Colosseum and I asked Colin Allen, sometime drummer with Zoot Money's Big Roll Band and Dantalian's Chariot, to join in his place. He first played with us when we recorded our next album, *Blues From Laurel Canyon*.

We started the album with a stereo recording of a jet plane, and then took the *Bare Wires* suite concept to a new level, making the entire album into a single segue. The story it told started with the flight ('Vacation'), the excitement of Sunset Strip ('Walking On Sunset'), the peace and solitude of the hills ('Laurel Canyon Home'), a depiction of life at Frank Zappa's log cabin ('2401'), and the highs and lows of my various affairs ('Ready To Ride', 'Medicine Man' and 'Somebody's Acting Like A Child'). Then I wrote about the move from Frank's house to stay with Canned Heat ('The Bear'), three songs about Catherine ('Miss James', 'First Time Alone' and

'Long Gone Midnight') and finally my sadness at having to leave Los Angeles ('Fly Tomorrow').

I did the artwork for the album myself, using photographs taken by Steve LaVere – who was later famous for putting together the recorded legacy of Robert Johnson – on top of the hill behind the Zappa house. I was into my full-on hippie and Apache Indian phase and was clad in pyjama bottoms plus a leather beaded vest that I'd made, topped off with a headband with an eagle feather. The images included a fire which I'd lit on the hill; I didn't know it at the time, but I could have been arrested for lighting a fire up there. At the time, all I could think of was being a primitive man in the wilderness… I did make sure I put out the fire very thoroughly.

On returning to the UK, we played our first live show with Colin, Mick and Steve in Haverfordwest; one gig later, we were off to Los Angeles again. Just before we left, I got a call from the guys in Canned Heat, who had arrived in London to start their European tour. I turned over our bandwagon and Bernie our road manager to them as an exchange deal, so that when we were in LA we could use their wheels. The arrangement worked very well for Bernie; while he was with them, he was in charge of carting two and a half tons of equipment all over Europe, superstar style!

Our first appearance at the Shrine Auditorium was a smash hit and did a lot for our collective morale. On the bill with us was Junior Wells, who was playing in a soul style rather than playing blues material. As a keen student of American blues, I had noticed this tendency for many black blues stars to move towards a James Brown influence; the times they were a-changing, all right.

The following week we drove up to San Francisco and did three nights at the Avalon Ballroom. Again, box-office records were broken on all three nights. Musically, I would sooner forget those shows ever happened. The equipment supplied to us was below par, and on top of that we played badly – somehow, we just couldn't get it together.

While in LA, I played on a recording session with Shakey Jake, the blues singer and harmonica player who had recently moved to the West Coast from Chicago. The session was a bit loose, but I enjoyed hearing his guitarist, Luther Johnson. It felt great to be invited to hang out while these legendary blues guys were in the studio. Mick Taylor even got to play on a session with Sunnyland Slim, another of my favourite boogie-woogie pianists. Muddy Waters was in town, too, and we had the privilege of being in the studio when he was laying down some tracks. This was the first time I got to meet Muddy; I was delighted to hear that he knew all about me and my British blues brethren.

After four weeks in LA, we flew to Chicago for the next leg of our tour. This was my first time there and the city seemed much larger than I'd imagined. I had previously met the blues artist Magic Sam when he was in LA, and he'd given me his number to call any time I was in Chicago, so I enjoyed a great afternoon there in his apartment. Ever the documentarian, I took my reel-to-reel tape recorder with me, and in addition to capturing the great conversations we had, he demonstrated some great stomping blues in his trademark style.

After one of our Chicago shows, Magic Sam's brother-in-law gave me a lift to Sam's club, but on the way we were pulled over by the police for having a faulty car with no exhaust silencer, exceeding the speed limit and having a Mississippi driving licence, which wasn't valid in Illinois. To add to the drama, the cop who pulled us over panicked when he saw me wearing a gun belt, which I wore on stage to hold my harmonicas (all non-lethal). He assumed that I was a long-haired hippie with a gun, and had us out of the car in seconds, holding us at gunpoint and calling for reinforcements. Five squad cars roared up and we were thoroughly investigated, until the facts were established and they let us go.

Once we got to Magic Sam's club, Mick Taylor was soon on stage, jamming with Sam himself. I was thrilled; this was where I truly belonged. To top things off, Otis Rush showed up, and I got my first look at the man responsible for the classic Cobra sides that Eric Clapton and I used to love so much. He was a soft-spoken gentleman and pleased to make our acquaintance. The blues rolled on, and new friends were made. Talking of Eric, when we played in Milwaukee, he was in town and sat in with us; it was great to play with him again.

In San Francisco, we were opening for Canned Heat. They were such huge stars that they had no trouble filling the 8,000-capacity venues, which were packed with hordes of blues freaks. A large number of them were on some form of illicit substance, and we were constantly being collared by admiring fans who could barely focus on what was going on. I still recall their bleary, vacant eyes, pawing hands and unintelligible ramblings.

Back in England, my landlord wanted me to move from Porchester Road – and having enjoyed some success in recent times, I was able to afford an upgrade. After looking around South Kensington, I found a house at the end of a cul-de-sac with two floors and a basement, plus a small garden out the back. The rooms were small, but in comparison with the two-room flat in Porchester Road, it was a palace. The address was 15 Billing Road and the rent was expensive, at £50 a week (around £800 a week these days). Fortunately, Steve Thompson helped out with the rent; he moved into the basement, where there was a small bedroom where he could practise the bass guitar.

The move had to be done fairly quickly because we now had a straight run of gigs all over the country, including a session for the BBC Radio One Club. This went very well; we recorded '2401', 'Long Gone Midnight', 'Walking On Sunset', 'It Hurts Me To Leave' and 'Ready To Ride', and we followed it up with a blues spectacular at the Royal Festival Hall.

We finished 1968 with another Scandinavian tour before I took three days off for Christmas. I was over at Pamela's for much of the time, so that I could be with the kids; I had been seeing them as often as I could at Billing Road, whenever Pamela was able to drive into town. Gary and Jason seemed to have accepted our separated situation, or at least taken it in their stride – although every time they had to go back to Lee Green, my heart ached.

On New Year's Eve, we played at Alexandra Palace along with Free and a host of other rock bands. It was great to see Andy Fraser holding down his big gig; the band sounded excellent. *Melody Maker*'s end-of-year polls were a cause for celebration when I read that I was voted the fifth best musician in Britain, sixth in the entire world, and also sixth in the British Male Vocalist category. I even beat Paul McCartney and John Lennon. Some things were clearly going my way.

CHAPTER 12

CALIFORNIA: LETTING THE GOOD TIMES ROLL

At the ripe old age of thirty-five, I began another love affair – this time not with another beautiful American girl, but with alcohol.

If you don't count the glass of cider I had in the army back in 1952, I had my very first drink after a show in Zurich on a Swiss tour in early 1969. I had recently read a long and detailed interview that the actor Rod Steiger had given to *Playboy* magazine. Rod – one of my heroes – talked about letting all his thoughts on life run free-form during a session of self-analysis; I think he said it was done under the influence of liquor. Perhaps I misunderstood his point, but I thought it would be interesting to record myself talking about life in general as I consumed a bottle of red wine, one glass at a time.

Out came a bottle, and I rambled on in what I thought was a very profound manner until it was empty and I was in a state of euphoria. I soon developed a liking for the effects of intoxication, and thus began my adventures with the demon drink, which would be a major part of my life for the next thirteen years.

After returning from Switzerland, the band situation was looking bleak, not because we had no gigs but because we had so many, stretching into the future. Our bassist Steve had been ill, requiring a series of replacements, which was difficult. I also had a mild touch of flu, and this – added to the stress I was under because of all the work – threw me into such a panic that I went to Rik Gunnell and told him that I simply couldn't go on.

He said, "Don't worry, John – I'll take care of it," and contacted the infamous Dr Robert, the subject of The Beatles' song of the same name, who was known in music circles as "the rock'n'roll doctor". He diagnosed me as suffering from stress and recommended that I lay off the gigs for a couple of weeks. The next fourteen shows were consequently cancelled; to fulfil legal obligations, Dr Robert supplied the required notes to say I'd had a nervous breakdown. We eventually rescheduled a lot of them.

I felt really weird, being grounded and having to think of the disappointed punters whose nights out had been spoiled. It was all for the best, though, because Steve was released from hospital and we were able to convalesce together in Billing Road.

'Convalescing', for me at least, meant romantic hangouts with a couple of new girlfriends. One of these was a really cute girl from Boston called Carol; we hung out together on a regular basis for quite some time. She had a good sense of humour and got on well with both Steve and me. He and I also went down to Marbella to catch some restorative sunshine, but returned to London after only two days because it was even colder and rainier there than in England. In any case, we were now feeling fit and anxious to get back to work. America was waiting for us, and on February 11 we flew to New York.

A few dates into our 1969 US tour, we played at the New York Fillmore East for the first time. Impresario Bill Graham was an extraordinary promoter. He ran his staff and the shows themselves like a drill sergeant; his attention to detail and care for his artists' needs were wonderful to behold. Along with the efficiency of the operation, the sound and light shows were a treat too.

Subsequent shows in Toronto, Winnipeg and Chicago were less sumptuous, despite the company of a wonderful girl who accompanied me for a few days; as usual, I grew tired of her company awfully quickly. Commitment seemed to be a weak point for me. I was more accomplished as a shopper than a partner, unfortunately; in Tucson, Arizona I went overboard on Native American jewellery, which was for sale everywhere.

After the concert that night, I was invited by a group of fans to a party up at a photographer's house in the hills. He wanted to take some photos of me while I was in town, and I agreed; they were used on the back cover of the *Empty Rooms* album the following year. As I fancied a blonde girl named Elizabeth, I needed little coaxing, although I didn't get close to her until the party was over. Sometime during the night I felt her come to my side and cuddle up under a blanket before passing out; we awoke together with the early morning sun streaming through the stained-glass windows. This was the story behind the song 'Sleeping By Her Side'.

I felt very connected to Arizona, and resolved to come back to go camping and to explore the Native American vibe. After headlining the Fillmore in San Francisco for three nights and then flying down to LA for a few days, I made up my mind that I wanted to move to America.

Obviously, Los Angeles felt like the place where I most belonged. I talked to Elmer Valentine about my idea, and he said he could definitely help me find a place to live. Laurel Canyon was my first and only choice, and as Elmer lived there, that's where he took me to look at houses. As he lived on the highest ridge in Los Angeles, with a breathtaking view of the whole city right down to the ocean, I reckoned Grand View Drive was the place to scope out.

I wasn't too keen on the first house we inspected, on the corner of Grand View and Kirkwood, because the access was on the steepest part of the junction and the place looked like a fortress, so he said, "Okay, let's take a look at this other one I know."

I was instantly smitten. The second property was only a year old and available for a good price, because the owner needed to shift it in a divorce settlement. The thing I most liked about it was that it was little more than a shell, with no established personality; I could visualise right away how I could remodel the interior to my needs. It had a big, L-shaped room with a kitchen on the street-level floor, with two rooms and a half bathroom downstairs, while the upstairs had the same L-shaped configuration with a bathroom over the kitchen and another bedroom over the garage.

The owner was asking $36,000 for it, and I didn't need to think twice before telling him I'd take it. Elmer said he'd help out with the arrangements while I was away, and I got on the phone to Rik Gunnell and told him my plans; he had dumped his Soho office and was now part of the Robert Stigwood Organisation. We began the paperwork and he sent me a cheque for the down payment of $12,000.

This was a huge moment for me. I'd have loved to get in right away with hammer and nails, but I had to wait out the escrow period, which was to take a couple of months. It felt great to be committed, and I was already making plans in my head for the alterations and possibilities. My friend John Judnich lived across the canyon on Brier Drive, and he let me move in with him until I could take occupancy of the new house. This was a godsend for me because we had a lot of time off in April – and apart from three shows up north in Vancouver, Seattle's Eagles Auditorium and the Sound Factory in Sacramento, we were based in Los Angeles.

It wasn't all peace and love in California. After a week's residency at the Whisky in March, we drove out to Palm Springs to the Sunair Drive-In, where a rock festival was being held on April 1. It was a chance to meet up with The Paul Butterfield Blues Band, who were on before us. It wasn't too happy a reunion, however, because I had been quoted in some rock newspaper as saying that I didn't care for Paul's band, or words to that effect. He had taken offence at this and gave me a piece of his mind, telling me that I should watch what I said to the press. He added that because we were all playing the same circuit, it was the role of a musician to stay away from negative statements about others in the same business.

He was right, and I've tried to heed those words ever since.

Once Paul had got all this off his chest, the rift was mended and we began playing. All was not well at the perimeter of the drive-in area, however, and it was soon apparent from the sight of numerous fires in the darkness that a riot was in progress. A number of people who apparently adhered to the popular hippie belief that music should be free had decided to tear down the fences and burn them. This quickly got out of hand, with police, fire engines and crowd control making it impossible for the show to continue. We played a short set, and I'm sure we didn't get paid because the promoter went bankrupt after paying expenses and settling legal battles. Ah well – this wouldn't be the last rock'n'roll riot of the era, or the worst.

After the Whisky run and gigs at the Shrine, Riverside and in San Diego, we closed out the month of April at the Avalon Ballroom in San Francisco. This was a disastrous gig for me because my passport was stolen from the dressing room while we were on stage. All our searching was in vain and I was in a total panic, because we were heading for Boston in the morning to play the last three dates of the tour before flying home. In order for me to leave the country, I had to have a temporary passport; this didn't come through until the very last moment, doing nothing to help my stress levels.

It had been a very long and fruitful tour, but I'm afraid I was reaching a saturation point with the traditional Bluesbreakers format. I felt that I had taken the lead guitar, organ, bass and drums line-up as far as it could go, and coupled with my imminent move to Los Angeles, it seemed that now would be a good time to change things up. I was also tired of enduring high volume levels on stage, and it struck me that if you removed the drums and electric guitar, this problem would be solved. But what would take their place?

I had been a fan of the horn player Jimmy Giuffre from the first time I saw the film *Jazz On A Summer's Day*, filmed in 1958 at the Newport Jazz Festival in Rhode Island. Jimmy had assembled a line-up of guitar, clarinet and trombone and made it work magically, so I thought of keeping Steve on bass and bringing in Johnny Almond, who played excellent flute in addition to tenor sax. I also planned to use the acoustic fingerstyle guitarist Jon Mark, who I'd met when he and I were doing a TV show and who was backing Marianne Faithfull at the time. I made the calls and all of them were up for the experiment, at least to see if it worked. I set up a time to rehearse at Billing Road.

Just around this time, I got a phone call from Mick Jagger. He told me that the Stones had been having increasing trouble with Brian Jones, who seemed continually distant from the rest of the band. He was always making excuses for not going out on the road when there was a need to do so. All in all, it just wasn't working out, so Mick asked me if I knew another guitarist who might fit the bill.

Of course, the timing was perfect. I wouldn't be needing Mick Taylor for my new venture, so he would be ideal. I gave his number to Jagger, and soon afterwards Mick became a Rolling Stone, leaving me free to make my next move.

Funnily enough, I got a message just after this that Brian Jones wanted to see me. When I called him, he said that he wanted to get some advice about putting a new band together so that he could record his own music.

One summer's day, Pamela, the kids and I made a trip to Brian's house in the country with our driver Mick Lawford at the wheel. It was a beautiful day, and when we arrived at the cottage Brian was in his music room, surrounded by an assortment of guitars, flutes and odd string instruments from the Middle East. We were shocked by how unwell he looked. He looked incredibly frail and had trouble walking; in fact, he seemed ready to fall over if he wasn't holding on to something.

I was sad to see the state that the excesses of the road with the Stones, the drugs and his own weaknesses had left Brian in. He was a shadow of his former self, and looked and behaved like a little old man. Still, he was totally serious and excited about putting some new music together, and told me that the reason he'd called me was that he'd always admired me and Alexis for our dedication to blues, unlike all the other musicians who'd abandoned the medium in search of fame and fortune.

While Pamela and the boys were outside playing on the lawn by the outdoor swimming pool, he and I tried to get a duet going – but it was sad and alarming for me to hear that he had lost all sense of rhythm and time. The musical hang didn't last too long as a result, but in our subsequent conversation I encouraged him to keep at it, because he was so obviously enthusiastic.

We went out to the garden and, using a walking stick to steady himself, Brian proudly showed us round. Although the pool wasn't heated, Gary and Jason borrowed some swimming trunks and went in. Brian told us that he found swimming to be helpful for his motor skills. We soon said our goodbyes and left.

It was a terrible shock to learn that Brian was found dead in that same pool just two days after our visit. I've heard so many theories about whether it was suicide or not, and although no one will ever know the answer for sure, I choose to believe that Brian died in an accident. He seemed so optimistic about his new life, separate from the Stones, that suicide simply makes no sense to me.

Back in The Bluesbreakers, I told Mick and Colin about the change in my musical direction, and we made a date to switch over to a new, drummer-less formation. Mick was covered, of course, and I knew that Colin would find new work without much difficulty.

The new line-up, featuring Jon Mark (guitar), Jonny Almond (flute and sax) and Steve Thompson (bass), began rehearsals at Billing Road and a repertoire started to take shape. For subject material, I drew on recent experiences from the last American visit, just as I'd done before; my mind was clearly firmly on my soon-to-be home country.

The first song I wrote was related to the late sixties counterculture, and was specifically directed at the popular hippie belief that there should be no laws against using drugs, and that all police officers were classified as 'pigs'. I had a personal interest in these points of view, having been somewhat involved in a riot at a free, impromptu concert by the pier in Santa Monica. Whoever put the event together didn't have a permit, and nearby residents soon summoned the police to break it up.

I had just sung a couple of songs as part of a loose jam session when the men in blue arrived in force and began making arrests for drug use. The crowd turned on them and the police were soon being pelted with rocks from all sides. Whatever you may think of the police forces of the world, this behaviour was wrong. I was one of the guys who got on the mike, urging the crowd to disperse quietly. The incident made the *LA Times*, with a photo that I later incorporated in the new album artwork.

I was inspired to write a song called 'The Laws Must Change', and drew on Lenny Bruce's message that when it came to drugs, the police were the wrong target. They were, after all, just doing their job; the issue of whether or not to legalise drugs was a decision that lay with governments, not law enforcement.

A renewed relationship with my Los Angeles honey became the subject of 'Thoughts About Roxanne'. During my last long stay in LA, I'd tried to be with her again, but by now she had a steady boyfriend, so a platonic friendship was all that she and I could manage. I went out shopping with her a few times, and we went to the zoo for an afternoon. In the end we resolved to wait until she was free before taking things any further. She was still the girl I wanted most in LA.

The new band soon assembled a set list of eleven songs, including one about Connie called 'Don't Pick A Flower' and the romping 'Don't Waste My Time', co-written with Steve and released as a studio single. Perhaps ironically, as we were getting the new act together at the house, the regular electric gigs were still being fulfilled by the old line-up, which was playing larger and more prestigious venues and sounding better and better.

We drew big crowds, especially when we went to Germany in June. The promoter Fritz Rau had put together a very important tour for us, and he was shocked to be told that midway through the tour I planned to abandon the line-up, drop The Bluesbreakers title and switch to an unlikely sounding drummer-less acoustic band, under the banner of John Mayall! Poor Fritz was desperate – and very fearful that I was going to sabotage all the success I'd built up. He pleaded with me to keep the band the way it was, at least for the first half of each concert; I could then introduce the new, weird line-up for the second half. But I was adamant, so he had no choice but to keep his fingers crossed that the German audiences wouldn't ask for their money back.

They didn't, fortunately; we played five sell-out shows in Germany and then travelled to Brussels, where we played our last gig together on June 24. Returning to England, Mick headed for The Rolling Stones and Colin picked up a permanent gig with Stone The Crows.

As for me, Aynsley Dunbar wanted me to produce his first album, *Retaliation*, as I mentioned earlier. We had a lot of fun with it;

I enjoyed the job of shaping the project without constricting the players. Aynsley later told me that he didn't make a dime from the LP – and I'm sure I didn't either. We suspected the usual managerial rip-off.

In July we flew to New York to finalise a new deal with Polydor Records; the old Decca contract was up, and Rik had come up with a better deal with Polydor, both financially and in terms of exposure. The new line-up made its first public appearance at the Newport Jazz Festival, and we were delighted with the reaction – especially at this historic event, which I'd only known from the *Jazz On A Summer's Day* movie.

I stood admiring the white wooden chairs on the lawns, and mused that I would never have imagined a few years before that I would one day be on this very stage. I took my Beaulieu movie camera with me and filmed some of the other artists, specifically a snippet of Frank Zappa & The Mothers Of Invention, as well as footage of Gary Burton warming up with his vibraphone in one of the rear tents.

As Frank was about to go on stage, someone came up behind me and tapped me on the shoulder. I turned around to see Miles Davis standing there.

"Hey man," he said. "I just wanted to tell you that I really dig what you're doing with your new band."

I thanked him, and he nodded and moved on. He was a man of few words, but very nice to talk to and evidently sincere. I was honoured.

A high point in my career came at the Fillmore East in New York, where we played on July 11 and 12, on the second night of which our live album *The Turning Point* was recorded. Eddie Kramer was the engineer; he had recorded demos for me a few years before, and was now becoming well-known in the American music business after working with Jimi Hendrix and Led Zeppelin. I was very nervous about recording live there, as each note and sound was so exposed, but we had a terrific audience who appreciated my trademark 'chicka chicka' sound in the song 'Room To Move'. That song is popular to this day, although I cringe when I hear my solo. To me it sounds really nervous and shaky, and I lose the beat several times.

These were our last shows before we broke up for a long summer vacation. I couldn't wait to get off the plane in Los Angeles and get into the new house. The escrow was pretty near completion, and in the meantime I stayed for a few days at John Judnich's again. The day I got the call telling me that I could take possession of 8353 Grand View Drive, I got busy right away.

My first job was to put up a dividing wall to break up the L-shaped upstairs area, keeping the larger section as the master bedroom and putting another bed in the smaller section. I bought a huge oak table from Olvera Street for the dining room and, using some old redwood railroad ties, converted the whole downstairs room into beams and wainscoting for an English Tudor look. I then changed the carpeting, hung my pictures and sent for my possessions to be freighted over from London.

I wanted a swimming pool and, assuming it would be cheaper if I asked a builder to create two at the same time, got together with Elmer, as he wanted a pool too. We both paid about $20,000 to a local contractor, appropriately called Dick, who seemed more interested in showing off to the ladies on the tennis courts than supervising the project. He had a couple of poorly paid Mexicans digging four holes, each twenty-five feet deep, in order to sink caissons that would be filled with steel and concrete. These were strong enough to support a deck and the pool itself, which was a concrete basin and a miracle of engineering. It was a long job and took up most of my vacation time, but when the pool was finished and filled with water, it was bliss to be able to dive in off the board and cool off from the blazing sun.

Why all this detail about my pool? You'll see – it plays an important part later on.

I still hadn't learned to drive, although I needed transport, so I bought a second-hand Ford station wagon and hired Gail Zappa's sister Sherry Sloatman to be my driver and housekeeper. She had been living in Hawaii and was a bit on the spaced-out side. Her housekeeping left much to be desired, but she tried her best and was useful for a while.

I wanted to explore the area, and when Pamela's friend Andee Cohen told Steve and me about a great place in the high desert town of Joshua Tree, I planned a visit. The place was a motel, run by an elderly couple known to the rock'n'roll elite as the Murphys. In due course, Sherry drove Steve and me out there.

We arrived in quiet, starlit darkness at the Joshua Tree Inn. We knocked on the office door, which was opened by Mr Murphy, who allotted us our rooms. The quiet was intense, and it was quite a shock to be in such silence. The air was intoxicatingly pure, and we sat out by the pool for a while before turning in.

The Inn was clearly a refuge for Hollywood's old school. We learned that only three or four rooms were occupied, and that the singer Scott McKenzie was a resident. After huge success with the song 'San Francisco (Be Sure To Wear Flowers In Your Hair)' two years previously, he'd dropped out of the LA scene and come out here to find some inner peace. We saw quite a lot of Scott in the days to follow; one night his friend Michelle Phillips of The Mamas & The Papas stayed over with a bunch of her friends. At night, Scott, Steve and I would sit outside, sipping drinks and watching the bats dip and dive around the lighted pool.

One night, we noticed a strange, ethereal figure in white robes and with a long grey beard. Asking who this was, we were told that it was John Barrymore Jr, a noted recluse who had been famous as an actor in TV shows such as *Gunsmoke* and *Rawhide*. He didn't speak much to anyone and soon drifted into the night like the ghostly hermit he had become.

I was in the mood for some experimentation, and the night before we returned to Los Angeles, I decided to repeat my earlier experiment of uttering my thoughts into a portable tape recorder while under the influence of alcohol. Sherry duly drove me out of town at twilight to a mountain of rocks in the desert, which I scaled carefully, holding my recorder and a bottle of port.

Once she had left, I took off all my clothes, perched in a niche high above the desert, popped the cork of the bottle and rolled the

DJ John Peel introduces me to a festival crowd somewhere in the USA. MICHAEL PUTLAND/GETTY IMAGES

Author Debby Chesher put together a book containing the artwork of musician artists. My work was fortunately documented before the fire that destroyed it all. Seen here are Klaus Voorman, Joni Mitchell and Commander Cody at a reception in 1979.
EBET ROBERTS/REDFERNS

The re-formed Bluesbreakers of 1982, featuring John McVie, Colin Allen and Mick Taylor. PAUL NATKIN/GETTY IMAGES

I never knew Robin Williams was a big fan till he showed up at one of my Los Angeles shows. A fine night for all.

When Maggie and I got married in North Yorkshire Alexis Korner and his wife, Bobby, attended the event along with my old friend Ray Cummings and his wife, Janet.

After John, Colin and Mick returned to their regular gigs, my Los Angeles band featured (l–r) drummer Willie McNeil, guitarists Coco Montoya and Kal David with bassist Bobby Haynes peeping through. TERRANCE BERT

Record producer Tony Carey and I take a break during our recording session for the album *Chicago Line* in Peter Maffay's studio in Tutzing, Germany. Peter was delighted to have us there.

Sharing a moment or two with harmonica-great Junior Wells at a festival show we headlined.

A rare occasion to be a guest on Jay Leno's *Tonight Show* where we got to perform a couple of songs too, 1990.
NBC/GETTY IMAGES

Shaking hands with Vice President Al Gore with President Clinton looking on at a benefit I was happy to be a part of.

Enjoying a backstage moment with New Orleans producer Allen Toussaint and guitarist Steve Cropper.

It was a big thrill for me to be playing on the same show as guitar god Stevie Ray Vaughan. We were a perfect musical match that night.

Backstage at a festival with Robert Cray and my delighted son Sammy posing happily for the camera.

A backstage moment with my son Zak, enjoying each other's hair adornments.

Posing with my granddaughter Ella outside a London hotel.

Drummer Keef Hartley sharing a moment with my mother, Beryl, at her home in Ripon.

My eldest son, Gaz, in full festival attire at one of the London gigs he performed at with his own band, The Trojans.

Sharing a backstage moment with guitar-great Peter Green during one of our joint British tours, 1997.

A happy family pose with wife Maggie and our two children, Sammy and Zak.

A nice shot of German promoter Fritz Rau on one of our many tours together.

Strange attire indeed as I was presented with an OBE outside Buckingham Palace, 2005. On a fashion note, you are unlikely to see me dressed like this again.

tape. I don't remember the words I recorded in that drunken ramble, although they seemed profound at the time, but I will never forget the sweetness of the experience. Imagine the scene: I was completely alone, more so than anyone for miles around. The only sounds were the cries of coyotes as darkness fell, and the moon and stars lit the rocks and Joshua trees with stunning luminescence. On my mountain of rocks, I felt as if I was the only human in the universe.

The experience lasted longer than I had planned; although I had arranged with Sherry to pick me up at a certain time, she didn't show up until later. Perhaps she couldn't find the right rock pile… Fortunately, she found me, or I'd be out there still.

When our time in Joshua Tree was up, we had to fly home from the tiny local airport as my station wagon couldn't be trusted to make the 120-mile trip back to LA. It was overheating and choking up constantly, so we let Sherry make the journey in her own time. It was no surprise that she got sidetracked and disappeared for a week. As for the car, we never saw it again.

After my vacation, Decca released *Looking Back*, a compilation of my non-album singles, and we were booked to play in Honolulu. We flew there on August 9, a black day in entertainment history; the newspapers ran headlines reporting the murders of Roman Polanski's pregnant wife Sharon Tate and four others in the most gruesome way imaginable. Charles Manson and his gang were the killers, and there was a tangible feeling of fear in Laurel Canyon. Steve was totally freaked out.

Fortunately, a major reception awaited us in Honolulu, which took our minds off the news. It was a real thrill to play, supported by Cheech & Chong, at the HIC Arena in front of our largest audience yet – 16,000 people. We had a couple of days to enjoy the island and it felt as if we had reached a career milestone. The *Turning Point* album was selling well, and our unusual line-up was getting a lot of attention in the press; we went on to play major venues such as Seattle's Eagles Auditorium, Pasadena's Rose Palace, the Phoenix Star Theatre and no fewer than three headlining nights at the Fillmore West.

Meanwhile, on the East Coast on 15 to 18 August, the biggest event in rock history – Woodstock – was taking place. This event profoundly influenced the culture in which I moved, with its assertions of anti-authoritarian rebellion, free love and anti-war sentiments – and to this day many people assume I played there. At the time, however, our own tour was in full swing. Keef Hartley was there with his band and told me afterwards how crazy it was.

Back in LA, I'd flown Pamela and the kids out for a couple of weeks while I was on the road, and, as Pamela now had local contacts, she was able to show them the sights. My mother Beryl flew in shortly afterwards; she was happily overwhelmed and wrote a glowing description of her first week's experience while waiting for us to return from the road. Once I was back at home, it felt a little awkward having Pamela under the same roof, even though we had separate rooms. Still, Beryl and the boys enjoyed their visit, which was the most important thing.

Our American tour finished up at the Whisky A Go Go for six nights in a row. At one of the shows I was flattered and impressed that my hero Rod Steiger had come to the gig and was sitting in the prime booth by the door. I was summoned to meet him, and he invited me to have dinner with him next door at Sneaky Pete's Steakhouse. We got on so well that I invited him to our house for an afternoon shortly afterwards. He absolutely bowled my mother over with his anecdotes. This was such a thrill for me, especially when he gave me his phone number and said I should come and visit his beach house in Malibu some time.

Once I was settled in at the new house, it soon became a hub for social activity. When it became known around town that my house was a late-night party place, all the waitresses from the local bars and restaurants regularly showed up to party after hours. I quickly became attracted to a girl from Virginia named Nancy, one of a regular gang of waitresses who would generally come up to the house after 3 a.m. Their preferred hangout was a platform which I'd made, with railings intended to resemble a western bar. I had some bullhorns and an antique western saddle hung over the rails; my reel-to-reel tapes and LPs were also stored there. On any given night,

I could look over to this part of the house to see Nancy and her friends Pam Robinson – who later married guitarist Terry Kath of Chicago – Donna Curry, Linda Lee Failing and Miss Cinderella of The GTOs. They all looked upon Nancy as their leader.

On crowded nights, the girls would sit up there, surveying the party animals as they streamed in from the street. There was a lot of pill usage in this after-dark social circle; the drugs of choice were downers, usually Mandrax or Quaaludes. Cocaine was also gaining favour at this time, but my visitors were interested in more or less any drug that was around. Nancy was mainly into Quaaludes; I hated this habit of hers because, when she took the stuff, her personality would change for the worse. The Quaaludes would kick in, she would become aggressive and then collapse. Those pills were my enemy.

One night she got into a parking-lot brawl with another female guest, with fisticuffs, scratching and tearing hair. Afterwards, she passed out on my bed. I put my feelings about this into a song I wrote for the next album, *Empty Rooms*; it was a solo monologue called 'Lying In My Bed'. Even so, I was totally captivated by her – the song, or rather a poem, sums up how it felt to love her unconditionally. Love has its own rules, I was learning.

CHAPTER 13

I'M A SUCKER FOR LOVE: AFFAIRS OF THE HEART

By the end of September, we were back on tour again. We worked mainly in Chicago and the Midwest. On one of the nights that we played Chicago's Kinetic Playground, Big Walter Horton came on stage with us – and even though he'd had one too many whiskies, he still had the magnificent electric harmonica sound that he and Little Walter had pioneered. In October, *The Turning Point* was released and I headed back to LA – and Nancy.

Ours was a very unpredictable relationship, and I was trapped in it for the next two years. It was an affair of great highs and jealous furies, both impossible to avoid. There was something so intense between us that we felt locked together, for better *and* worse. The relationship alternated between love and hate, and yet we couldn't imagine breaking up because most of the time we seemed like a perfect match. I was blinded by romance.

The night before I left for a British tour, Nancy and I had a very tender night together; it felt as if the world didn't exist outside the bedroom door. The scent of her perfume and the candlelight inspired me to write a song about her called 'To A Princess'.

The British tour was booked all over the country; we were enjoying a very high profile. We even had another show at the Royal Albert Hall, where Keef's band opened for us; he also shared the stage for our final show on November 30 at the Cambridge Regal Theatre. We did a total of twenty-one shows back to back, but still found time to go into a London studio to record tracks for the next album. I recorded with Jon, Steve and Johnny on 'Counting The Days' – inspired by how hard it was to be away from Nancy this whole month – and other tracks called 'Waiting For The Right Time' and 'Something New'.

Once again, I was starting to get fidgety with the limitations of my band. As I saw it, we had explored the musical possibilities to the limit and yet we still only had a repertoire of around ten songs. Furthermore, as I was going to be living permanently in California, I knew it would soon become impractical to have a band of British-based musicians. The idea of forming a band of Americans was much more appealing.

For now, we still had concert tours booked into the next year – and in fairness to all, I decided we'd stick it out till they were done. I announced a disbanding date for June 1970, and that was that. The next afternoon I was on the plane back to Laurel Canyon and my lover.

At first Nancy and I were inseparable, so much so that I asked her to give up her apartment and move in with me; she did so very happily. It was nice to be close, but the bliss didn't last, with cracks starting to appear when I followed up on Rod Steiger's offer to visit him in Malibu. We arrived one afternoon and were soon relaxing on the beach that adjoined his backyard. He was a very voluble host and kept us entertained with tales of his recent adventures in Russia, where he'd spent months working on the Napoleon movie, *Waterloo*. Rod's actor neighbour Jack Warden dropped by, as did Rod's girlfriend, and we all went to the market to pick up wine and groceries for dinner.

After our meal – and well into the wine – Rod embellished his stories with excellent character impressions, notably of W. C. Fields, who he had also portrayed on film. I got into the act and we developed a cockney dialogue together, much to everyone's amusement. Unfortunately, this perfect day and evening ended poorly; we'd been invited to stay the night and were shown to a guest bedroom, but Nancy decided that she needed to go and sort something out with one of her ex-boyfriends at the Whisky, where the band Chicago were playing that night. She said she'd be back in an hour and drove off.

I was left to hang out with Rod, who talked about his first marriage to Claire Bloom and how much he loved their daughter, who was supposed to come out to California. When it was clear that Nancy wasn't going to be back any time soon, he retired to bed, leaving me in the guest room to finish the last of the wine. Alone, unable to sleep and thoroughly miserable, with my jealous mind imagining all sorts of situations, I waited and waited. At 5 a.m. Nancy came back, heavily drugged; she couldn't tell me what had gone on for all those hours, and was pissed off that I would even ask.

Perhaps it sounds ridiculous, but I still loved her so much that on a trip to the Joshua Tree Inn in December, Nancy and I exchanged marriage vows while watching the entertainer Tiny Tim get married to Victoria Budinger on *The Tonight Show Starring Johnny Carson*... yes, that does sound ridiculous.

I'd planned to spend Christmas in Cheadle Hulme with Beryl, and invited Nancy to come too. She accepted, but only if she could bring her best buddy Donna with us. It bugged me that Donna was never too far away from Nancy, because I felt that we were both battling for Nancy's favour, but I agreed. The three of us duly flew to England.

Beryl was very happy to have us with her for Christmas; we filled the house with life and consumed home-made mince pies and bottles of wine. As we woke up on Christmas morning, Nancy was overwhelmed by the huge sack of presents I had bought her. Perhaps I should have got something for Donna, who obviously felt left out. As the days went on, Donna got more and more antsy, evidently out of jealousy, and she went home early. Things were a lot less tense after she'd gone.

In order to add another dimension to our US tour in 1970, I decided to ask a British one-man-band musician called Duster Bennett to join the show. He was an excellent, dedicated bluesman, and I thought the American musicians in my band would be greatly impressed by him.

Duster's equipment was fairly primitive, consisting of a bass drum that travelled without a case, a hi-hat, cymbals, foot pedals and a harmonica rack which went round his neck. He was a devout Christian, never swore and carried a Bible with him all the time; as such, he was a stark contrast to the hard-drinking Bluesbreakers.

On the plane from London to New York, Jon Mark did so much drinking that when we arrived at JFK he was legless. Somehow he managed to bypass customs and immigration, having wandered unnoticed through some door. We alerted the airport officials that he was missing; later, they found him wandering around in a daze, pissed out of his brain.

It was Jon who coined the phrase "Give me a glass of brain damage!" when he ordered a drink from a bartender; this inspired my Brain Damage Club, the bar I set up at home on Grand View Drive. One of the regulars was Rik Gunnell, who had moved out to LA; he found an expensive rental at the top of Trousdale Estates. He didn't care about the cost as it was all being paid for by the Robert Stigwood Organisation.

My band members were characters, to say the least. In the spring of that year, one of them met a young lady and was smitten enough to invite her to our gigs. Oddly, he was a happy family man at the same time, complete with his wife at home. Still, he pursued this road romance – and the longer it went on, the more convinced he was that he was in love. Eventually he phoned his wife and told her that he was bringing home another woman once the tour ended! She was not amused, but, believe it or not, the other woman did indeed move in with them. It didn't last more than a few months; his wife emerged as the winner in this domestic triangle.

From New York we flew west to Edmonton and Vancouver in Canada and then rented a couple of vans to take us down the West Coast. Dates in Texas followed and then we were back to Los Angeles for a four-day residency at the Whisky. As I'd expected, Duster was a big success with our audiences; he also loved the opportunity to see America for the first time. Once we were back in LA, Nancy had had enough of the road and stayed home for the next leg of the tour.

Later, up in Eugene, Oregon, I was feeling a bit homesick, so I decided to surprise Nancy by flying home unannounced. This was more difficult than I thought it would be, because there weren't too many planes flying at night and there was a connection involved. Still, I left a note for the band, took a cab to the airport after the show and caught the last flight out of Eugene. After sitting around an empty airport in San Francisco waiting for the first plane out, I stumbled in at about 8 a.m. Because I'd had no sleep, my surprise arrival really didn't accomplish much other than me writing the song 'Night Flyer'.

The second leg of the tour began with a return one-nighter at the HIC Arena in Honolulu and continued with a direct flight to New York, where we set up a base. This enabled us to do the Fillmore and other East Coast venues throughout March, with time off during the week. While there, we recorded songs for the new album. One of these, 'To A Princess', featured a bass guitar duel between Steve Thompson and Larry Taylor, who was in town working with Canned Heat. I loved the way it came out, with its escalating scale movement.

We then completed a European tour, the last for the *Turning Point* band, with fourteen British concerts including Manchester's Free Trade Hall, the Liverpool Philharmonic and the Royal Albert Hall. Germany, Austria and Holland followed, and we played our final gig in Lyon, France on June 1. I was so glad that it was over at last and I could move on, not least because my love affair with alcohol had now developed into a fairly toxic relationship.

I remember one particularly turbulent evening after a show in Copenhagen. The evening had started pretty well with a good gig, and we celebrated afterwards at the Palace Hotel in honour of my brother Philip and his wife, Lesley, who had come over to see the show. The drinking quickly escalated out of control; I was downing endless Pernods, while Nancy was falling about on Quaaludes and brandy. The inevitable yelling followed, and I staggered out of the hotel, desperate to escape. I found refuge in the gutter behind the hotel and lay there semi-comatose for I know not how many hours. It was dawn when I woke to face a truly biblical hangover.

After the tour, Nancy and I stayed on in England a bit longer because we wanted to go up north to visit my mother and her family. We had tickets to fly home on June 30 and were all set to leave when I was offered a last-minute slot on the bill at the Bath Festival Of Blues And Progressive Music – the event that later inspired Glastonbury – three days before our departure. It was good money, and too prestigious an opportunity to miss, with Led Zeppelin, Pink Floyd, Jefferson Airplane, Yes, Santana and Fairport Convention on the bill alongside many other huge bands of the day. There was just one snag; I didn't have a band, having just split up the musicians for good. I didn't relish the thought of calling up Jon, Johnny and Steve so soon after we'd said our professional farewells, so I decided to put together a last-minute line-up.

We had a publicist at that time named Mike Housego, who later wrote: "I couldn't believe it. Just twenty-four hours before the show and John didn't have a band! How the hell is he going to get a band together, rehearse, and ship them all down to Bath? He made his first phone call. 'Hello – is that Peter Green? Hello Peter, it's John. Fancy a blow down at Bath this weekend?...' Ten minutes later a new John Mayall band had been formed and was on the road to Bath. They walked on stage and played an incredible set."

Despite Mike's kind words, our set wasn't as together as most people thought. Peter was in a strange mood and was drifting around in a red, floor-length kaftan, looking very biblical with his flowing hair and full curly beard. Apart from Peter, the other musicians were Aynsley Dunbar on drums, Blind Faith's Ric Grech on bass and violin, and my half-brother Roderick on Hammond organ. We had the right instrumentation to make any jam session work, but the problem was that the original schedule was so delayed that we didn't get on stage until 5 a.m. We were so knackered that it was hard to breathe much life into the set, especially as a lot of the audience had fallen asleep hours before.

Back in Los Angeles, the situation between Nancy and me was more volatile than ever, with constant rows and flare-ups, usually triggered by some trivial incident. For instance, if I so much as smiled at an airline stewardess, I faced sulks and accusations for hours. I admit that, on my side, I was drinking a whole lot more and was very unsociable unless I had a drink in my hand.

My alcoholic excesses were now seriously out of control. After most gigs I would find myself in the hotel bar with the band, challenging all comers to drinking contests. Johnny Almond and I would often try to outdo each other with shots of Pernod. I was usually the winner, but after my brief euphoria I usually found myself in a dizzy, swirling haze, or throwing up violently – or both. Still, I kept drinking. I was having too much fun to stop.

My greatest pleasure in 1970 came when I worked on the new house. The Californian weather was beautiful; it felt so great to be off the road and able to get down to the new designs and renovations. I owned a half lot adjacent to the main house, so I drew up a design that would extend the living area into the bar to beat all bars. I also bought three adjoining lots on the other side of the house for less than $3,000 each, so that no one else would be able to build there.

I'd decided to make the smaller section of the upstairs level into my bedroom, vacating the large room and making it into a library for my book and magazine collections. The new expanded building also featured an indoor balcony that would overlook the bar below; I also found a place for a large tree sculpture.

Rik, now settled in at his new house and living high on the hog, threw quite a few parties, and it was at one of these that I met The Staple Singers, who had been signed to Robert Stigwood's label. It was such a treat to actually meet and talk to the bandleader Pops Staples, and particularly his daughter Mavis, whose soulful voice had haunted me for years. Here they were, just ordinary family folk, enjoying cocktails by the pool and mingling with friends. It was a paradise in many ways, one connected to the various strands of the entertainment industry. Of course, dubious people populated this world, but I enjoyed myself anyway, usually accompanied by a trusty flask of vodka.

Rik's assistant Eddie Choran, who we called Fast Eddie, also moved out from New York. Nancy had always gone on about what a fine actress she could be if given the chance, and through Eddie she was now given that shot, helped by the influence of Stigwood's office. Eddie set up a lunch with a top film and TV producer called Beryl Vertue at the Beverly Hills Hotel, and a few days later the word came back that Nancy could start right away in a daytime soap opera. It was just the opportunity she needed – but she turned it down, saying that she didn't consider soaps to be 'real' acting. This was odd, as she seldom missed an episode of her favourite soap opera. She never had another chance again.

It was now July, and I had to get a new band together. I'd already talked to the bassist Larry Taylor, and since he was no longer with Canned Heat, he was interested in joining me in my latest drummer-less configuration. Ever since hearing the guitarist Harvey Mandel's solo LP *Cristo Redentor* in 1968, I thought he'd be ideal for my band, as he had an electronic sound that sounded like no one else I'd ever heard. He said yes to my offer – so now it only remained for me to track down the elusive Don 'Sugarcane' Harris, whose searing violin had floored me when I first heard Don & Dewey's instrumental single 'Soul Motion' over at Frank Zappa's house.

Sugarcane had recently appeared on Frank Zappa's *Hot Rats* album, and Frank was my means of locating him – by leaving messages on his mother's phone. He wasn't working at the time and my project was ideal for him, as it would provide him with a steady income that would – unfortunately – then be swallowed up by his heroin habit. The poor guy had been a junkie for years; it was this tragedy that had prevented him from receiving the recognition he deserved as the most soulful violinist in rock history.

Despite his habit, he was a gentle person with a great sense of humour; he was a constant source of entertainment for us all as the tracks for my new album, *USA Union*, were laid down. Hearing him in the studio was unbelievable, and the sessions went by very smoothly. His virtuoso playing on the song 'Crying', which I'd written in the midst of remorse following a fight with Nancy, was stunning. Originally he'd wanted to play electric violin, as he had on all the other songs, but I insisted he should perform this one acoustically. On the road, the song was always a high point of our set.

The album's songs 'My Pretty Girl', 'You Must Be Crazy', 'Possessive Emotions', 'Deep Blue Sea', 'Took The Car', 'Night Flyer' and 'Off The Road' were all related to Nancy and me in some way, while the remaining two songs were 'Where Did My Legs Go' – a boogie-woogie piece saluting my alcoholic lifestyle – and 'Nature's Disappearing', inspired by an article about ecology that I'd read in a magazine. As a supplement to this song, I reprinted the original text, which listed ten ways in which one could help ease the gradual destruction of our planet. In retrospect, this was pretty progressive – the modern ecological movement didn't really take hold for at least another decade.

When the album was finished, I contacted the famous jazz critic Leonard Feather, and took a copy of the tape to his home, also in Laurel Canyon, at the top of Mulholland Drive. He reviewed it so favourably that we printed the entire review on the back of the album. When the album came out, Polydor even put up a billboard on Sunset Boulevard opposite the Chateau Marmont. My American profile was close to its peak at this point.

With the new album completed, it was time for a break from the road and the chance to bring over the family for a vacation. In mid-July, Beryl, Gary, Jason, Tracey and Ben got off the plane with beaming faces, looking forward to seeing the house and soaking up some California sunshine. For a few days we hung out at home, watched movies, visited the beach and lay by the pool. I had hung a rope from the top balcony and this was the kids' favourite activity, swinging from one side of the pool to the other.

We'd planned to go on a camping trip, and duly rented a Winnebago motor home. Nancy's sister Patty and her boyfriend Eddie were also coming along, so we needed a pretty big vehicle to accommodate all nine of us. We loaded up with provisions and set off on the San Bernardino freeway towards Barstow, where we'd planned to make our first stop.

We didn't really have much of a plan; we were hoping that we'd find an ideal spot where it would be hot enough to get a tan but mild enough at night to sleep in our tents. However, we got more heat than we bargained for when we veered off on a hundred-mile detour to stay the night in Death Valley. The sun was setting when we got there and we settled down for the night after a restaurant dinner.

It's hard to describe the insane heat we experienced the next morning. Nancy and I were sleeping on the Winnebago roof when the sun rose over the mountain ridge – and within half an hour the temperature was over a hundred degrees and rising. We leaped down, rounded up our belongings and got out of there as quickly as possible. Fortunately, Beryl was in her element – being so deprived of hot weather in England – so there were no complaints from her, but when we next tried camping at Lone Pine, the temperature dropped to near freezing at night. We just couldn't seem to get it right.

One great thing that came out of that holiday was that Gary and I began work on a horror film that he wanted us to make. It was based on a story from the *Tales From The Crypt* comic called 'Only A Dream'. The plot was that a guy (Gary in this case) falls asleep and dreams he is ravenously hungry. He looks in the refrigerator, but there's nothing in there. In a trance, he finds himself walking in a forest – and comes upon a fresh grave. Unable to control his urges, he starts digging at the earth until he pulls out an arm and starts eating the rotting flesh. He gags and vomits, but wakes up in his own bed, relieved that it was only a dream. Going downstairs to the kitchen, he opens the fridge... and a rotting corpse tumbles out. The movie ends with his scream of horror.

We'd already shot the sequence of Gary in the bedroom reading a copy of *Tales From The Crypt* and dozing off. I then filmed the scene where he wakes up in a daze and sleepwalks out onto Grand View Drive, and then we worked on the forest shot. After dark, on the perimeter of the campground, we dug a trench and, with the camera on a tripod and remote control, I lay down out of frame and we buried my arm – to which I'd previously applied bits of latex rubber and paint.

When Gary pulled out my forearm from the earth, he lunged at it and tore off the strips of latex; it really looked like rotting skin. He was so into his performance that he actually choked. With those shots finished, the only part left to do was the scene of him opening the refrigerator and having me fall out. We took out the food and shelves so that there was room enough for me to squeeze in. I wore some ragged clothes that we got from a swap meet and made up my face and hands to resemble a very convincing corpse. I filmed three separate takes of this scene at fast camera speed so that it could be looped together in slow motion. For the soundtrack, which we roughly synchronised on a cassette, I used all sorts of pieces, mainly from Pink Floyd's album *Meddle*. Gary did the extended scream of horror that closed the film, which we watched at every opportunity.

Back on the road, we found a much better place to camp in Sequoia National Forest, where we actually used the tents by day and night. My mother was captured on film, frolicking about in the glade by the redwoods, picking flowers and generally being at one with nature. Socially, however, things were deteriorating rapidly; during the drive north, Nancy hit Jason with a slipper for being overactive. He never forgave her and avoided her for the rest of the stay in Los Angeles. Things were never the same after this. Gary naturally sided with his younger brother, Ben shut down completely, and only Tracey, who was Nancy's favourite, would associate with her. The trip descended into bickering and fights, with Beryl doing her best to keep the peace. On August 10, we had an eleventh birthday party for Jason, and the next day – when our new American tour was to start – I sadly saw the family off at the airport.

By the autumn I had completed the remodelling of the house, and I really felt like a king in his castle. The most dramatic part of the job was installing a huge picture window that looked out over the canyon. It was actually a plate-glass shop window turned on its end so that it was two storeys high. A crane mounted on a heavy-duty truck struggled up the narrow winding streets and carefully lowered it into place.

The Brain Damage Club was now up and running. I'd got hold of a shipment of old redwood railroad ties, which I split down the middle with an industrial table saw; I decorated the new wing and the bar with these in a Tudor style. The front of the bar incorporated tree branches that reached the ceiling, and the shelves behind it were filled with liquor of all kinds. Vodka, rum, bourbon, scotch, gin and tequila were contained in huge, pump-topped bottles which had been manufactured by Smirnoff as a promotional gimmick. I soaked off the Smirnoff labels and replaced them with labels from the correct brands; each held more than a gallon of spirits. Once the bar was complete, Rik Gunnell was my most regular companion; we both loved the English pub ambience. Our glasses were never empty.

In late October, I was asked by Polydor to come up with a double album. My plan was to call it *Back To The Roots* and to round up as many of my previous colleagues as possible for an all-star package. I wrote all the songs fairly quickly to meet the deadlines and began planning the artwork, which would include a twenty-four-page booklet.

There were certainly enough candidates for the job, but because of where they all lived, the project would involve doing some sessions in LA and the rest in England. My American rhythm section revolved round Larry Taylor and his friend Paul Lagos on drums, while in England we'd have Steve Thompson and Keef Hartley. The featured players would be Johnny Almond on saxophones and Sugarcane on violin. As for guitarists, Harvey was central to the LA tracks, and fortunately I was able to get a commitment from Eric Clapton, who happened to be in LA at the time.

The sessions went really well. It was a big moment for me to actually get Eric to come into the studio, so I didn't want to put him off with too many rehearsals. Essentially, I ran down the songs' chord sequences and had him overdub his guitar on the tracks 'Prisons On The Road', 'Looking At Tomorrow', 'Accidental Suicide', 'Force Of Nature' and 'Goodbye, December', all in the space of one afternoon.

Throughout the session Eric didn't appear to be too animated, and for most of the songs he had his guitar volume turned down a bit too much for my liking. I was hoping that the more aggressive approach that he used on 'Prisons On The Road' would appear on the other songs he recorded, but no matter; I felt really lucky just to have him on the album. Before Eric left, Larry Taylor came by and the three of us recorded a basic blues and boogie piece called 'Home Again' – the end of a perfect day.

I then took the tapes to England to add Mick Taylor to some of the existing tracks, as well as cutting new ones to include the British brigade; Keef Hartley took up the beat just like old times. The recording, overdubbing and mixing took a couple of months; I did the mix with engineer John Judnich at Larrabee Studios in LA. We were both pretty new at the game and learning as we went along. Surrounded by boxes of tapes and trying to fit all the pieces together, we captured the performances from all the great musicians who rolled up to add their contributions.

However, after the album was released in spring 1971, I wasn't happy with the finished results. I felt that I'd crammed too much of everything on the tracks and that a simpler approach would have been better. Trying to fit in three different guitarists, all soloing on the same song, resulted in what I considered a traffic jam in which you couldn't focus on any one player. Years later, I located the original twenty-four-track reels in a warehouse in New Jersey, copied everything onto fresh tape and, with my drummer Joe Yuele adding new drum tracks, we remixed most of the songs. This kept the solo focus on one player at a time. I called the album *Archives To Eighties* and it was released in 1988.

At the end of 1970, Rik organised a short tour of Japan for me. The only drag was that we couldn't take Sugarcane Harris with us due to his extensive drug and prison records. The Japanese are most particular about that. For me, it would be the first time since the army days that I'd been back there. We picked up a gig in Hawaii on the way over on December 12, and two days later we were in Tokyo.

How it had grown since 1953! The Ginza market, which I remembered as being a place you could walk around and see in an hour or less, was now a sea of flashing neon lights. The promoter was Tats Nagashima and he hosted us at a couple of great restaurants. It was the first time I'd experienced *teppanyaki* cooking – where the food is cooked on a hot griddle at the table – and I recall how fussy I was about not having any kind of spices on my steak. I was evidently a picky eater in those days, but the meat was out of this world and like nothing I'd ever tasted.

Before we came home for Christmas, Rik and I were very impressed with a gallery of paintings that hung in the Hilton hotel gift shop. We paid many thousands of dollars for several of them, but when we examined them closely back in our rooms, we realised they were reproductions rather than originals. It took a lot of Rik's high-powered bulldozing to return them and get our money back.

CHAPTER 14

HOWLIN' MOON: THE BRAIN DAMAGE CLUB IS OPEN!

I realise that I may come across in this period as a bandleader who changed his musicians a lot. I admit that I did exactly that, but you have to realise two things. Firstly, my record label – Polydor at the time – asked me for new albums every few months, it seemed. To achieve this I needed to keep the music fresh, and that meant rebuilding my line-up from time to time, particularly after long, exhausting tours. Secondly, I was now in my commercial and creative prime; songwriting ideas came thick and fast to me back then, as indeed they do today, and I needed the right people to express those ideas for me.

For these reasons I assembled a mostly new band in early 1971, ahead of that spring's block of gigs in Europe. Sugarcane had to be given money to get his violin out of hock, but at least he'd managed to stay out of jail in our absence. This time I felt that the band would be enhanced if we had a drummer, so I called up Paul Lagos, whom Larry had suggested; Paul had played on my song 'Blue Fox'. He was an amusing character with an unusual style. When we had a song with a drum feature, he would begin his solo on sticks or brushes, and then set them aside to play with his hands.

Our European tour commenced in February. The opening act was a fun bunch of guys from New York called Randall's Island, whose frontman was constantly roaring about on a unicycle and playing the flute at the same time. I once tried to mount the unicycle, but never even got close to anything but a tumble.

Most of February was devoted to Scandinavia and Germany; while in Munich, we played the song 'My Pretty Girl' for the *Ohne Filter* TV programme, and it looked and sounded great. Before the British leg, the journalist Chris Welch came over to Hamburg to review the show for *Melody Maker*. He wrote:

> "John opened up with a slow, swinging ditty called 'Devil's Tricks', a track from his forthcoming *Back To The Roots* album, and set the trend for a rather low-keyed performance. Paul stuck mainly with the brushes, as they moved into 'Get Well Soon' featuring the genius of Sugarcane Harris, one of the finest in jazz and blues. John switched from ancient guitar, to keyboard and harp, singing his own compositions with casual ease and actually stirring up the most excitement with his harmonica. Paul took a solo on 'Took The Car' which proved interesting if restricted, and Harvey, the self-effacing little guitarist, took off on 'Nature's Disappearing'. The encore was 'Full Speed Ahead', a loose jam which John ended by the expedient of shoving a microphone into the amplifier to simulate an automobile collision."

We had a tour manager named Art Satren, who Rik appointed from the Stigwood office. He reminded me of Groucho Marx in that he was always somewhat in a hurry, darting round, giving orders and always on the phone. He was constantly busy and up to his ears in work. If you knocked on his door and asked for anything, it was always the same response: "I can't deal with it now – I've got all this paperwork." Always paperwork – but he got the job done.

However, towards the end of the European tour the band started to show signs of strain. As usual, Sugarcane was constantly on the lookout for drugs, and his playing became erratic to say the least. In Paris, he and Paul scored some heroin, which led to an embarrassingly shaky performance. After a few other dodgy incidents, we finally made it to England to finish the tour. Now that they were away from their European drug connections, the guys were playing better, and behaving themselves. I was relieved, because on March 20, the *Empty Rooms* LP was released and the live dates were attended by a lot of press.

An American tour was next; fortunately, there was time for a break at home. I was weary and longing for Laurel Canyon. Nancy would be waiting and I'd get to chill out and catch up with my movie-going. Stanley Kubrick's *A Clockwork Orange* was playing on Hollywood Boulevard and attracting huge crowds; another biggie was *The French Connection*. Since the movie ratings system had changed, more mature subjects were being covered and there was no limit to what kind of language was permitted in these films. Lenny Bruce would have loved it!

From our opening show at Maryland University on April 21, until we closed at the Whisky A Go Go on June 2, we racked up twenty-six shows – and by now I'd really had enough. Three days before our final Los Angeles date we did a show at Oklahoma City Civic Center as the opening act for Alice Cooper, and we were heartily booed during our set. I understood the crowd's sentiments; our live chemistry had gone all to hell, and I wanted out. I needed a whole new concept.

Looking back, it's amazing how many albums I put out in those days. It seemed like *Empty Rooms* had barely had a chance to sell – and, indeed, it didn't sell many copies – before *Back To The Roots* was released. The reviews of the latter were mixed; I think the critics seemed to like it better in England than in the USA. Even so, despite the effort we put into the project, its elaborate twenty-four-page booklet and the high-quality paper, its sales didn't match up to expectations.

What to do, then? Push forward, of course! After all, Polydor seemed to have a constant appetite for more John Mayall albums. With my mind racing ahead, I set to with fresh ideas. The next album was to be a chronological story called *Memories*, covering tales from my family history. The new songs included 'Home In A Tree', in which I recalled my lonesome teenage years when I despaired of ever finding a girlfriend; my wasted army days in 'The Fighting Line'; and the death of my grandfather and thoughts of returning to civilian life after Korea with the songs 'The City', 'Separate Ways', 'Nobody Cares' and 'Play The Harp'.

I used Larry Taylor as my anchor, and teamed up again with Jerry McGee, who was a regular member of The Ventures and still doing occasional trips to Japan, where they were still one of the hottest acts ever to play in that country. Jerry was such a beautiful player that I didn't need anyone else to record the new suite; between the three of us we cooked up magic that didn't require a drummer. I remember mapping out the album with lyrics and music; I chose the stories, followed the appropriate moods and tempos to match, and then fitted the lyrics into each piece.

Beryl came over for the summer and the three of us went to Kona Village in Hawaii. Things were tense again, of course; I can remember another great row between Nancy and me, with Beryl in the middle of it comforting each of us and trying to repair the rift. Although Kona Village is such an enchanting place that nothing could spoil it entirely, it seemed apparent to me that our relationship wasn't going to work out.

On the other hand, there appeared to be no way to get out of it. Each time we had a fight and she said she was leaving me, I welcomed the threat – but it never came close to reality. Conversely, if I threatened to kick her out of my life she would fly into a rage. There was one horrible night, close to the end of the year, when she grabbed a kitchen knife and came at me. It was like a scene out of *Psycho*. I turned around and ran out of the front door to escape her fury. In despair, I wondered how on earth my life could have come to this.

Music was always there to soothe me, fortunately, and in August I received a call from the legendary gravel-voiced radio DJ Robert Weston Smith, better known as Wolfman Jack. His radio programmes had turned countless legions of listeners into blues fans over the previous decade. Jack had been given the go-ahead from Stax Records to set up a recording session for the great Albert King – and as I was a friend of Albert's, he thought I might be interested in producing it.

I was thrilled with this opportunity. I'd grown bored with the way Albert's recent albums were all starting to sound the same, and I thought I could do better by getting my guys in and throwing him into different styles. I set to work on finding my supergroup. Larry was the starting point, and through his contacts we got hold of Clifford Solomon for alto saxophone. Clifford had been a long-time member of Ray Charles' band, and through him I also got trumpeter Blue Mitchell on board.

We needed a drummer and came up with Ron Selico, who was basically a jazz drummer but who had a powerful style and would fit very well. We then located guitarist Lee King – said to be a relative of Freddie King – and finally an enthusiastic young organist from San Francisco named Kevin, whose last name seems to have been lost since then. Another hot tenor player on the jazz scene was Ernie Watts, and he was booked to solo on a couple of tracks. So there it was.

I felt as if I were truly living among the mighty. If someone had told me at a fifties jazz-listening party in Manchester that one day I'd be hiring these legends, I would have laughed. All we needed now was the man himself.

On August 28, when we met at Wolfman Jack's studio, I discovered that Albert couldn't read, and therefore any song that I proposed to write words for would be no use at all. We set up and jammed for a while, but as it didn't seem to be going anywhere, I sent Albert out for lunch and in his absence composed the songs on guitar, piano and organ. On Albert's return, he plugged in his guitar, took the pipe out of his mouth and made up the lyrics. It was great to hear him respond to the different keys and moods.

The songs weren't released until 1986, when Stax issued them as *The Lost Session*, but the experience gave me an idea for putting my next band together. By the end of the King sessions, I'd got to know Ron, Blue and Clifford well enough to make them an offer to join me after I came back from Europe. I also got in touch with a guitarist who I revered – Freddy Robinson. Freddy had recorded a couple of albums on Warner Bros that knocked me out, and he had his jazz chops down in addition to being a noted blues guitarist on the Chicago circuit, where he'd paid his dues as part of Little Walter's regular band. In my head, a jazz–blues fusion idea was already a reality.

Soon after the *Memories* album was released, Polydor asked me to do a tour of Europe and the UK. The only snag was that Jerry backed out at the last minute, saying he didn't want to go on the road any more – although this didn't stop him from going out with The Ventures later on. They must have offered more money! I decided to give Keef a call, and even though there were no drums on the record, he was up for doing the tour, especially as it would give him a chance to work with Larry Taylor.

When we got talking about guitarists, he suggested I call Chas Chandler, who recommended an eighteen-year-old Scot called Jimmy McCulloch, who had played in Speedy Keen's band Thunderclap Newman, as well as gigging with Harry Nilsson and Klaus Voormann. Jimmy was now in the process of rehearsing his own group, Bent Frame, which Chas was looking to manage, and he would later go on the road with Paul McCartney – but for now he had time to do a short tour with me. I was impressed by his playing and jolly personality.

The start date of the tour was set for September 12 in Germany. Larry and I were scheduled to fly over to England to meet up with Jimmy and Keef for a rundown of what we'd be playing, but before that could happen, I was in for a shock.

My father Murray's second wife Gwen called me on the eighth of the month to say that he had died suddenly the day before. He was only sixty-seven. Apparently he'd come home from work, and over dinner complained of indigestion. Soon afterwards he suffered a stroke; an ambulance was sent for, but he died on the way to the hospital.

The news of a parent's death always leaves you stunned. I was completely taken aback, especially as I was so far away and had had so little to do with my father in many years. I left the next day to fly to London; from there I took the train to Manchester. The funeral was held in a crematorium in Stockport, and I attended with Gwen, Roderick and Stephen and several drinking friends of Murray's.

Throughout the service I felt numb, and as detached as the minister. I couldn't feel any emotion as I listened to this sanctimonious guy spouting all this rhetoric about what a pillar of strength Murray had been in the community. None of it had anything to do with the actual person.

Tears finally came in the car on the way back to my father's bungalow, accompanied by a couple of his pals who were also upset at the way the service had gone. It suddenly felt real when they began talking about how Murray would have hated it. He would much rather have been remembered as a man who was happiest when surrounded by his friends, with Django Reinhardt records playing in the background and a drink in his hand. That's how I'll remember him.

In a daze, I returned to London to connect up with the band, and we set off to play eight shows in Germany before coming back to England for the final leg of the tour. Reviews were mixed, and one particular article about our Croydon concert gives you some idea of what it was all about. It was Chris Welch again, who was very disappointed by the laxness of our set; he commented on my rambling harmonica solos and almost arrogant attitude throughout. He mentioned me pouring drinks, clinking glasses and lighting cigarettes during Larry Taylor's bass solo, which he considered the high point of the show among the endless jammed twelve-bars.

I agreed that we were a bit rough and untogether, and I didn't care for my own singing or playing. The new songs were too full of weird changes to play guitar comfortably while a harmonica harness was strapped to my chest, but the fans didn't appear to notice. However, Jimmy's lead guitar playing was much applauded, helped by his diminutive size. All those wild blues licks, coming from someone who – at a distance – looked as if he was fourteen years old!

By the beginning of October, when the tour finished, I was ready to go back home and get on with the next album. I recruited harmonica player Shakey Jake Harris, Ron Selico, Larry and Freddy Robinson into the line-up. We recorded at Larrabee with John Judnich engineering it, and we had a blast. Shakey was great on harp and vocals – but for me, Freddy was the shining star. There were a few extra musicians to vary the styles, and we even had someone play spoons on one song. The album, *The Devil's Harmonica*, sank without trace on its release early in 1972, but it later became a collector's item.

Back home for Christmas, things were finally coming to a head with Nancy. We both knew it was over, and we had discussed how best to make the transition. I was prepared to agree to anything to get her out of my life, and in the end the only solution I could think of was to buy her a place to live.

There was a house on Kirkwood up for sale, and she agreed that if I bought the house, she would pay me rent as soon as she got settled in and found a job of some sort. I had doubts about this, of course, but I felt there was a light at the end of the tunnel and began the escrow proceedings. I think the final price was about $30,000, and once I became the legal owner, she packed up her stuff and moved in.

As a final Christmas present to Nancy, I forked out for a handmade fur coat from Ventura Boulevard. It was expensive, so I had her name sewn into the inside of the lining to prove her ownership if it were ever stolen. However, she either sold it or lost it. I also gave her my Pontiac Firebird, which she or a friend totalled soon afterwards. God, the hoops I jumped through to get rid of that woman!

Once free of Nancy, I spent a lot of time with Rik Gunnell in my house and out on the town in Los Angeles. With Ron Selico now gone, I made the call to Keef and he came over to take residence in the bachelor pad that was now my domain. Rik was a constant companion most nights as we made the rounds of the restaurants before heading home, where we spent the hours until daybreak – and beyond – reminiscing at the bar with those huge pumps of liquor enhancing our ramblings.

In retrospect, it was amazing that we were able to formulate, and then stick to, a business plan. Our idea for 1972 was that we would debut in Los Angeles, playing warm-up shows at the Whisky for two nights, and then begin a three-month world tour in Hawaii, Australia and beyond. It was a risk, given that there were only two shows dedicated to preparation, and to add to this, Larry Taylor told me that he couldn't do the tour. He'd been moody and in poor health for a while; he was also thinking of taking two years off the road to concentrate on his upright bass studies. With the long string of dates looming, we were in a bind.

Fortunately, Larry suggested a replacement, a guy called Putter Smith, who agreed to come on board for the Australian part of the tour. I trusted Larry's judgement that Putter would be able to do the gig, even though I hadn't met him myself or heard him play. When he joined us, I was taken aback, because Putter had become famous the previous year as an actor, having played a villain called Mr Kidd in the latest James Bond movie, *Diamonds Are Forever*. I'd seen the film, and it felt weird to look up from my piano and see him standing there in the rhythm section. Keef felt the same way, and we gave Putter a lot of good-natured 'Kidd'-ing as we travelled across Australia and New Zealand.

After five weeks of successful shows, we flew to England where Putter quit and was replaced by Victor Gaskin, who had impressed me with his bass playing on The Cannonball Adderley Quintet's live *Mercy, Mercy, Mercy! Live At 'The Club'* LP back in 1966. Our first gig with Victor took place at the Royal Festival Hall on April 3; this was an important show for us, because the critics were always out to review whatever new musical project I had for them.

On our arrival in London, there was no opportunity for a rehearsal, so we met Victor at the soundcheck. Fortunately, that was all that was needed. He alternated upright bass with bass guitar and we played a funky, improvised set; the audience really came alive, leaving their seats and leaning on the front of the stage, where they smoked cigarettes and cheered our individual solos – much to the chagrin of the hall's management.

My new album, *Jazz Blues Fusion*, came out in May, as we travelled through the rest of the UK and all through Europe. One incident sticks in my memory of a club in Belgium, where some drunken punter decided to pick a fight with Victor for some unknown reason. Our noble bassist was holding his own until he tripped backwards. Chairs went flying everywhere, and I jumped into the fray to assist my friend. Victor was on the floor, with this maniac punching him from above, so I pulled the guy away. Victor stood up, handed me his pipe, and was then able to take care of his attacker. I'm not usually a violent man, but when I dusted myself off I noticed several clumps of our assailant's hair between my fingers. Together we won the day!

It was a very weary but triumphant bunch of guys who boarded the plane back to the USA to finish off the tour, right where we'd started so many months before. After our final show at the Whisky on June 2, the mission was completed and we went our separate ways for the summer.

After being on the road for so long, it was a real treat to be back in the lovely Laurel Canyon. There was still a lot to be done around the house; my next big project was to do something with the hillside garden. I had plans to carve out pathways and do major planting, so I got busy with axes and spades and cleared the way through the foliage. I enlisted the help of a gardener called Frank Gallego, who knew all about which plants would work best. I built an archway and gate, and during the next month or two, our builder Ernie Mayer built me a summer house to my specifications. I had expectations of female company somewhere in the future, so we installed a water bed, an antique mirror and a mirrored ceiling. It was the seventies, come on!

I'm recalling all this because my house came to a sad end not long afterwards. It was truly the end of an era – one that will not come again.

After the positive reaction to *Jazz Blues Fusion*, Polydor was quick to request a live album; we arranged to record a set at the Whisky. Keef had been back in England working on an album and came over; Victor joined us from New York; Freddy travelled from Chicago; and the rest of the gang were already here. I wrote a whole slew of new songs with jazzy chord changes and lined up some extra horn players to fatten up the arrangements and vary the soloing. We had Fred Jackson on baritone and tenor saxes, Charles Owens on tenor, soprano and flute, and the great Ernie Watts came in to do a solo on the song 'High Pressure Living'. Victor played upright bass and Larry returned to the fold on bass guitar, which made for an interesting experiment. Eddie Kramer came in from New York as engineer and Rik managed to persuade none other than Bill Cosby – sadly fallen from grace all these years later – to introduce the gig on July 10.

Most excitingly for me, Victor had set up an introduction to my revered hero Cannonball Adderley, who agreed to come and sit in on the session. This was a major coup as far as I was concerned. He lived in Beverly Hills, and I was invited to a party at his house a few days before the gig. Cannonball was every bit as hospitable and humorous as I'd expected and I looked forward to having him on stage with us.

I guess it was too much to hope that all would go without a hitch... On the night of the show, the Whisky was packed, and the stage was crowded with musicians as we kicked off with the first shuffle. I blanked out on some of the lyrics and the songs ended up longer than I'd anticipated. Normally this wouldn't have been a problem, but when Cannonball came on, Clifford was so in awe that he took it upon himself to blow chorus after chorus, with no room for Cannonball to jump in. He played at least two dozen choruses of repetitive nonsense. Finally, when Cannonball took over, it was fabulous – but the reel-to-reel tape ran out dead in the middle of his solo! Most of it was lost during the tape changeover, and none of it was usable.

Indeed, when I finally heard the tapes of the show, most of the songs were so scattered and overlong that I couldn't use them, despite Eddie Kramer's skill and effort. The only way of saving the day was to go into the studio and re-record about half of the songs, and then loop the live applause in under the opening and closing bars of the live versions. That was the story of the cursed *Moving On* album.

Still, life was good in other ways. During August the family came over, and Keef stayed on to party as usual. We went to the beach a lot because the weather was beautiful that year; our favourite was Leo Carrillo Beach. We would stock up with fried chicken and go have fun in the surf; I wrote the song 'California Campground' about our days there. Beryl and Keef were a good team, and after

Gary, Jason, Tracey and Ben went back to England at the beginning of September, the three of us headed west on a camping trip.

With summer over, it was time to go back to work. We had a two-month tour of the States starting in early October, and because I wanted a fuller horn section for the new songs, I added a baritone sax player named Fred Clark. He was a little older than the other musicians, and a nice enough guy, but eventually he angled his way into taking solos and got rather upset when I edged him out. Improvising wasn't one of his strong points and so he was relegated back to section work. By the end of November I'd definitely had enough – and had to tell him he wouldn't be needed in the future.

Fred wasn't the only casualty of this tour. Clifford's solos were getting longer and longer; I grew tired of it and decided that we needed a change. I hadn't the heart to tell him my future plans, as he'd been such an integral part of the band for such a long time. I decided to wait until my head was clear and I'd had time to unwind from the road.

In the final stages of the tour we attempted to record a live album at two shows, but the results weren't very good, thanks to numbers with no coherent lyrics to speak of and long rambling solos that dragged everything down. Back at home I cobbled together some lyrics and overdubbed them on 'Sitting Here Thinking' and 'Burning Sun', while the other tracks stayed as instrumentals. With some judicious editing the masters remained on the shelf for nearly a year before finding a home as a bonus LP to go with the next studio package. Why live albums were so difficult for me at this time, I have no idea.

In December, I let Clifford know the bad news; fortunately, he took it pretty well and said how much he'd enjoyed the ride. I had thought how great it would be if I could get a saxophone player like one of my early idols, Red Holloway, who'd knocked me out with Jack McDuff's 1963 album *Brother Jack McDuff Live!* It was my good luck that Blue knew him well, and agreed to vouch for me when we located Red at his regular Los Angeles venue, the Parisien Room, a jazz venue that specialised in live music every night of the week.

I know how awkward I must have sounded on the phone to Red, trying to explain what my offer was all about. With Blue, Freddy and Victor already on board as reliable references, he said yes – and from that day on I was a frequent customer at the Parisien. I will never forget taking a table at the front and the friendly ribbing by the comedians from the stage because I was a white blues singer.

Red was a superb host and we became friends from the moment we met. It's hard to remember the complete list of who I saw there in such informal surroundings, but it did include Dizzy Gillespie, Sonny Stitt, Big Joe Turner, Kenny Burrell, Jimmy Smith and another of my heroes, Eddie Harris. These were incredible nights that I will always treasure.

Just as things were going smoothly for me, with Christmas at home coming up and the prospect of an exciting new band, I was struck by a bombshell. Rik Gunnell, who had been out on the road with us collecting the money, did more than collect it. He – and the cash – disappeared without warning.

I recall it exactly. One night we were all out at dinner together, but the next morning when his wife Lynn awoke, Rik was nowhere to be found. She called me to see if he had come over to my place for a nightcap, but I said no. It was a complete mystery.

Phone calls to friends and acquaintances shed no light on the matter. Rik had quite simply disappeared. I couldn't help but wonder if he'd been murdered. After Robert Stigwood's office investigated the accounts, it was revealed that Rik had absconded with a huge amount of money. An estimated $250,000 was gone, which in 2019 is more than £1.5 million.

Quite apart from the loss of the money, it was a sad situation for me because I really missed Rik's larger-than-life presence. It was like losing a brother, and it took me a long time to adjust to the fact that I might never see him again. It also left my professional future up in the air. Fortunately, because I was contracted to Robert Stigwood, and Rik was Stigwood's employee, I was not held responsible for the embezzled money.

Stigwood remained my management company, and when they'd taken out a warrant for Rik's arrest, they sent out a young executive named Jeff Tornberg to be considered as my new business manager. I was horrified. How could this guy take the place of Rik, the roaring giant? There was nothing about him that I could relate to, and I phoned Robert and told him that Jeff was not the guy. I suggested Rik's brother John, who I thought could get the business back on track. Robert agreed to come to LA to discuss it in person.

It so happened that Ahmet Ertegun – the legendary head of Atlantic Records – was also in town, and I was invited to dinner with him and Robert. We dined at a restaurant on Larrabee and the wine flowed freely. By eleven o'clock we were all in a pretty loose state and, full of the moment, decided to go to the Parisien Room.

For reasons that I didn't grasp until later, Robert suggested that I go along in their car and leave mine parked in town, but I countered that I wanted to take my car as well. A wild chase followed; it was lucky we weren't stopped by the police for speeding.

Ahmet, as the world's biggest jazz fan, was much impressed that a club as great as the Parisien existed in our city. By the time we departed for further drinks at the Beverly Hills Hotel, where Robert had a suite, it was getting pretty late. Ahmet didn't stay long, leaving Robert and me to finish the wine.

After a while, Robert – by now with bleary eyes bulging out like poached eggs – started to put the make on me. I was taken aback, and when he disappeared into the bathroom, intent on slipping into something more comfortable, I seized my opportunity to escape. As I jumped into my Toyota and sped off with a roar, I realised why he'd suggested leaving my car at home.

Typically for Stiggy, the incident was not mentioned at the next day's meeting, or indeed ever again. Still, I persuaded him that John Gunnell should be transferred to Los Angeles, thus beginning another chapter in the unpredictable saga that is Mayall management. Booze helped to cement the relationship back at my house, now truly earning its name as the Brain Damage Club. I designed and printed a new batch of membership cards to reward anyone who claimed some sort of outrageous behaviour under the influence of alcohol.

The year ended with a big New Year party. Did the booze bottles take a hammering at the Brain Damage Club? I think you know the answer by now.

CHAPTER 15

ROOM TO MOVE: BROKEN BONES – AND A FIERY TRAGEDY

Our first tour of 1973 was to be in Australia; we didn't bother rehearsing before we set off, so there was a party atmosphere as we congregated at LAX with our instruments and baggage. John Gunnell had gone ahead to make sure all the gigs were set up and the money coming in as it should be, and he threw a party for us at the first hotel. It was here that I met his fiancée, Fran, who overwhelmed me; I felt that she was attracted to me, and it was a sad moment for me when the party drifted to a close and she left with John, who hadn't been paying much attention to her all evening.

Meanwhile, there were one or two other women circulating, and our boys were trying their best to make an impression. By now I was fairly tipsy and decided to pair up with Blue Mitchell; he and I took turns making out in relay fashion with one of the women. Before I staggered to my room and passed out, the last vision I had was of Blue lying on this female, too tired to move, and snoring intermittently as his strokes got ever weaker. It was a hell of a way to start a tour – and a shameful contrast to the noble way I'd felt about Fran earlier that evening. How could I be so shallow?

At the end of the tour, Fran and I drove out to Bondi Beach, where we had the most romantic of afternoons, sitting together on the rocks, kissing and talking about life and love. She was committed to John, though, and it was a very bittersweet day. I later wrote the song 'Better Pass You By' for the next album...

"You knock me out, but you belong with another guy / so before you drive me crazy I'd better move and pass you by

You're the one that's got no place for me / no way I can have you unless you set your main man free

It's my bad luck I didn't meet you long ago; it's too late now for me to hang around your door

I'll be leaving her, won't be bothering you nohow

I can't be living with you, so I'll learn to live without you now."

On February 9 I stopped smoking, having got to the shameful point where I was getting through four packs a day. I remember the exact time – 2 p.m. At first, I decided to hold off for one hour without a cigarette. Usually I would have smoked two or three in that time, so it was more of a challenge than you might think, but I tried to keep busy in the office, filing papers and tidying up. After an hour I felt terrible, but the worse the deprivation got, the more I was determined to continue, one hour at a time.

At 6 p.m. Eddie Choran came by to fill me in on our touring plans, and I wondered if he would notice that I didn't have a cigarette burning. He didn't, which gave me more encouragement. By now I was looking at it as a scientific experiment and kept up with the abstinence for the rest of the day. By the early evening my sense of smell had returned; I could actually smell the roses and other garden scents. I'm proud to say that from then on I have never touched another cigarette.

Life remained tranquil for several months. Between dates with the band, I spent my time with various girlfriends; a wonderful woman called Joyce was my partner in a passionate, if brief, affair; many air stewardesses came and went; and I developed a serious crush on a glamour model called Roberta Pedon. I often visited the cinema for extended periods; sixteen hours of unbroken viewing was my record. My friends were always at the Brain Damage Club, and we drank, and drank, and drank...

I suppose the end to all these good times had to come sooner or later, and on March 9, 1974 a rather serious full stop marked the end – at least temporarily – to the partying. We were in LA, recording a new album, *Ten Years Are Gone*, and in the evening John Gunnell,

Fran, our friends Mutt and Kathy and I went out for dinner. Mutt was into exotic beverages, so we moved on to the Athenian Gardens on Canoga and Franklin, where we drank Greek schnapps that tasted like you imagine creosote would. As a result, when we went up the hill to my house, we were far from sober.

My dear friend Kansas J. Canzus and our chum Marty had been there a while, cooking up a big dinner, and they'd invited their friends Susan and Doug over to join in the festivities. It soon became yet another all-night drinking social club, with everyone involved in something of their own choosing. Kathy and I were lying under a floor lamp discussing careers; John and Fran were having one of their many arguments; Susan and Doug were lying out on the beanbag; and Mutt was passed out on the couch. Kansas noted later that everyone was "high on a personal level", which is a diplomatic way of putting it.

I decided, on a whim, to perform a daredevil jump from the balcony into the pool. Now, the balcony was only around twelve feet above the water, which wasn't a big deal, but in order to clear the concrete surrounding the pool, you had to jump at least six feet forwards when you made your leap. As I took off, I suddenly saw Kansas climbing out of the water at the exact spot where I was aiming to land. This led to a fatal split second of indecision as I took off. My brain told me to cancel the leap, but it was too late.

Over half a century later, I can still feel the two massive impacts: the first when my left heel hit the concrete, about two feet short of the water; and the second when my body pitched forward and my kneecap shattered on the edge of the pool.

By the time I surfaced at the other side of the pool, Kansas and the others had rushed over to help. I lifted my kneecap from the water and saw that it was visibly changing shape. It was clearly in two pieces under the skin, and as I watched in horror, the whole area began to swell up like a balloon. The pain was literally indescribable.

Kansas later recalled: "I was in the pool, chatting to Kathy, when I happened to look up and saw Mayall coming straight toward my head at a forty-five-degree angle. I instinctively ducked under the water and felt him land close to me. He immediately surfaced with shock on his face, and said, 'Fucking hell, I've broken my goddamn leg!'"

He and Doug pulled me out of the water and, after a moment of indecision as I writhed in agony, they decided to take me upstairs, get me dressed and take me to the emergency room. I was loaded into the car and we headed to an emergency clinic on Santa Monica Boulevard near La Brea.

Kansas says: "We arrived at 3.20 a.m., and the nurse's first question was 'Do you have insurance?', which really pissed me off because Mayall was moaning in agony. I finally convinced her that John Gunnell would pay in cash, and they reluctantly brought out a roller stretcher and wheeled him in. I filled out the form at the desk, and they asked, 'How much money do you want to deposit?' I asked, 'How much do you want?' She asked in return, 'How much do you have?' I couldn't believe it!"

They bandaged my leg, which was good, but gave me no pain medication, which was less so. I was told to return at 9.30 a.m. to see the doctor, so, back at home, I lay on my bed with bags of ice on my knee and ankle. I was in terrible pain; at one point I tried to get up and fainted.

The following morning, the doctor finally gave me some pain relief, telling me that a pin would need to be inserted in my heel to fix it – but that nothing could be done until the swelling subsided. I was told to return two days later, so it was back home to the ice packs. The pain was so excruciating that a lot of this is a blur to me. My self-esteem plummeted. What a stupid, stupid thing to happen – and the more my leg swelled and hurt, the more serious and hopeless it all seemed to become. We'd all been so carefree just a few hours before.

There was no way I could remain at home for two days, given the state I was in. In addition, it turned out that the doctor at the clinic hadn't even noticed that my kneecap was shattered! John spent some time on the phone and eventually got through to Dr Lewis Cozen, the top surgeon for all the major sports injuries in Los Angeles. Cozen wanted me in hospital as soon as possible, so I was admitted.

He told me that my kneecap was shattered into several pieces – and as for the heel, the bones were crushed beyond repair.

I would have to remain in the hospital and be on major pain medication until the swelling went down. The plan was then to remove all the chunks of bone that used to be my kneecap, while what was left of my heel would be compressed, so that the particles of bone could graft together. He also said that my running days were over – and that I would probably have to walk with a cane for the rest of my life. What a horrible prospect to add to the pain.

I lay there, powerless. Pills were administered every six hours, and while they didn't kill the pain nearly enough, a higher dosage would have been dangerous. I used to count the minutes till my next pill.

A few days later Cozen performed the operation, removing my kneecap and refashioning a heel. When I awoke on a gurney, I looked down to see my leg encased in plaster up to the hip with my toes sticking out of the end. As the anaesthetic wore off, it was back to the pain again.

I'd asked the doctor to keep the pieces of kneecap for me; they were preserved in a little jar at my bedside for posterity. Why not?

As the days passed, friends came by to visit me. We would work our way through bottles of wine; I still wonder why the patrolling nurses didn't call a halt to our casual imbibing. I also took my first steps assisted with crutches, and by March 19 I was deemed roadworthy. I was wheelchaired to the front desk and signed off, given a codeine prescription and driven home by Kansas.

One of the hardest things to deal with during and after the hospital confinement was the absence of a bath; by now, I was feeling like a leper. The itching inside the cast was also driving me nuts – so, with my leg wedged along the top rim of the tub, I scooted into the bliss of a hot bath. The relief didn't last long, unfortunately; shortly afterwards, I attempted to climb up and down the stairs on crutches, and fell all the way down the staircase. It was a painful business, and from then on I opted to slide downstairs on my butt.

When most people have a cast, they usually graffiti it with signatures and other scrawls, but because I knew I'd be on the road soon and would need album art, I dug into the comic art of *Tales From The Crypt* and spent a few days copying and colouring the Old Witch and various other horror characters on mine. The hard part was doing it with mirrors to reach behind my leg, and it took days to finish. The results can be seen on the cover of *The Latest Edition* album, released that May.

By the middle of April, I had tentatively resumed playing music and staying up late – hindered, of course, by my injury. Mixing and press duties took up my time, too, and Beryl and the kids came for a welcome visit. I remember Gary, now a robust teenager, set himself the task of concocting a Brain Damage punch, one cup of which laid my mother out.

A European tour in May and June passed without incident, although doing it on crutches represented a challenge! When the tour was over, I decided to rest up and head to southern Spain for some welcome sunny weather.

It was there that, following a lead from Bob Hind at the booking agency, I finally tracked down the elusive Rik Gunnell, who was working at a little beach bar in the quiet seaside resort of Marbella. He explained away his actions of the previous year, and while I don't recall details of the story, I was convinced enough to ask the Stigwood office to loan him some money – perhaps foolishly, in retrospect.

Of course, there was quite a lot more catching up to do and, although Rik vowed with tongue in cheek to pay me back the money he'd run off with, I knew I wouldn't ever see a nickel of it. However, it didn't stop us from enjoying the rest of the week by the beach where I sunbathed by day and drank by night. Here I became quite well known for my notorious alcohol capacity. One night in a bar after closing time, the bartender watched in wonder as I knocked back a record thirty-seven vodka screwdrivers; I still had enough composure to walk out of there. However, I suffered later, decorating the toilet bowl before I passed out for the night.

Back home in one piece, I signed a record deal with ABC Blue Thumb Records, as my contract with Polydor had expired while we were on the road. Apart from that, life went on in its usual fairly insane way. Everything in the Brain Damage Club days was way over the top, in every direction. At my pool parties, my male and female guests lay nude all round the sun deck, with endless joints passed around. Several of the usual suspects chose to repeat my balcony jumps into the pool, although without the consequences I had suffered. It seems that we never learn from our mistakes, I told myself, as I fixed my regular breakfast vodka and orange…

★★★

The remaining years covered in this book pass swiftly, dear reader.

In 1975 I recorded an album whose title pretty much explained my situation – *New Year, New Band, New Company*. Sugarcane Harris and Larry Taylor stayed on board, but I added guitarist Rick Vito, keyboardist Jay Spell, drummer Soko Richardson and singer Dee McKinnie for a different sound. We hit the road with a vengeance that year, starting at our beloved Whisky A Go Go in Los Angeles and heading through Canada, the UK and America. In the autumn we played the Royal Albert Hall; I recall I was wearing tight yellow leather shorts, which I'd made myself, accessorised with Indian silver. Don't forget, it was the seventies!

The following year was even more productive, with two albums released by ABC – *Notice To Appear* and *A Banquet In Blues*. We toured America, and around the same time I received my official Green Card. The USA had welcomed me in at last!

Perhaps this explains my productivity in 1977, or maybe it was just that the arrival of punk rock had inspired me. Two live albums – *Lots Of People* and *Primal Solos*, the latter made up of shows from 1965 and 1968 – plus a studio LP, *A Hard Core Package*, kept the Mayall flag flying. I toured the USA and Europe once again, taking the whole summer to do it. It wasn't all fun, with a former girlfriend suing me unjustly for a petty financial issue – but on the other hand, I had a darn good time. I estimated later that I enjoyed the company of somewhere between seventy and a hundred women that year.

In 1978 I released a live album, *The Last Of The British Blues*, toured America once again, and without warning fell in love with a beautiful woman from Chicago called Maggie Mulacek, who I met at Stone Lake, Wisconsin. Maggie sang backing vocals in my band, adopting the stage name Maggie Parker, and we had some great times on that first tour, hanging out with Joe Cocker among other artists. She came over to the house in Laurel Canyon after Christmas and we were inseparable from then on.

The next year, 1979, was mixed to say the very least. On the upside, I was so happy to be with Maggie, to whom I was married until 2011. Two albums appeared, both of which I'm proud of to this day: their titles are *Bottom Line* and *No More Interviews*, the second of which reveals the attitude I had developed to the press at the time!

The *Bottom Line* album, produced by Bob Johnston, had a whole list of fantastic guest musicians on it – the Brecker Brothers, Paul Shaffer, Cornell Dupree, Tim Drummond, Steve Lukather and Jeff Porcaro among them. Our European dates, which we named the Brain Damage Tour, were a success too. The band at this point was Maggie and me with Kathryn Fields, Ruben Alvarez, Chris Cameron, Angus Thomas and Christiaan Mostert, although I sent Kathryn home after a while as her vocal harmonies weren't meshing with Maggie's. Afterwards we embarked on a camping trip with the family; these are all great memories of wonderful times.

However, fate was soon to intervene once again, and the end of that first golden era in Laurel Canyon was on its way. On September 16, 1979, Maggie, Beryl and I got up for a morning swim and a drink by the pool, and then went to our indoor cinema to see *The French Connection*. Just as the film had started, a friend called Terry Smith came in and alerted us that he'd seen smoke rising above Laurel Canyon and that helicopters were circling the area.

We went outside to see the sky full of black smoke, ash fluttering around and a nearby helicopter announcing through a loudhailer that all residents had to evacuate the area immediately. The entire hillside was on fire. I turned on the garden hose to begin wetting the garden and house exterior, but there was no water pressure.

By now, the houses near mine were starting to burst into flames, and a tree just outside my front door was beginning to smoulder. We had no choice but to climb in the car and get the hell out of there.

We drove down the hill, negotiated a traffic jam of emergency vehicles and panicked residents, turned up a parallel road and parked close to a nearby house, which was emitting clouds of black smoke. As we watched, an airplane flew over and deposited a few tons of water on it, to little effect. I knew then that my house was doomed.

When the smoke cleared a few minutes later and I looked over at my home, I saw nothing but a pile of rubble; the entire property must have been consumed by flames in less than half an hour.

I felt sick to my stomach and sat down on the kerb. I had no possessions with me, and neither did Maggie or Beryl. Everything we owned had been in the house, not to mention all the handmade furniture and fittings that I had laboriously constructed and which could never be replaced. Maggie told me later that I simply repeated to myself, "It can't be true. It can't be true."

One of our neighbours, a Beverly Hills salon owner named Soo Nee, insisted on giving us some shoes, clothes and cash, as we sat there in disbelief. I have never forgotten her kind gesture.

A total of twenty-four houses were destroyed that day; luckily, no one was killed. We found out later that the fire was started by a couple of teenage kids playing with fireworks.

In the evening, we went out for a meal and sat quietly, trying to process what had happened. The scale of the loss was impossible to grasp. I had lost diaries belonging to my grandfather; uncountable personal possessions; music; art; photos; instruments; even a collection of vintage erotica from my father. That night, Maggie and I slept on the living-room floor at Terry's apartment, and through the hours of darkness, I wept for the loss of so much of my past. The golden years were truly over.

★★★

In 1979 I was forty-six years old, and two decades into a successful career that, I'm happy to say, is as busy as ever today. In 2019, it's forty years since the Laurel Canyon house burned down, but I've never forgotten the great times we had there. The last part of this chapter runs through some of the high points of my life since then, and if you want more detail than that, you'll have to wait for the next book I'm working on.

In the aftermath of the fire, we retrieved what we could from the ruined house – which was almost nothing – and dealt with the legalities, which were complex because the house below mine was alleged to have been damaged by a mudslide from my property.

The bigger loss was the contents rather than the house itself. You can always rebuild a house, and we did that, on the same foundations, but when you lose all your books, photographs, memorabilia and music, you really have to start again, mentally. You never really recover from that. To this day I still wish I had the tapes that I used to make on the road. I have memories of what those days were like, but no physical records. I'm a collector, though, and I started right away to build up various things, just to feel at home and rebuild a semblance of my previous life.

Musically, I was as driven as ever. When I put the old instrumentation back together in 1985 and recorded the *Return Of The Bluesbreakers* album, that kicked off a new wave of blues for the eighties, and then I continued the band with different line-ups including guitarists Coco Montoya, Walter Trout, Buddy Whittington and Rocky Athas.

Each band line-up I've had has worked well together, and we've enjoyed all the great responses we've had to what we do. I always remain good friends with them all and still enjoy consistent relationships with my booking agents in London and California.

I have my own cottage industry, I suppose. I manage myself and stay in touch with my fans through our website, www. johnmayall.com, and I obviously write the music – usually on a keyboard. I feel very fortunate that I'm able to go out and earn a living through my creativity and playing the music that I love for my fans.

I'm proud of my catalogue too, which I think is important, because it's going to last and that's something that I hope will continue as time goes by. My music is always from the heart and it's always nice to know that it's reaching people who can connect with the emotions I put out there. I always celebrate the people who have been in my life and when I listen back to the music, it brings those people to life.

Today, my current band – guitarist Carolyn Wonderland, bassist Greg Rzab and drummer Jay Davenport – is the most productive and enjoyable that I've ever had. I love touring with them and, even after so long on the road, I'm not tired of it yet. We perform around a hundred shows every year all over the world, and the response and communication with the fans is so stimulating and exciting that we always enjoy and appreciate it so much.

My mission is to celebrate life through the blues and it always has been. Many people in this busy world might be new to this music, so it's my job to share the work of the great people who shaped the blues that I play. I hope that you will respond to it and find a connection between it and the feelings and events in your own lives. That's what it's all about!

Songwriting still flows pretty easily for me. I think it was Big Bill Broonzy who was quoted as saying that when you're writing a song, you might think of a kitchen, for example. Then you think of all the things you can do in that kitchen – you can cook, you can eat and so on – and then you've got a subject for a song. There's no great secret to it. Life is good and I celebrate it.

On a related note, I'm sure you've read a lot of the booze-related stories in this book – I know I enjoyed them all at the time – but fortunately for my liver and sanity, I stopped drinking alcohol for good on April 10, 1982. Without alcohol, you become a more sensible person and you take care of business better. I've been totally focused on my career since I gave up. Enthusiasm is better directed too. It was a challenge, but not as tough as I'd thought, once my mind was made up.

During the last few years I have been fortunate enough to form a strong working relationship with my co-producer Eric Corne, who has the expertise to capture any of the ideas that I come up with. When we collaborate in the studio, everything runs very smoothly, and the great albums we have made on his label Forty Below Records attest to that working ethic. Notable examples of the CDs we've done together are *A Special Life, Find A Way To Care, Three For*

The Road, *Talk About That* – which featured the great Joe Walsh – and two volumes of unreleased live shows from 1967 featuring Peter Green.

The latest release, *Nobody Told Me*, blazes new trails for me, with guest contributions from guitarists Joe Bonamassa, Alex Lifeson, Todd Rundgren, Larry McCray, Steven Van Zandt and Carolyn Wonderland, and will hopefully delight all my fans. Since this recording, Carolyn has joined Jay, Greg and I as a regular member on our touring schedule and is sure to be thrilling audiences everywhere.

In my life I'll continue to move forward and hope you'll continue to travel this journey with me. Life is good.

DISCOGRAPHY

STUDIO ALBUMS

1965
John Mayall Plays John Mayall (Decca)

1966
Bluesbreakers With Eric Clapton (Decca)

1967
A Hard Road (Decca)
Crusade (Decca)
The Blues Alone (Decca Ace Of Clubs)

1968
The Diary Of A Band Volume 1 (Decca)
The Diary Of A Band Volume 2 (Decca)
Bare Wires (Decca)
Blues From Laurel Canyon (Decca)

1969
Looking Back (Decca)
Primal Solos (Decca)
The Turning Point (Polydor)

1970
Empty Rooms (Polydor)
USA Union (Polydor)

1971
Back To The Roots (Polydor)
Memories (Polydor)

1972
Jazz Blues Fusion (Polydor)

1973
Moving On (Polydor)
Ten Years Are Gone (Polydor)

1974
The Latest Edition (Polydor)

1975
New Year, New Band, New Company (ABC One Way)
Notice To Appear (ABC One Way)

1976
A Banquet In Blues (ABC One Way)

1977
Lots Of People (ABC One Way)
A Hard Core Package (ABC One Way)
Primal Solos (Decca)

1978
The Last Of The British Blues (ABC One Way)

1979
Bottom Line (DJM)
No More Interviews (DJM)

1980
Road Show Blues (DJM)

1985
Behind The Iron Curtain (GNP Crescendo)

1988
Chicago Line (Entente Island)
The Power Of The Blues (Entente)
Archives To Eighties (Polydor)

1990
A Sense Of Place (Island)

1992
Cross Country Blues (One Way)

1993
Wake Up Call (Silvertone)
Return Of The Bluesbreakers (AIM Australia)

1994
The 1982 Reunion Concert (One Way)

1995
Spinning Coin (Silvertone)

1997
Blues For The Lost Days (Silvertone)

1999
Padlock On The Blues (Eagle)
Rock The Blues Tonight (Indigo)
The Masters (Eagle)
Live At The Marquee 1969 (Eagle)

2000
Time Capsule (Private Stash)
UK Tour 2K (Private Stash)

2001
Boogie Woogie Man (Private Stash)
Along For The Ride (Eagle)

2002
Stories (Eagle)

2003
No Days Off (Private Stash)
70th Birthday Concert (Eagle)

2005
Road Dogs (Eagle)

2006
Essentially John Mayall: Live Rarities (Eagle)

2007
In The Palace Of The King (Eagle)

2008
The Second Decade (Secret Records)

2009
Tough (Eagle)

2011
Live In London (Private Stash)

2012
Historic Live Shows Volume 1 (Private Stash)
Historic Live Shows Volume 2 (Private Stash)
Historic Live Shows Volume 3 (Private Stash)

2014
A Special Life (Forty Below)

2015
Find A Way To Care (Forty Below)
John Mayall's Bluesbreakers Live In 1967 Volume 1 (Forty Below)

2016
John Mayall's Bluesbreakers Live In 1967 Volume 2 (Forty Below)

2017
Talk About That (Forty Below)

2019
Nobody Told Me (Forty Below)

SINGLES (UK)

1964
Crawling Up A Hill / Mr James (Decca)

1965
Crocodile Walk / Blues City Shakedown (Decca)
I'm Your Witchdoctor / Telephone Blues (Immediate)

1966
Lonely Years / Bernard Jenkins (Purdah)
Key To Love / Parchman Farm (Decca)
Looking Back / So Many Roads (Decca)

1967
Sitting In The Rain / Out Of Reach (Decca)
John Mayall's Bluesbreakers With Paul Butterfield EP (Decca)
Double Trouble / It Hurts Me Too (Decca)
I'm Your Witchdoctor / Telephone Blues (Immediate, reissue)
Suspicions Part 1 / Suspicions Part 2 (Decca)

1968
Jenny / Picture On The Wall (Decca)
No Reply / She's Too Young (Decca)
The Bear / 2401 (Decca)

ACKNOWLEDGEMENTS

My gratitude and respect go to the many fine musicians with whom I have been privileged to perform and record, both those departed and those still with us.

Many thanks to Jane Ebdon for helping to get this book into the right place for publishing, Matthew Hamilton at Aitken Alexander, David Barraclough and the team at Omnibus Press, Mick Fleetwood and my co-writer Joel McIver.

INDEX

All songs and albums are by John Mayall except as indicated.